FREDERICK COUNTY, VIRGINIA, MARRIAGES

MARRIAGES

1771-1825

Compiled and Edited by

ELIZA TIMBERLAKE DAVIS

CLEARFIELD

Originally published
1941

Reprinted
Genealogical Publishing Co., Inc.
Baltimore, Maryland
1973, 1975

Reprinted for
Clearfield Company, Inc. by
Genealogical Publishing Co., Inc.
Baltimore, Maryland
1989, 1996, 2003

Library of Congress Cataloging in Publication Data
Davis, Eliza Timberlake.
Frederick County, Virginia, marriages, 1771-1825.
Reprint of the 1941 ed.
1. Marriage licenses—Frederick Co., Va. 2. Registers of births, etc.—
Frederick Co., Va. 3. Frederick Co., Va.—Genealogy. I. Title.
F232.F75D3   1973   929'.3755'992   72-11714
ISBN 0-8063-0545-2

Made in the United States of America

TO MY BELOVED HUSBAND,

CHARLES E. DAVIS,

Whose encouragement has been
a stimulant to my every purpose.

PREFACE

These records of marriages in Frederick
County, Virginia, beginning with the earliest,
1771, and continuing to the year 1825, should
be of unusual interest and value to libraries,
historians and genealogists everywhere. Be-
cause of the transitory nature of many of the
early settlers, these marriages are the only
records that remain.

Frederick County was formed in 1738 from
a portion of Orange County, Virginia; and, with
Augusta County, was all that country west of
the Blue Ridge Mountains. In 1763, by the
treaty with France, its western boundaries were
limited by the Mississippi River and it embraced
what is now the states of West Virginia, Kentucky,
Ohio, Indiana, Illinois, Michigan and Wisconsin.

Two streams of migration flowed through
Frederick County, The first came from New Jersey,
Pennsylvania and Maryland. Among these were
the German, Dutch, Welsh and Scotch-Irish. The
second were the English people from Tidewater,
Virginia, who became large land owners.

Winchester, the County Seat of Frederick
County, was at one time the furthest western
outpost, and much early history was made in and
about it.

MARRIAGE BONDS

Alexander, Joseph & Sarah Bell, Widow   November 14, 1777.
   Surety, - Robert Kenny

Alexander, Morgan & Sarah Snickers   January 19, 1773.
   Surety, - Edmund Taylor. Father, Humbil Janant.

Allensworth, Amanuel & Kitty Black   October 28, 1798.
   Surety, - Luke Garratt. Parents Simon Allensworth
         & Catherine Butler Allensworth.

Amick, Philip (Eamigh) & Catherine Huffman   June 25, 1793.
   Surety, - Conrad Crebs.

Anderson, Jacob & Jane Cochran   September 4, 1793.
   Surety, - George Somerville.

Babb, Abner & Susannah Robinson   May 27, 1793.
   Surety, - Thomas Babb. Parents James & Mary
         Robinson.

Babb, Peter & Jane Bell   November 2, 1797.
   Surety, - William Williams.

Baker, Joseph & Elizabeth Weaver   December 30, 1797.
   Surety, - Jacob Weaver.

Bainbridge, Absalom & Elizabeth Taylor   May 28, 1793.
   Surety, - Gilbert Meem. Consent of John Taylor.

Barber, James (widower) & Mary Harper   September 11, 1793.
   Surety, - Thomas Harper

Barnett, John & Drusilla Rowland   September 14, 1793.
   Surety, - Abner Gossett. Mother Martha Dawson (nee
         Rowland), wife of George Dawson.

Barton, Galbrath & Eleanor Talbott   September 4, 1798.
   Surety, - Hezekiah Young.

Bartlett, Henry & Elizabeth Davis   January 2, 1797.
   Surety, - William Davis, father.

Bell, George & Elizabeth Catlett   August 19, 1777.
   Surety, - Robert Rutherford. Father Robert
         Catlett.

Bishop, Bailey & Arrianna Spurrier   April 13, 1793.
     Surety, Elisha Spurrier.

Bougher, Jacob & Mary Whetsel   April 20, 1773.
     Surety, - Sam May

Bowman, Daniel & Judith Good   August 4, 1798.
     Father, Peter Good.

Boxell, Robert & Elizabeth Orr   July 6, 1793.
     Surety, - Aaron Bonham.   Mother Ann Cave.

Britton, Joseph & Margaret Martin   March 17, 1793.
     Surety, - Wilson Britton.   Parents John & Elizabeth
                           Radenour.

Brown, John & Elizabeth Curlett   May 17, 1793.
     Surety, - Peter Helphenstine.

Brown, Joseph & Mary Smith   July 10, 1793.
     Surety, - John Boxell.

Brownfield, Thomas & Elizabeth Fisher   April 29, 1793.
     Surety, - William Adams.

Buckley, Job & Susannah Newcomb   April 22, 1793.
     Surety, - James Simpson.

Burwell, Philip & Elizabeth Page   November 9, 1797.
     Surety, - Nat Burwell.

Eyrnand, John & Mary Ann Earle (spinster) October 30,1777.
     Surety, - Benjamin Elkins.

Cain, John & Chloe Horton   October 3, 1797.
     Surety, - John Chapman.

Carver, Valentine & Barbara Hoier   May 20, 1793.
     Surety, - Henry Lewis.

Catlett, Peter & Mary Bell   August 13, 1774.
     Surety, - George Bell

Catterlin, Joseph Jr. & Sarah Brecount   June 4, 1793.
     Surety, - Joseph Catterlin.   Father David Brecount.

Chapman, Thomas & Mary Stone   December 22, 1797.
     Surety, - Walter Watson.

Childs, Alex. & Ann Maria Griffith   November 6, 1798.
     Surety, - David Griffith, father.

Christ, Jacob & Ragina Cartmell   October 18, 1798.
Surety, - Martin Cartmell.   Father Nathan Cartmell.

Christ, Thomas & Agnes Rogers   August 25, 1798.
Surety, - John Ritter.   Mother Catherine Rogers.

Clark, George (batchelor) & Daicey Farmer (spinster)
Surety, - William Farmer.   May 7, 1793.

Clayton, Philip & Mildred Dixon (spinster) March 7, 1777.
Surety,- Thomas Moore Jr.

Clevenger, George & Rachel Cooper   October 23, 1797.
Surety, - Vincent Crabb.

Cole, Daniel & Elizabeth Wilcocke   September 18, 1798.
Consent of Abigail Burk

Conrad, Frederick Jr. & Frances Thruston April 21, 1793.
Surety, - David Holmes.

Conrad, John & Grace Stuart (widow)   November 3, 1777.
Surety, - Mitchell Reed.

Coffman, Harman & Margaret Hickman   November 27, 1798.
Surety, - John Senseney.

Cooley, Peter & Sarah Adamson   April 11, 1793.
Surety, - John Reynolds.

Corbett, John & Margaret Stanford (widow) December 7, 1797.
Surety, - William Stanford

Cowan, Nathaniel & Sarah Rice   November 16, 1797.
Surety,- Alexander Simrall.

Craig, Hugh & Elizabeth Thompson   October 27, 1798.
Surety, - John Craig.

Crampton, John & Sidney Barrett   April 23, 1798.
Surety, - Jacob Crampton.

Crider, John & Elizabeth Lemly   November 29, 1797.
Surety, - Isaac Jennings.

Cryder, John & Mary Johnston   June 20, 1793.
Surety, - John McGinnis.

Cryser, Jacob & Leah Garrett   October 25, 1798.
Surety, - Luke Garot.   Parents Luke & Mary Garot.
                 (Garrett)

Cunningham, Thomas & Mary Keller   September 25, 1793.
Surety, - Charles Helzel.

Daingerfield, Henry & Elizabeth Mynn   August 9, 1793.
        Thruston (spinster)
    Surety, - David Holmes.
Davis,Henry M.& Hannah Wilson   August 22, 1798.
    Surety, - Jermemiah Wilson, father. Daniel Davis
    father of Henry.

Devoe, David & Margaret Jewell   May 13, 1793.
    Surety, - Seth Straton. Father William Jewell.

Dillon, Daniel & Sarah Gay   June 13, 1793.
    Surety, - Amos Paxon. Father David Gay.

Dues, Samuel & Sarah Loftin   Nov. 8, 1777.
    Surety, - William Owens. Father Daniel Loftin.

Dunn, Thomas & Rebecca Wickersham   May 8, 1793.
    Surety, - William Wickersham.

Edwards, Joseph & Elizabeth Abrell (widow) July 30, 1776.
    Surety, - Adam Nable.

Elbon, Reuben & Mary Gorley   October 24,1778.
    Surety, - John Gorley, father. Ann Gorley, mother.

Emett, John & Mary Meldrum   October 15,1773.
    Surety, - John Nicewanger.

Ewing, Thomas & Ediah Crawford   September 24,
    Surety, - John McGinnis. Father John   1798.
        Crawford.

Farflinger, Jacob & Barbara Kline   April 12, 1798.
    Surety, - Jacob Kline.

Farling, Thomas M. & Mary Stump (spinster) June 16, 1794.
    Surety, - James Eddy.

Fawcett, David & Phebe Lupton   Sept. 13, 1798.
    Surety, - John Jamison.

Flaugherty, James & Ginnie Graham   April 20, 1793.
    Surety, - James Compton.

Folke, Charles & Jane Farmer   November 16,1797.
    Surety, - Thomas Farmer.

Freestone, Daniel & Lydia Decker   March 25, 1793.
    Surety, - Henry Decker.

Funk, John & Jemima Britain   July 22, 1793.
    Surety, - Joseph Britain.

Funk, Michael & Lavinia Slusher   August 11, 1798.
    Surety, - Frederick Slusher, father.

Gains, Absalom & Patty Scarff   September 11, 1797.
    Surety, - Samuel Griffin.

Garrett, John & Ann Allenworth   June 14, 1793.
    Surety, - Philip Allenworth.

Gelkeson, Samuel & Susannah Heth   July 3, 1777.
    Surety, - John Peyton Jr.   Father Henry Heth.

Glascock, Jesse & Dilly Lewis   May 19, 1798.
    Surety, - Reuben Elliott.

Gordon, Francis & Mary Barger (orphan)   June 17, 1793.
    Test.- Daniel Overacre & John Gordon.

Gossett, Abner & Mary Mercer   December 23, 1797.
    Surety, - William Gossett.

Grahm, Thomas & Jane Riley.   November 15, 1797.
    Surety, - Mark Harper.

Gray, Hannums & Mary Craig   October 27, 1798.
    Surety, - John Craig.

Green, George & Charlotte Babb   April 25, 1798.
    Surety, - Thomas Babb.   Blanche Babb mother to
                                  Thomas Babb.

Griffith, David Jr. & Priscilla Griffith November 27, 1798.
    Surety, - David Griffith, Sr.

Grigsby, Jesse & Betsy Northern   May 11, 1798.
    Surety, - Jonathan Northern.

Groves, Michael & Elizabeth Booker   May 14, 1793.
    Surety, - Jacob Booker.

Groves, Solomon & Fanny Marquis   May 9, 1798.
    Surety, - Isaac Marquis

Grubs, Eli & Nancy Robinson   September 6, 1793.
    Surety, - George Cooper.   Father William Robinson.

Harmon, Jacob & Christanna Mock   October 28, 1797.
    Surety, - George Mock.

Haynie, Edward & Betsy Anderson   January 1, 1803.
    Surety, - Adam Anderson.

Heide, John & Jane Sterlings   September 16,1797.
    Surety, - Hutchenson Sterlings.

Henry, John & Clarkey Reiley   August 8, 1798.
    Surety, - Hugh Reiley

Holdenby, William & Nancy Helphenstine   April 14, 1798.
    Surety,- Philip Shearer.   Father Henry Helphenstine.

Hicks, Samuel & Agnes Latty   July 29, 1793.
    Surety, - Joseph Latty, father.

Hicky, David & Catherine Cohagin   June 15, 1793.
    Surety, - John Noldin.

Hodge, Robert & Ruth Perrill   June 21, 1793.
    Surety, - Joseph Perrill, father.

Hodson, Nicholas & Elizabeth McAnnully   September 25, 1793.
    Surety, - Peter Chrisman.

Hogan, Samuel & Jane Murphy   November 20,1797.
    Surety, - John Cunningham.

Hoyle, Christian & Mary Davis   September 18,1797.
    Surety, - Zachariah Murphy.

Holmes, Hugh & Elizabeth Thomas   -- - 1797.
    Surety,- Fred Conrad, Jr.

Homes, Thomas & Rachel Read   June 30, 1793.
    Surety, - John Read.

Hooper, John & Polly Bailey   April 12, 1798.
    Surety, - William Clements.

Hotsinbeller, Jacob & Milly Seagle   Sept. 14, 1793.
    Surety, - George Marks.

How, James & Peggy Dean   January 1, 1803.
    Surety, - Nathan Smith.

Humphries, John & Sally Berry   February 11,1775.
    (Surety torn off)

Hutchinson, James & Jane Duffield (spinster) Sept. 6, 1776.
    Surety,- John Duffield.

Hutton, William & Catherine Municks   January 3, 1798.
    Surety, - Henry McFarden.

Jacobs, William & Jemima Mulliken   June 7, 1792.
     Surety, - John Jones. Mother Elizabeth Mulliken.

Jenkins, Jonathan & Ann Hog (spinster)   Sept. 4, 1777.
     Surety, - Trystam Ewing.

Jewell, Samuel & Rachael Painter   June 14, 1798.
     Surety, - Seth Stratton. Father Isaac Painter.

Johnston, Stephen & Lydia Clevenger   November 11,1797.
     Surety, - Jacob Anderson.

Jolliffe, John & Mary Dragoe (spinster)   April 7, 1773.
     Surety, - John Rogers.

Jones, John & Eleanor Alexander (widow)   October 18, 1777.
     Surety, - Robert Boyce.

Jones, William & Ann Blakemore   August 11, 1792.
     Surety, - Abraham Neill. Father Thomas Blakemore.

Jones, William & Polly Pine   January 2, 1798.
     Surety, - Nicholas Hanshaw.

Jones, Zachariah & Mary Jennings   May 31, 1793.
     Surety, - Gary Robertson. Father Edward Jennings.

Kearnes, Edward & Rachel Barnett   Sept. 17, 1793.
     Surety, - Patrick Kearnes, father.

Kegley, Robert & Mary Simpson   June 30, 1798.
     Surety, - John Simpson, brother.

Kendall, John & Verlinda Sandbury   October 17,1797.
     Surety, - Peter Speers.

Kenlin, William & Lydia Littler   October 16, 1798.
     Surety, - James Bruce.

Kyger, Jacob & Mary Overacre (spinster)   August 31, 1776.
     Surety, - George Kyger.

Kinkead, William & Agatha Chinn (spinster) February 7,1777.
     Surety, - James G. Dowdall.

Kuntz, Jacob & Dolly Boman   January 30, 1798.
     Surety,- Humphrey R. Johnston.

Lambert, Christopher & Catharine Crider (widow) Nov. 25,1777.
Surety, - Frederick Conrad.

Lang, William Simpson & Elizabeth Smith   November 8, 1798.
Surety, - Tobias Walters.

Langley, Curtis & Susannah Ridgeway   October 17, 1798.
Surety, - Jesse Britton.

Langley, William & Elizabeth Cochran   October 9, 1798.
Surety, - Benjamin Langley.

Larrick, George & Rebecca Brinker   November 7,1798.
Surety, - George Brinker.

Larue, John & Hannah Jackson   July 8, 1798.
Surety, - Jacob Edinborough.

Lee, John & Eleanor Ellis   August 10, 1793.
Surety, - Jonas Likans.

Lewis, Evan & Ann Marple   October 1, 1793.
Surety, - Enoch Marple.

Lindsey, Jacob & Mary Everns (spinstress)   November 11, 1797.
Surety, - William Cottrell.

Little, William & Margaret How   January 26, 1773.
Surety, - Robert Rutherford.

Littler, Elijah & Margaret Williams   March 26, 1793.
Surety, - Samuel Littler & Ann Littler. Barnett
Williams, father.

Long, Nimrod & Eleanor E. Williams   September 3, 1793.
Surety, - William C. Williams.

Lyles, John & Sarah Glass   March 20, 1793.
Surety, - Robert Glass.

McAlester, John & Elizabeth Joliffe   October 4, 1797.
Surety, - Amos Joliffe.

McBride, James & Catherine Frisbee   October 8, 1798.
Surety, - Simon Rodgers.

McClun, Thomas Jr. & Elizabeth Bailey   April 10, 1793.
Surety, - John Barrow. Margaret Bailey, mother.

McDonald, Charles & Jemima Carter   December, 1797.
Surety, - William Gilles.

McGuire, Edward & Milisent Doby   July 27, 1774.
    Surety, - Henry Peyton Jr.

McKay, John & Elizabeth Sugars   August 1, 1798.
    Surety, - Samuel Sicks

McKee, Robert & Jane Cather   September 3,1793.
    Surety, - Joseph Cather.

McKeewan, Thomas & Rachel Harny   October 10, 1797.
    Surety, - James McDonald.

McKee, John Ferguson & Jane Marple   January 29, 1799.
    Surety, - Ezekiel Marple.

McKinsey, James & Susannah Bruin   April 25, 1798.
    Surety, - Arthur Carter.

McVicker, William & Dinah Mercer   September, 1797.
    Surety,- Moses Hercer.

Madden, John & Catherine Bonham   May 11, 1793.
    Surety, - Thomas Jones.

Malin, Job & Ann March   May 11, 1793.
    Surety, - Michael March, father.

Maloney, John & Elizabeth Keys   April 12, 1793.
    Surety, - James Dowdell.& John Morgan.

Mark, Henry, & Katy Stone   April 18, 1798.
    Surety, - Lewis Stone, father.

Martin, James Lee & Mary Fry   May 21, 1793.
    Surety, - Christopher Fry.

Mason, John & Hannah Frost   June 8, 1773.
    Surety, - John Frost.   Father William Frost.

Matheny, John & Martha Brown (widow)   October 17, 1797.
    Surety, - William Harper.

Meers, Joshua & Tabitha Stephens   June 26, 1793.
    Surety, - John Windsor Driver. Parents Joseph
                    and Celea Stephens.

Meem, Gilbert & Frances Sumrall   August 1, 1793.
    Surety, - George Beatty. Father James Sumrall.

Mercer, Edward & Mary Dinah Steer   April 29, 1793.
    Surety, - Thomas Babb. Joseph Steer and Grace
    Steer, uncle and aunt of Mary Dinah Steer.

Mercer, Robert and Hannah Mercer   Nov. 30, 1797.
    Surety, - Thomas Babb & Lewis Benett.

Middleton, William & Milly McFesson ? Surety, - John Knester. (?)	October 12, 1797.
Miller, Jacob & Lucy Hicks Surety, - David Hicks.	September 15, 1798.
Millhorn, John & Elizabeth Cackley Surety, - John Cackley.	December 21, 1797.
Mills, Eli & Esther Beaty Surety, - David Beaty.	May 4, 1793.
Monmouth, Jacob & Elizabeth Alexander Surety, - Benjamin Rutherford.	March 9, 1798.
Morley, John & Elizabeth Shepherd Surety, - Richard Shepherd.	June 4, 1792.
Morris, Samuel & Rebecca McDonald Surety, - Jacob Lindsey.	November 2, 1797.
Murphy, Daniel & Susannah Daugherty (widow) Nov. 9, 1797. Surety, - John Daugherty.	
Nabell, Adam & Mary Dunes	June 17, 1791.
Navel, Wennery & Susannah Gray	____ __ 1794.
Neff, Francis & Elizabeth Cooley Surety, - Peter Cooley.	October 5, 1797.
Neill, Charles & Elizabeth Cullen	April 3, 1787.
Neill, Thomas & Abigail Dunn	June 27, 1787.
Newton, Isaac & Hannah Cooper	January 17, 1799.
Nicewanger, John & Sarah Grove	October 8, 1795.
Nulton, John & Christiana Spour	December 13, 1790.
Nelson, John & Catherine Washington	November 3, 1789.

Neill, John & Liddy Abrill   September 30, 1774.
    Surety, - Thomas Smith. Mother Elizabeth Abril.

Nicewanger, Abraham & Lydia Nicewanger   June 22, 1793.

Noblar, John, & Elizabeth Campbell   December 28, 1798.
    Surety, - Jacob Kiger. Parents John & Jane
                                    Campbell.

Noble, John & Mary Perselar (Pickslar) July 2, 1798.
    Surety, - Daniel Miller. Father Jacob Perselar.

Noland, Obed & Priscilla Bailey (widow) September 22, 1798.
    Surety, - Dillan Bridges.

Oglevie, David & Hannah McKay   August 5, 1798.
    Surety, - Joseph Irwin. Parents Job & Ann McKay.

Owens, Nimrod & Bady Smith   August 3, 1793.
    Surety, - Daniel Grubs. Parents Humphrey and
                                    Elizabeth Grubs.

Overstake, Benjamin & Elizabeth Wenkland July 20, 1793.
    Surety, - Henry Wenkland.

Palmer, John & Elizabeth Kendall   June 3, 1793.
    Surety, - Thomas Biggs.

Parker, John & Hannah Millner (spinster) March 27, 1793.
    Surety, - John Jackson & John Ball. Father John
                                    Millner.

Parrell, Joseph & Mary Nixon (spinstress) September 25,1797.
    Surety, - John Clutter.

Paull, William & Elizabeth Bowen   November 2, 1772.
    Surety, - Bartholomew & Thomas B. Bowen.

Payne, James & Elizabeth Overton   December 12, 1797.
    Surety, - Stephen Miller.

Peck, Samuel & Elizabeth Drake   September 18, 1797.
    Surety, - Gershom Drake.

Pender, Daniel & Jane Sill   April 23, 1798.
    Surety, - Aquilla Dyson.

Perry, John & Nancy Anderson   August 31, 1793.
    Surety, - John Hayney.

Phleazer, Abraham & Margaret Goodekuntz   December 8,1797.
    Surety, - George Phleazer.

Price, Benjamin & Rebecca Fisher   August 4, 1798.
    Surety, - Barak Fisher, brother.

Purcell, George & Priscilla Nokes   October 8, 1798.
    Surety, - Baldwin Copping.

Raimey, Isaac & Margaret Dearmont   December 19,1797.
    Surety, - Peter Dearmont.

Rea, Allen & Eleanor Fisher   April 25, 1793.
    Surety, - John Rea.   Consent of Susannah Fisher.

Reed, Thomas & Jane Bonard   July 22, 1793.
    Surety, - Joseph Johnston.

Reeder, Abel & Elizabeth Marquis   November 10,1798.
    Surety, - Mary Marquis.

Reiley, George & Sarah Brown   October 28, 1797.
    Surety, - James Henry.

Rennols, Samuel & Peggy Gilkeson   May 9, 1798.
    Surety, - Edward McGuire.

Reynolds, Thomas & Mary Smith   July 21, 1774.
    Surety, - William Clancy.

Richards, John & Mary Bean   May 31, 1798.
    Surety, - Mordecai Bean.

Roach, Richard & Sarah Lindsey   Sept. 6, 1773.
    Surety, - Jacob Lindsey.   Parents Edmond & Mary
                                       Lindsey.

Roberts, Thomas & Sarah Rankin (spinster)   March 17, 1774.
    Surety, - Mordecai Redd.

Rogers, Owen & Eleanor Nelson   Sept. 1, 1798.
    Surety, - Jacob Jenkins.

Rogers, Robert & Mary Bealer   April 12, 1798.
    Surety, - Jacob Jenkins.

Roper, Nicholas & Mary Horn   October 9, 1797.
    Surety, - James Walker, Esquire

Rout, William & Ann Staze   December 12,1797.
    Surety, - Isaac Chrisman.

Rowzey, William & _____ Hoff (spinster) Nov. 4, 1797.
    Surety, - Morgan Hoff.

Rudolph, George & Christianna Hotsinfiller   May 16, 1793.
Surety, - Joseph Fry.

Rust, Mathew & Deborah Undrell   May 20, 1793.
Surety, - Dale Carter.

Samsell, John & Anna Groves   Sept. 28,1797.
Surety, - Casper Cline

Scoggins, Turner & Elizabeth Archy   May 30, 1793.
Surety, - James Elkins. Mother Ann Archy.

Scroggins, William & Mary Clark   Nov. 28, 1797.
Surety, - Hugh Johnston

Seagler, George & Mary Scell   October 30,1797.
Surety, - Jacob Seagler.

Secrist, George & Ann Fry   August 3, 1793.
Surety, - Benjamin Fry

Scott? Jacob & Eleander Oglesby?   May 31, 1793.
Surety, - William Tate. Father George Oglesby.

Sharp, Spencer & Nancy Arnold   April 9, 1793.
Surety, - James Strother.

Smith, Edward & Elizabeth Bush   June 27, 1777.
Surety, - John Cox. Father Philip Bush.

Smith, Jonathan & Lydia Korcheval   May 4, 1793.
Suarty, - Henry Beatty.

Smoot, James & Mary Cahoon   June 4, 1793.
Surety, - Daniel Cahoon, father.

Snickers, William & Frances Washington   May 28, 1793.
Surety, - Robert Macky.

Snodgrass, James & Mrs. Elizabeth Cusyck   July 8, 1793.
Surety, - Captain John Brady.

Sparks, Elijah & Eliza.Weaver   August 8, 1793.
Surety, - John B. Tilden. Father Frances Weaver.

Spencer, Richard & Mary Malin (Melon)   Sept. 29, 1798.
Surety, - William Malin, brother. Jacob Malin,
father.

Sprout, Thomas & Jane Melton   May 23, 1798.
Surety, - Joseph Carter.

Stickley, Joseph & Peggy Harman   April 12,1798.
Surety, - Mathias Harman.

14.

Strosnider, Casper & Sarah Cyphet   September 9, 1797.
    Surety, - Adam Strosnider.

Stump, Lewis & Hannah Shambaugh   June 22, 1793.
    Surety, - John Stump. Parents Philip & Margaret
                          Shambaugh.

Sumrall, Alexander & Sally Donaldson   December 2, 1797.
    Surety, - Gilbert Meem.

Taylor, William & Alsey Kean   August 1, 1793.
    Surety, - John Kean, father.

Taylor, William & Elizabeth Dunlap   October 19, 1797.
    Surety, - Benjamin Taylor

Thomas, George & Elizabeth Freeman   November 10, 1798.
    Surety, - William Freeman, father.

Trowbridge, David & Mary Grady   September 25, 1797.
    Surety, - Michael Grady.

Vance, James & Ruth Glass   October 1, 1798.
    Surety, - William Sumrall.

Vance, Robert & Mazy Beall   October 24, 1798.
    Surety, - Robert White, Jr.

Vaughan, Vincent & Mary Shite   December 9, 1797.
    Surety, - Stephen Hotspellar.

Wall, Richard & Dosie Griggsby   July 21, 1798.
    Surety, - Original Vroe.

Washington, Fairfax & Sarah Armistead   October 15, 1798.
    Surety, - Alexander Balmain.

Way, Stephen & Mary Richardson   April 24, 1793.
    Surety, - Samuel Richardson, father.

Watkins, Nicholas & Mary Freeman   November 15, 1797.
    Surety, - William Freeman

Watson, James & Lettice Burnett   October 14, 1797.
    Surety, - Rachel Carter.

Watson, Thomas & Martha Moffett (spinster) Nov. 4, 1797.
    Surety, - Walter Moffett.

Weaver, Leonard & Ingle Slusher   August 5, 1793.
    Surety, - Fred Slusher, father.

Weiner, John & Ann Wharf   October 2, 1792.
    Surety, - Michael Humble.

West, Thomas & Elizabeth Dailey   October, 1797.
    Surety, - Province McCormick

Williams, Enoch & Lydia Fulton   September 14,1797.
    Surety, - Thomas Fulton.

Williams, William & Elizabeth Brenan   November 2,1797.
    Surety, - John Brenan.

Willingham, George & Sally Stewart   August 16, 1798.
    Surety, - George Stewart.

Willis, Robert Carter. & Martha Sedwick   December 21,1776.
    Surety, - Valentine Crawford. Father Benjamin Sedwick.

Wolfe, Peter & Anne Cornwell   July 28, 1777.
    Surety, - Jeremiah Garner.

Wood, Robert & Comfort Welsh   April 1, 1774.
    Surety, - Matthew Glenn & Allen McDonald.
    Comfort Welsh daughter of Thomas Welsh, Sr. of
    the Province of Maryland.

Wall, Richard & Nancy Miller   June 7, 1798.
    Surety, - James Cheek. Father Adam Miller.

OMITTED BOND

Henry, Aaron & Ann Aires   September 28,1798.
    Surety, - John Kean & James Henry. Mother Judith
                                        Aires.

Blackmon, Lawrence Owen & Mary Wilson   April 2, 1793.
    Surety, - James Hickman.

MINISTERS' RETURNS.

Abercromby, Robert and Elizabeth Phillips March 14, 1793. C. S.
Acre, John and Catherine Fetherling, Sept. 8, 1789. C. S.
Adams, David and Leannah DeHaven, July 18, 1794. A. B.
Adams, John and Ann Colville, January 9, 1787. J. M.
Adams, Jacob and Rachel Adams, March 19, 1801. J. B.
Adams, John and Catherine Dish, November 18, 1815. G. M. F.
Adams, Joseph and Edah Lupton, Sept. 14, 1816. G. M. F.
Adams, Mathias and Martha Hersha, January 15, 1799. J. W.
Adams, Peter and Eliza Fisher, July 1, 1818. J. D.
Adams, William and Alice Austin, March 15, 1783. A. B.
Adams, William and Sarah Dawson, October 7, 1801. J. W.
Abernathy, John and Susannah Babb, April 26, 1810. C. S.
Ackerman, John and Anna D. Shaver, August 28, 1810. C. S.
Afflick, James and Catharine Hotzenpiller, December 31,1822.J.W.
Ager, William and Elizabeth McFadden, Jan. 30, 1812. J. W.
Albert, Michael and Sarah Anderson, Jan. 9, 1800. J. W.
Albert, Michael and Sarah Kile, Feb. 10, 1817. G.M.F.
Albert, William and Sarah Brewer, April 3, 1792. C.S.
Albin, Andrew and Martha Sutton, October 11, 1796. A. B.
Albin, Elijah and Susan Dalby, Sept. 30, 1812. G.M.F.
Albin, James and Ann Ellis, January 8, 1809. J. W.
Albin, Robert and Elizabeth Carter, Dec. 31, 1821. J. W.
Albin, Samuel and Sarah Smith, Dec. 31, 1806. J. W.
Aldred, Henry and Elizabeth Whipple, June 22, 1786. C.S.
Aldredge, John and Sybilla Reiley, Jan. 27, 1799. C. S.
Ale, John and Elizabeth Sell, March 13, 1788. C. S.
Alexander, James and Jane Peyton, Dec. 27, 1821. T. L.
Alexander, John and Mary Nutt, October 30, 1807. W. H.
Alexander, John and Jemimah Crigler, Jan. 14, 1810. S.O.H.
Alexander, Patrick and Elizabeth Eckstine Oct. 24, 1787. C.S.
Alexander, William and Sarah Cafford, June 2, 1786. C. S.
Alexander, William and Jane Sherrard, Jan. 6, 1789. J. M.
Alexander, William and Mary Green, Feb. 15, 1809. S.O.H.
Alexander, William and Elizabeth Powers, Jan. 12, 1815. J.B.T.
Aliff, John and Catharine Allison, Nov. 20, 1822. G. R.
Allamong, John and Rosannah Snapp, March 6, 1806. C. S.
Allamong, William and Charity Lewis, April 12, 1808. J. W.
Allen, Aquilla and Sarah Ann Trenary, Aug. 1, 1822. J.B. Jr.
Allen, David and Sarah Taylor, Sept. 23, 1808. W. H.
Allen, Jacob and Hannah Shephard, Jan. 5, 1804. J. W.
Allen, Robert and Nancy Rowland, May 1, 1814. J. B. T.
Allen, William and Sally Scroggin, Dec. 29, 1796. W. W.
Allensworth, Amanuel and Kitty Black, Oct. 28, 1798. W.W.
Allensworth, James and Eliza Catlett, Jan. 16, 1810. W.N.
Allison, Rozin and Mary Weer, April 18, 1800. J. W.
Alsaff, Jacob and Mary Shores, Feb. 21, 1811. T. L.
Ambler, John and Catharine Norton (widow), Nov. 21, 1799. C. S.
Amiss, Lewis and Elizabeth Mastin, July 25, 1805. L. C.
Anders, George and Anna White, Sept. 25, 1792. C. S.
Anderson, Abraham and Hannah Howell, Sept. 1, 1791. C. S.
Anderson, Elijah and Miriam Anderson, Nov. 6, 1794. C.S.
Anderson, Eliakim and Jane Anderson, Dec. 30, 1799. J.I.

Anderson, Jacob and Jane Cochran, Sept. 4, 1793. C. S.
Anderson, James and Mary Watson, April 11, 1811. A. B.
Anderson, James and Sarah Bean, Sept. 12, 1811. J. W.
Anderson, Jesse and Catherine Sands, Jan. 7, 1802. J.W.
Anderson, John and Sarah Dawson, April 16, 1807. J.B.T.
Anderson, Nathan and Mary Fridley, May 24, 1786. A.B.
Anderson, Peter and Hannah Boacht, May 27, 1801. J.B.
Anderson, Richard and Sueresa Howell, Dec. 7, 1795. A.B.
Anderson, Richard and Nancy Dowell, Dec. 18, 1789. A. B.
Anderson, Robert and Elizabeth Cryder, Nov. 16, 1820. J.B.T.
Anderson, William and Lydia Morgan, July 24, 1800. J.B.
Angel, Nathaniel and Margaret Francis, Dec. 18, 1792. C.S.
Antrim, James and Ann Pratt, March 8, 1820. T.B.Jr.
Anson, William and Elizabeth Lucas, Feb. 20, 1788. C.S.
Antle, Peter and Deborah Hinton, May 30, 1789. C.S.
Antrim, Joshua and Ann Collins, Feb. 15, 1788. C.S.
Archer, James and Achsah Clevenger, Jan. 26, 1809. J.B.T.
Arisman, Jacob and Elizabeth Babb, August 7, 1812. J.W.
Armistead, Addison Bowles and Mary Howe Peyton, Nov. 15,1804.
                                                        A. B.
Armstrong, William and Ann Blair, March 8, 1791. A.B.
Arnett, Thomas and Lydia Allaway, July 30, 1792. W. H.
Arrington, Richard and Ann Henning, April 29, 1792. C. S.
Arterbourn, Jacob and Levi Williams, Dec. 10, 1801. W. W.
Ash, Francis and Betsy Hand, Feb. 12, 1789. A. B.
Ash, John and Elizabeth Carpenter, Feb. 12, 1787. C.S.
Ashby, Edward and Margaret Penticost, Jan. 15, 1788. J. M.
Ashby, William and Elizabeth Britain, Oct. 28, 1785. A.B.
Ashburn, Henry and Susannah Vincent, Feb. 25, 1794. A.B.
Ashenhurst, John and Nancy Scott, Nov. 4, 1799. J.W.
Ashley, John and Sarah Lanham, Feb. 15, 1810. C. S.
Ashby, Rezin and Maria Davis, May 12, 1820. T. L.
Ashby, Robert and Elizabeth Ash, Nov. 16, 1815. J.B.T.
Ashton, Peter and Mary Ann Shutt, April 15, 1819. J. D.
Ashton, Charles H. B. and Sarah Anderson, Dec. 23,1819. A.B.
Atwell, Samuel and Nancy Ferguson, August 31, 1820. T.L.

Babb, Baley and Deliverance Horner, Sept. 20, 1785. A.B.
Babbs, Charles H. and Rebecca Alloway, Jan. 27, 1789. J.M.
Babb, David and Mary Hensell, Jan. 10, 1805. J. W.
Babb, Henry W. and Grace McCoole, Nov. 10, 1796. A. B.
Babb, Henry and Elizabeth Walker, Jan. 31, 1793. C. S.
Babb, James W. and Rebecca Scarf, Jan. 28, 1813. S. B.
Babb, Peter and Jane Bell, Nov. 9, 1797. A. B.
Babb, Peter and Jane Scarf, March 29, 1819. G.M.F.
Babb, Thomas and Margaret Wilson, Nov. 27, 1788. J. M.
Babb, Thomas and Liddia Dillon, July 24, 1804. W. H.
Babb, Robinson and Rachel Bailey, Nov. 29, 1817. G.M.F.
Badcock, William Henry and Nancy Porter Williams, Feb. 19,
                                                  1793. A.B.
Bailes, John and Elizabeth Lawyer, Oct. 26, 1809. W. H.
Bailes, Moses and Rebecca Stanford, Dec. 29, 1822. T. L.
Bailey, Joel and Rachel Moore, May 3, 1788. J. M.
Bailey, John and Elizabeth Long, Dec. 3, 1785. C. S.
Bailey, Thomas and Elizabeth Albert, June 13, 1802. C. S.
Bailey, William and Phebe Ridgeway, Feb. 9, 1792. C. S.

Baker, Andrew and Mary Wendel, December 3, 1792. C.S.
Baker, Christian and Sarah Slough, Feb. 20, 1789. C. S.
Baker, Hilarius and Mary All'emong, Sept. 28, 1820. J. D.
Baker, John and Alcinda Louisa Tapscott, Dec. 5, 1815. A.B.
Baker, Joseph and Elizabeth Weaver, Dec. 30, 1797. A. B.
Baker, Joseph and Sarah Lockhart, Sept. 10, 1807. C. S.
Baker, Thomas and Sarah Hyland, March 22, 1800. A. B.
Baker, William A. and Elizabeth Foster, July 11, 1809. J.W.
Baldwin,Cornelius and Mary Briscoe, October 16, 1783. A.B.
Baldwin, Cornelius and Nelly Conway Hite, Nov. 28; 1809. A.B.
Baldwin, Cornelius and Susan Pritchard, August 31, 1819. A.B.
Baldwin, Henry and Susannah Manloby, Oct. 21, 1790. C. S.
Baldwin, Joseph C. and Eliza Baldwin, June 6, 1810. A. B.
Baldwin, Joshua and Elizabeth B. George, Feb. 26, 1823. G.M.F.
Baldwin, Robert T. and Sarah Macky, May 14, 1818. A. B.
Baldwin; Thomas Jr. and Mary Kurtz, Jan. 7, 1802. J. W.
Baldwin; William and Elizabeth Mann, Nov. 28, 1805. A. B.
Baldwin, William and Margaret Mahaman, March 26, 1813. J.W.
Ball, George Lewis and Catherine Kerfott, Nov. 12,1816. S.O.H.
Ball, John and Susannah Parkins, Feb. 23, 1804. W. H.
Ball, William and Drusilla Singleton, July 18, 1790. A. B.
Ball, William and Ruth Tracey, Nov. 29, 1792. A. B.
Ball, William and Susan Greggory, Nov. 14, 1814. J. W.
Ballard, Richard and Nelly Hill, Oct. 12, 1786. A. B.
Bar, James and Sarah Price, April 17, 1814. J. W.
Barber, James and Mary Harper, Sept. 11, 1793. C.S.
Barbi, Thomas and Patty Braham, Oct. 17, 1786. A. B.
Barr, Francis and Nancy Willington, Sept. 10, 1801. A. B.
Barley, Adam and Lydia Merber, May 9, 1807. J. W.
Barley, Daniel and Catherine Stump, Oct. 17, 1805. C. S.
Barley, David and Sarah Bostion, Nov. 30, 1800. C. S.
Barley, John and Sarah Marsh, Oct. 30, 1803. A. B.
Banks, Edward and Barbara Hott, June 16, 1807. J. W;
Barnes, Edward and Mary Moore, Feb. 27, 1788. C. S.
Barns, Joseph and Mary Sham?, Sept. 24, 1817. J.B.T.
Barnet, Lewis and Mary Iles, Sept. 4, 1788. C. S.
Barpoe, Jacob and Catherine Thomas, Feb. 4, 1790. C.S.
Barker, Moses and Margaret Brison, July 23, 1807. J.B.T.
Barr, Michael and Grace Jones, March 4, 1799. J. W.
Barr, William and Elizabeth Yoe, Dec. 24, 1818. J.B.T.
Barnett, Ambrose and Margaret Helm, June 8, 1791. W. H.
Barnett, John and Drusilla Rowland, Sept. 17, 1793. A. B.
Barnett, John and Mary Severns, Sept. 6, 1812. W.H.
Barrack, Jacob and Jane Harrison, Oct. 5, 1802. J.W.
Barrack, John and Margaret Lawyer, ___ 1, 1796. A.B.
Barrett, Benjamin and Sarah Ward, June 18, 1801. A. B.
Barrett, David Jr. and Winifred Kirby, Feb. 28, 1807. W.H.
Barrett, Jonathan and Rachel George, Nov. 9, 1787. C. S.
Barrett, Thomas and Margaret Warden, May 15, 1799. J. W.
Bartlett, Henry and Elizabeth Davis, Jan. 2, 1799. J. I.
Bartlett, James and Sally R. Lambkin, March 12, 1789. J.W.
Bartlett, William and Eleanor Grubbs, Jan. 20, 1823. J.B.Jr.
Barton, Galbraith and Eleanor Talbot, Sept. 6, 1798. T.B.Jr.
Bassey, Jeremiah and Mary Clevenger, April 17, 1792. E.P.
Bateman, Henry and Grace Alsop, July 10, 1782. J.M.
Batt, Moses and Sarah Edwards, Feb. 28, 1790. W. H.

Baylis, John E. and Modlin Snapp, Feb. 1, 1813. S.B.
Baylis, Thomas B. and Mary K. Wilson, Feb. 3, 1825. J.B.T.
Bazer, Asaph and Ruth Wood, May 13, 1788. S.O.H.
Beagler, James and Ann Hess, April 16, 1795. A.B.
Beales, Benjamin and Sarah Curlett, Nov. 9, 1801. J.W.
Bean, Eli and Sarah Hall, Nov. 23, 1822. G.M.F.
Bean, John and Eve Sinsinning, October 27, 1789. A.B.
Bean, John and Molly Ledford, March 8, 1789. A.B.
Bean, William and Polly Mauck, Aug. _ 1804. J.B.T.
Bear, Frederick and Molly Shrack, April 5, 1798. C.S.
Bear, Peter and Susannah Burchell, Jan. 29, 1798. A.B.
Beaty, James and Sidney Riley, Oct. 31, 1805. J.W.
Beatty, Joshua and Edith Cleavenger, Aug. 3, 1802. W.W.
Beatty, Samuel and Mary Steel, Aug. 3, 1820. T.B.Jr.
Beaty, William and Maryann Romine, Jan. 11; 1803. L.C.
Beavers, Moses and Hannah Halbert, Nov. 17; 1803. A. B.
Beavers, Robert and Mary Marquis, March 23, 1826. T.L.
Beck, James and Nancy Jones Mustin, Dec. 29, 1825. T.L.
Beckley, Charles and Elizabeth Tapp, April 3, 1816. J.B.T.
Beddow, George and Elsey Lewis, April 4, 1805. J.W.
Beddow, George and Hester Tucker, Jan. 8, 1813. W. H.
Bedinger, Daniel and Sarah Rutherford, April 26, 1791. A. B.
Beemer, John and Elizabeth Kerns, March 19, 1818. J.B.T.
Belfield, John Wright and Mary Beall Daingerfield. May
                                26, 1814. A. B.
Bell, Anthony and Mary McCool, May 29, 1800. J. W.
Bell, Ferguson and Rebecca Eskridge, Feb. 9, 1797. A.H.
Bell, George and Elizabeth Weaver, April 7, 1825. J.B.T.
Bell, James and Mary Ferguson, Dec. 19, 1796. J. I.
Bell, John and Elizabeth Sherrard, Oct. 20, 1796. A.B.
Bell, John and Mary Campbell, Jan. 14, 1792. W. H.
Bell, Samuel and Jane Smith, Dec. 10, 1789. A. B.
Bell, Squire and Elizabeth Bazzell, April 11, 1824. T.L.
Berlyn, Jacob and Polly Krouse, Nov. 16, 1822. T.K.
Benn, Robert and Franky Riley, Dec. 27, 1807. W. H.
Bennegar, George and Mary Bennett, Feb. 8, 1787. C. S.
Bennet, George and Margaret Parrell, Feb. 30, 1814. J. W.
Bennet, Henry and Eury Morgan, April 18, 1805. A. B.
Bennet, Robert and Lydia Anderson, March 28, 1805. A. B.
Bennett, John and Elizabeth Long, Oct. 28, 1792. A. B.
Bennett, William and Sarah Oglesby, Feb. 26, 1788. C.S.
Benson, William and Isabella Eliche Calmes, Jan. 13,1788. J.M.
Benson, William and Mary Irvin, Oct. 11, 1782. J.M.
Bentley, John B. and Elizabeth Hollinback, Oct. 13, 1811. C.S.
Beohn, Mr. and I. Watson, Dec. 26, 1816. A.A.S.
Berkel, William and Mary Sherndorfer, Nov. 1, 1785. C.S.
Berkley, Reuben L. and Nancy D. Hancock, July 28, 1818. W.H.
Berlin, Jacob and Sarah Handle, Sept. 10, 1807. L.S.
Bernerd, Frederick August and Dorothea Helm, Oct. 17,1785.C.S.
Berry, Benjamin and Winney Berry, Dec. 21, 1789. A. W.
Berry, George and Lucinda Settle, Jan. 22, 1807. J.B.T.
Berry, Isaac and Debby Perfater, Dec. 24, 1791. A.B.
Berry, John and Lettice McKay, Oct. 31, 1785. A. B.
Berry, John and Margaret Cook, Oct. 7, 1790. A. B.
Berry, Samuel and Sarah Kendall, Oct. 26, 1799. A.B.
Berry, Thornly and Betsy W. Kendal, May 16, 1800. J.I.

Bertelow, Joshua and Margaret Smith, Dec. 23, 1818. J. D.
Beveridge, John and Nancy Jones, Aug. 26, 1809. A. B.
Biggs, Thomas and Eve House, Sept. 11, 1790. W. H.
Binegar, John and Ann Merl, April 10, 1800. J. B.
Bishop, Elisha and Elizabeth Ellis, April 13, 1786. A.B.
Bishop, Greenbury, and Mary White, April 5, 1807. A.B.
Bishop, Joseph and Ann King, Nov. 13, 1792. A. B.
Bishop, Joshua Jr. and Margaret Limes, Nov. 18, 1806. T.A.
Bishop, Lloyd and Elizabeth Bishop, Nov. 13, 1803. A. B.
Bishop, Thomas and Elizabeth Spurrier, Oct. 13, 1796. A.B.
Bixler, Abraham and Sara Rhodes, March 12, 1807. J. W.
Black, George and Rhody Anderson, Aug. 31, 1786, C. S.
Black, John and Catherine Weaver, Nov. 9, 1786. C. S.
Blackart, Luke and Rebecca Albin, July 30, 1808. J. W.
Blair, Beverly and Ann Beverly Whiting, Jan. 12, 1812. A.B.
Blair, William and Elizabeth Bryan, July 11, 1800. A.B.
Blakemore, George and Elizabeth Mauzey, May 26, 1783. J.M.
Blakemore, Marquis Q. and Rebecca Winston Chandler, March
                                        14, 1813. W. Hill
Blakemore, Thomas and Elizabeth W. Brooke, Aug. 30, 1825. W.H.
Blundell, William and Peggy Marcus, Feb. 19, 1795. A. B.
Blythe, William and Mary Hueston, Feb. 15, 1799. A.B.
Boarer, George and Mary Tolman, July 23, 1797. A. B.
Bogan, John and Catherine Lewis, June 12, 1788. A.B.
Boling, George and Mary Stewart, Sept. 12, 1822. T. L.
Boling, William and Margaret Moore, Aug. 15, 1826. T. L.
Bolton, Isaac and Charity Norman, Nov. 9, 1811. J. W.
Bond, John and Mary Bennett, April 6, 1788. A. B.
Bond, Samuel and Mary Longacre, May 29, 1787. C. S.
Bonde, Rudolph T. C. and Elizabeth Ewing, Jan. 28, 1819. J.B.T.
Bonecutter, Christopher and Elizabeth Loy, Sept. 14, 1812. J.W.
Bonecutter, George and Phoebe Wright, Dec. 31, 1806. J.W.
Boneham, Hezekiah and Ann Christian, July 15, 1792. E. P.
Bonham, Nathan and Elizabeth Dean, June 8, 1790. A. B.
Bonham, Samuel and Maria Ann Sowers, Nov. 22, 1805. W. Hill
Bonham, Smith and Ann Cleavenger, May 24, 1807. L.C
Bonsell, Joseph Jr. and Phebe Adams, June 4, 1805. J.W.
Bookless, David and Mary Balentine, Aug. 26, 1782. J.M.
Booling, John and Jenny Hood, Oct. 24, 1803. J. I.
Booth, George and Elizabeth Washington, June 11, 1795. A.B.
Booth, Isaac and Sarah Henshaw, Jan. 27, 1803. A. B.
Borders, Matthias and Nelly Awbrey, April 7, 1796. A. B.
Boram, William and Mary Brooks, Aug. 26, 1800. W. W.
Borden, James and Winney Hankins, Dec. 25, 1806. L. C.
Borders, George and Rebecca Fred, May 18, 1803. C. S.
Borer, Martin and Caty Kelley, Sept. 17, 1792. C. S.
Boucher, Abraham and Margaret Mackley, March 5, 1812. J.W.
Bowen, Charles and Nancy Howard, Feb. 8, 1803. A. B.
Bowen, Maredith and Lucy Drake, Nov. 15, 1810. G. M. F.
Bowen, Meredith and Catherine Carper, May 24, 1819. G.M.F.
Bowen, Morton and Elizabeth Greenlee, Dec. 16, 1819. W. Hill
Bowen, Richard and Elizabeth Lindsay, June 18, 1788. A.B.
Bowers, Adam and Elizabeth Wetzell, May 29, 1808. W. Hill.
Bower, George and Kitty Albert, Nov. 9, 1788. C. S.
Bowland, David and Elizabeth Rumduc, July 16, 1801. J.B.
Bowman, Daniel and Judith Good, Aug. 4, 1798. C. S.
Bowman, Elias and Eve Rickert, Nov. 10, 1789. C. S.

Bowman, Henry and Susannah Suberly, Aug. 1, 1790. C. S.
Bowman, Isaac and Mary Cline, Dec. 7, 1792. N. L.
Bowman, John and Mary Ann Grim, March 16, 1822. J.B.T.
Boxer, John and Elizabeth Rutter, Nov. 18, 1792. C. S.
Boxell, John and Jane Orr, Jan. 27, 1793. A. B.
Boxwell, Joseph and Senrah Bonham, May 31, 1796. A. B.
Boxwell, Robert and Elizabeth Orr, July 6, 1793. A. B.
Boyce, John and Catherine Lowry, Jan. 16, 1815. J. W.
Boyer, Jacob and Susan Ritenour, Feb. 21, 1824, R.F.F.
Boyers, Jacob and Elizabeth Lauck, April 14, 1805. J. W.
Boyse, David and Ann Williams, Aug. 27, 1795. A. B.
Brabham, Joseph and Nancy Wiley, May 18, 1820. T. L.
Bragg, Thomas and Edy Cockrell, Nov. 15, 1816. S.O.H.
Brahan, Henry and M ry Suberly, Aug. 20, 1797. C. S.
Braithwaite, Benjamin and Maria Hoffman, Nov. 7, 1824. J.D.
Branner, William and Susannah Smith, Nov. 12, 1817. G.M.F.
Branson, Robert and Bulah Painter, Nov. 14, 1787. C. S.
Branson, William B. and Elizabeth Frances Hale, Oct. 24, 1822. J. W.
Branton, Alexander and Rebecca Shull, May 9, 1822. J.B.
Bray, Isiah and Mary Frazier, Dec. 30, 1806. A. B.
Bredine, Henry and Jane Kidd, March 5, 1807. W. Hill
Breedlove, Charles and Theodosia Clevenger, May 28, 1787. C.S.
Breige, James and Amanda F. Shepherd, Oct. 6, 1824. J.B.T.
Brent, George and Susannah Anderson, Dec. 10, 1812. A. B.
Brew, Henry and Catherine Suberly, April 18, 1791. C. S.
Brewbaker, Ronimus and Elizabeth Fustnerin, May 9, 1787. A.B.
Briel, Henry and Elizabeth Orndorff, Nov. 12, 1796. C. S.
Briell,-Michaell and Eve Foss, Oct. 16, 1787. C. S.
Briley, William and Jane Atwood, Jan. 13, 1825. T. L.
Brill, George and Elizabeth Bachelor, June 30, 1789. C. S.
Brill, Joseph and Rebecca Orndorff, April 4, 1822. J.B.T.
Brinker, George and Elizabeth Haney, Oct. 30, 1810. S.O.H.
Briscoe, Cuthbert and Elizabeth Thompson, July 6, 1800. A.B.
Briscoe, James and Catherine Bazzle, May 8, 1822. T. L.
Brison, Benjamin and Ann White, Oct. 14, 1805. J.B.T.
Brison, Robert and Elizabeth Bowlen, Sept. 16, 1784. J. M.
Brittain, Jacob and Margaret Martin, Aug. 19, 1793. N. L.
Britton, Jonah and Patsy Lauck, Dec. 30, 1820. G.M.F.
Britton, Lesse and Susannah Noland, April 1, 1802. J.B.
Broce, Joe and Elizabeth Rice, Feb. 25, 1790. E. P.
Brook, Stephen and Anne Hart, Oct. 25, 1791. C. S.
Brookover, Asael and Margaret Griffin, Oct. 13, 1796. A. B.
Brookover, John and Elizabeth Pertley, Jan. 10, 1787. J. M.
Brooks, William and Susannah Congrove, March 30, 1803. R.F.
Brotherton, John and Mary Hodge, April 24, 1823. G.R.
Brown, Adam and Christiana Zuber, June 6, 1799. A. B.
Brown, Daniel and Sarah Southward, Jan. 1, 1788. C. S.
Brown, Daniel and Rachel Henson, Dec. 22, 1793. E. P.
Brown, David Jr. and Mary Parkins, May 1; 1799. C. S.
Brown, David and Janey Hancher, March 22, 1804. A. B.
Brown, Francis C. and Mary Ann Newman, July 16, 1822. W. M.
Brown, James and Jane McNeill, Dec. 13, 1787. A. B.
Brown, James and Elizabeth Cunningham, Feb. 8, 1807. W. Hill
Brown, James and Betsy Hess, Feb. 17, 1811. S. O. H.
Brown, Jesse and Kitty Poe, Nov. 20, 1791. C. S.
Brown, John and Harriet Johnson, May 6, 1817. T. L.

Brown, Joseph and Mary Smith, July 10, 1793. A. B.
Brown, Joseph and Winifred Headly, Sept. 21, 1806. B. D.
Brown, Thomas and Martha Myers, Feb. 2, 1808. G. R.
Brown, Thomas and Sarah Williams, July 25, 1810. J.B.T.
Brown, Thomas and Ann Carter, Dec. 4, 1812. W. Hill.
Brown, William and Sally Bucher, June 6, 1799. C. S.
Brownfield, Thomas and Elizabeth Fisher, May 16, 1793. C.S.
Browning, Charles D. and Rebecca Moore, Sept. 21, 1824. G. H.
Bruce, James and Lydia Joliffe, Nov. 6, 1783. A. B.
Bruce, John and Sidney Smith, April 6, 1820. A. B.
Brualey, Lewis and Mary Swartz, Feb. 10, 1816. G.M.F.
Bruner, John and Mary Coe, Nov. 1, 1818. T. K.
Brunner, Jacob and Alley Capper, Jan. 31, 1805. C. S.
Brure, James and Bythe Vincent, March 22; 1791. I. L.
Bryan, Charles and Mary Walters, Nov. 28, 1785. C. S.
Bryant, James and Hannah Sample, Aug. 5, 1794. C. S.
Bryan, Joseph and Ann Carter, Feb. 9, 1812. E. H.
Bryant, Samuel and Anne Williams, Jan. 2, 1794. A. B.
Bryarly, David and Jane Murray, May 22, 1806. W. Hill
Bryarly, David and Matilda Ann Gordon, June 16, 1814. A. S.
Bryarly, David and Eliza Brent, Dec. 12, 1816. A. S.
Bryarly, Samuel and Lucy Helm, March 7, 1793. N. L.
Bryce, John and Catherine Mayhew, Sept. 15, 1796. A. B.
Bryson, Benjamin and Mary Stephens, August 29, 1820. J.B.T.
Bryst, Henry, and Catherine Wax, August 14, 1787. A. B.
Bucher, Jacob and Caty Snyder, Dec.9, 1802. C. S.
Bucher, John and Polly Schneider, Oct. 25, 1804. C. S.
Buchanan, Alexander Pitt and Sarah Hite, Jan. 14, 1794. A.B.
Bucher, Jacob and Margaret Crum, March 15, 1795. C.S.
Buck, Warner and Barbara Slusher, March 26, 1782. J. H.
Buckingham, Charles and Fanny Smith, Feb. 4, 1788. A. B.
Buckley, Job and Susannah Newcomb, May 13, 1793. N. L.
Buckley, Joshua and Mary Catterlin, June 10, 1790. A. B.
Buff, John and Eleanor Vanort, Dec. 17, 1795. A. B.
Bulger, James and Elizabeth Madden, April 5, 1806. W. Hill
Bull, Samuel and Betty Waldon, Oct. 19, 1793. E. P.
Bulger, Reuben and Sarah Tilman, April 19, 1820. J. W.
Bulger, William and Catherine Castleman, March 18, 1823. T.L.
Buringer, Charles R. and Margaret McCormick, Dec. 7, 1826. T.W.
Burk, John and Susannah Shuler, Aug. 9, 1787. A. B.
Burk, Isaac and Lydia Woodrow, Jan. 6, 1791. A. B.
Burke, Isaac and Sarah England (widow Friedley) June 22, 1792.
                                                       C. S.
Burk, Thomas and Rachel Pickering, Jan. 16, 1810. W. Hill
Burke, Thomas and Elizabeth Eddy, July 2, 1807. W. Hill
Burkhammer, Philip and Sarah Dick, Jan. 29, 1799. A. B.
Burkley, Abraham and Sally Peters, April 29, 1822. J.B.T.
Burton, Benjamin and Eliza H. S. Ship, Sept. 14, 1820. J.L.D.
Burton, Samuel and Mary Fulk, Oct. 5, 1795. A. B.
Burlyn, Philip and Fanny Gantt, Sept. 12, 1813. W. H.
Burroughs, Philip and Susannah John, Jan. 17, 1802. R. F.
Burwell, Philip and Elizabeth Page, Nov. 10, 1797. A. B.
Bush, Andrew and Mary Correll, Sept. 13, 1815. G.M.F
Bush, Caspar and Patience Adams, April 26, 1786. A. B.
Bush, Cornelius and Abigail Wilcox, Aug. 23, 1790. W. H.
Bush, William and Eva Maria Barley, Jan. 24, 1802. C. S.
Bushman, Henry and Libby Houseman, Oct. 25, 1792. W. H.

Butcher, Jeremiah C. and Hannah Thompson, April 6, 1816. G.M.
Butterfield, John and Edith Cloud, Oct. 10, 1808. J. W.
Butterfield, Thomas and Lydia White, Feb. 16, 1795. C.S.
Butterfield, Thomas and Ann Newbury, April 24, 1788. C.S.
Butler, Jacob and Rebecca Hott, Dec. 12, 1814. G.M.F.
Butler, John and Elizabeth Ward, Aug. 16, 1796. A. B.
Butler, John and Catherine Pingstaff, Oct. 24, 1803. A. B.
Butler, John and Susannah Grice, April 13, 1811. J. W.
Butler, Joseph and Lydia Rees, April 25, 1815. J. W.
Butler, Thomas and Susannah Baker, Sept. 4, 1794. C. S.
Buzzard, David and Louisa Baker, Feb. 1, 1822. J. D.
Byland, James and Sarah McCrittan, Feb. 28, 1802. J. W.

Cable, Jacob and Phoebe Crupper, April 18, 1808. A. B.
Cackley, Abraham and Christina Whissend, Nov. 26, 1793. C.S.
Cahoon, Samuel and Polly Anderson, Aug. 13, 1804. J. W.
Cain, John and Chloe Horton, Oct. 3, 1797. W.W.
Cain, Levi and Ruth Vance, Jan. 3, 1793. S. H.
Caldwell, Joseph and Jane Holliday, Dec. 18, 1792. A. B.
Caldwell, Joseph and Mary Griffith, (Widow) Sept. 8, 1788. A.
Callen, James and Elizabeth Montgomery, April 19, 1820. J. Mc
Calvert, John and Ann Parrell, Jan. 21, 1821. J. McC.
Campbell, Iver and Elizabeth Kiger, Jan. 8, 1804. A. B.
Campbell, Jacob and Polly Hinton, Dec. 20, 1788. C. S.
Campbell, James and Mary Rogers, Jan. 27, 1790. A. B.
Campbell, John and Eliza Buchannon, Feb. 12, 1791. W. H.
Campbell, John and Ruth Hodgson, May 17, 1800. J. B.
Campbell, John and Dolitha Catlett, March 10, 1803. W. Hill.
Campbell, Thomas and Ann Hall, March 19, 1811. J. W.
Campbell, William and Mary Johnston, Nov. 5, 1799. J. W.
Campbell, William and Amey McNelly, Oct. 14, 1802. A. B.
Campbell, William and Harriet Reed, April 3, 1811. J.B.T.
Campbell, William and Esther Fisher, Nov. 25, 1819. J. D.
Canron, John and Sarah Ducker, April 4, 1791. W. H.
Canavan, William and Ann Vanort, April 15, 1798. W. W.
Candy, James and Elizabeth Lion, Feb. 15, 1791. B. S.
Cannister, John and Hannah Breech, Oct. 8, 1787. A. B.
Cape, Joseph and Hannah Davis, Oct. 27, 1803. A. B.
Capper, David and Hannah Wingfield, Dec. 29, 1808. J.B.T.
Capper, William and Mary Coulter, March 13, 1803. A. B.
Carlile, John D. and Sarah Holliday, Sept. 25, 1812. A.A.S.
Carmichael, Daniel and Nancy Lions, June 11, 1792. B. S.
Carmer, Christian and Mary Ehrheart, Dec. 11, 1787. C. S.
Carn, Edward and Elizabeth Light, Jan. 30, 1787. C. S.
Carol, Daniel and Elizabeth Emett, Dec. 1, 1791. L. C.
Carpenter, James and Peggy Alexander, April 13, 1797. A.B.
Carpenter, Matthew and Harriet Benson, Feb. 27, 1817. T. L.
Carper, Frederick and Mary Sheaer, Jan. 1, 1788. C. S.
Carper, Jacob and Eliza Keller, Nov. 28, 1822. G.M.F.
Carper, John and Nancy Bowles, Dec. 1, 1811. C. S.
Carper, John and Christiana Lawyer, March 12, 1816. G.M.F.
Carper, William and Margaret Ritter, March 28, 1786. C. S.
Carrell, Lemuel and Sophia German, Oct. 18, 1819. G.M.F.
Carroll, Colin and Ann Littler, Sept. 4, 1792. W. H.
Carroll, Dempsey and Jane Arnold, Jan. 4, 1822. J. W.

Carroll, Jesse and Jenney Nutt, Feb. 18, 1800. J. W.
Carroll, John and Philadelphia Ashby July 25, 1822. T. L.
Carroll, William and Elizabeth Morgan, Oct. 16, 1800. A. B.
Carson, Beaty and Elenor Crockwell, April 6, 1801. J. W.
Carson, Joseph and Mary Fisher, July 15, 1792. A. B.
Carson, Joseph and Mary Ann Reed, July 15, 1812. J.B.T.
Carson, Simon and Eliza Rogers, Oct. 8, 1785. J. M.
Carson, Simon and Jane Anderson, May 22, 1817. J. B. T.
Carter, Adam and Barbara Shafuer, Nov. 9, 1822. G.M.F.
Carter, Alexander and Tracy Settle, Nov. 25, 1802. R. F.
Carter, Arthur and Mary Kerfoot, Oct. 23, 1792. C. S.
Carter, Arthur W. and Ruth M. Noble, Sept. 3, 1822. D.D.
Carter, Benjamin and Sidney Peach, March 18, 1806. C. S.
Carter, Edmond and Elizabeth Pierce, Dec. 7, 1796. A. B.
Carter, Ezekiel and Ann Brookover, Nov. 2, 1785. C. S.
Carter, George Washington and Mary Burwell, October 3, 1812.
A. B.
Carter, James and Margaret Pickens, March 22, 1804. W. H.
Carter, James and Charlotte Raworth, Oct. 12, 1809. J. W.
Carter, John and Rebecca Rowland, Dec. 30, 1806. J. W.
Carter, Joseph and Elizabeth Pierce, Nov. 13, 1791. R. S.
Carter, Joseph and Ann Williams, March 28, 1797. J. I.
Carter, Joseph and Ann Simpson, April 14, 1805. A. B.
Carter, Joseph K. and Elizabeth Carter, Nov. 6, 1816. W.H.
Carter, Joseph and Elizabeth Lupton, Jan. 1, 1817. G.M.F.
Carter, Joseph W. and Elizabeth Barnett, May 2, 1826. T.L.
Carter, Richard and Esther Rogers, June 29, 1815, J.B.T.
Castleman, Alfred and Margaret Milton, Sept. 29, 1825. T. L.
Castleman, George and Jane Burchell, April 26, 1818. T.L.
Cartmell, Edward and Porsinna Bailey, March 22, 1791. S. H.
Cartmell, John and Christiana Frye, April 23, 1782. J.M.
Cartmell, Joseph and Sally Lintz, April 19, 1804. A. B.
Cartmell, Martin and Ann Ball, July 10, 1808. A. B.
Cartmell, Nathaniel and Sarah Bean, April 23, 1807. C. S.
Cartmell, Solomon and Elizabeth Rife, Jan. 26, 1792. C. S.
Carty, William and Polly Weaver, Nov. 9, 1799. A. B.
Carver, Valentine and Barbara Hoier, May 21, 1793. A. B.
Carver, William and Franky Howell, Sept. 16, 1784. J. M.
Cashmore, Edward and Delia Clevenger, Aug. 29, 1810. A. B.
Cassady, Thomas and Barbara Fulk, Nov. 15, 1787. C. S.
Carter , Thomas and Mary Stanbury, Nov. 12, 1794. C. S.
Castleman, Benjamin and Elizabeth Goff, Feb. 5, 1801. C.S.
Castleman, Thomas and Hannah Bushrod Frost, Feb. 26, 1807. A.
Cather, David and Delila Williams, May 2, 1824. T. L.
Cather, Jasper and Sarah Moore, March 27, 1786. C. S.
Cather, John and Elizabeth McKee, Feb. 13, 1800. A. B.
Catlett, Elijah and Peggy Sperry, Feb. 4, 1816. W. N.
Catlett, Horatio and Molly Ann Catlett, Dec. 22, 1809. W.H.
Catlett, Jesse and Ruth Bonham, Feb. 9, 1792. E. P.
Catlett, Joseph and Nancy Allensworth, Jan. 6, 1801. W.W.
Catlett, Nimrod and Sarah Poyles, Jan. 13, 1807. W. H.
Catlett, Thomas and Polly Poyles, Jan. 20, 1808. W. H.
Catlett, William and Lucy Ashby, Nov. 30, 1803. W. D.
Catterline, Darby and Thurza Elkins, March 9, 1799. J. I.
Catterline, Joseph and Sarah Brecount, June 6, 1793. N.L.
Caterlin, William and Rachel Drake, Nov. 12, 1788. J. M.
Catterlin, Joseph and Mary Mercer, June 10, 1801. A. B.

Cauthorn, Dabney and Caroline Lloyd, Sept. 6, 1821. T. L.
Cave, John and Elizabeth White, Jan. 31, 1812. J. W.
Chamberline, Joseph and Susannah Dannel, Jan. 6, 1812. A.B.
Chamblain, Ezekiol and Elizabeth Romine, Dec. 8, 1792. N.L.
Chapin, George and Elizabeth McDonald, Nov. 9, 1794. A. B.
Chapman, Elias and Sarah Gibons, Jan. 23, 1791. R. S.
Chapman, John and Jane Caldwell, March 14, 1794. A. B.
Chapman, Jehosaphat and Eleanor Gibbons, Jan. 4, 1791. A.B.
Chapman, Joseph and Polly Mulinex, Sept. 17, 1807. A. B.
Chapman, Thomas and Mary Stone, Dec. 24, 1797. A. B.
Chapman, Thomas and Catherine Lemley, Oct. 20, 1820. J.B.T.
Chapman, Valentine and Ruth Stevens, Feb. 12, 1783. A. B.
Chapman, William and Fanny Rust, Sept. 14, 1786. J. M.
Chapman, William and Sarah Royer, Sept. 12, 1812. J. W.
Charlton, Thomas and Elizabeth Haymaker, Sept. 13, 1801. J.B.
Chastain, Lewis and Alice Sherman, Sept. 25, 1801. J.W.
Chenowith, James and Rebecca Bruce, Sept. 21, 1790. W.H.
Chenowith, John and Susannah Seal, Feb. 4, 1807. J. W.
Cheshire, John and Jooly Grubbs, Dec. 19, 1803. J. I.
Chew, William and Lydia Hanshaw, March 31, 1803. J. W.
Childs, Alexander and Anna Maria Griffith, Nov. 9, 1798. J.W.
Chiles, Griffin and Mary Ann Cole, Nov. 2, 1821. J. W.
Chiles, Mason and Elizabeth Cain, Feb. 20 1822. G. R.
Chitter, Joseph Powett and Margaret Reid, Dec. 18, 1792. C.S.
Chrisman, George and Dorothea Saunders, March 14, 1818. J.F.
Chrisman, Joseph and Jane Chrisman, April 4, 1826. J. A.
Chrisman, Peter and Jane Hobson, Dec. 27, 1787. A.B.
Christey, Hugh and Catherine Rogers, Aug. 27, 1804. J. W.
Christy, Samuel and Elizabeth Light, Jan. 4, 1821. J. P.
Churchman, Edward and Edith Clevenger, Aug. 30, 1792. E.P.
Chusick, David and Rachel Craven, Nov. 14, 1791. R. S.
Clabough, Robert and Sarah Perine, Jan. 22, 1794. C.S.
Clair, Edward and Eliza Gibbs, May 29, 1790. C. S.
Clark, Edward and Mary Clark, Nov. 7, 1811. A.B.
Clark, George and Daisey Farmer, May 9, 1793. C. S.
Clark, John and Sarah Jacobs, Oct. 20, 1796. A. B.
Clark, John Payne and Stacy Glasscock, Sept. 28, 1799. A.B.
Clark, John S. and Catherine Ewing, May 19, 1818. J.B.T.
Clark, Joseph and Mary Hampton, Jan. 1, 1784. J. M.
Clark, Nathan and Elizabeth Matson, April 4, 1786. C. S.
Clark, Septimus and Jane Opie, July ? 1806. J.B.T.
Clark, Thomas and Sarah Crockwell, Sept. 5, 1787. A. B.
Clark, William and Margaret Lewis, Nov. 7, 1806. J. W.
Claspill, Robert and Elizabeth Smith, Sept. 26, 1809. J.W.
Clawson, Cornelius and Betsy Harrison, April 25, 1801. J.W.
Clavenger, John and Peggy Garner, March 11, 1788. A.B.
Clear, Thomas and Julia Minser, Nov. 5, 1823. J.W.
Clements, Samuel and Margaret Mayhew, Nov. 30, 1796. A.B.
Cleveland, Samuel and Mary Stephens, Sept. 1, 1791. L. C.
Clevenger, Enos and Christena Crouse, March 28, 1824. T.K.
Cleavenger, David and Polly Trenary, Sept. 17, 1807. L.C.
Clevenger, Aden and Sally Beadles, Sept. 27, 1801. L.C.
Clevenger, Asa and Rebecca Danks, Oct. 8, 1809. J.B.T.
Clevenger, George and Polly Fawcett, June 2, 1790. A.B.
Clevenger, George and Rachael Cooper, Oct. 23, 1797. A.B.
Clevenger, Isaac and Catherine Whitman, April 24, 1792. C.S.
Clevenger, Jacob and Catherine Thomlin, Aug. 26, 1795. E.P.

Clevenger, Jacob and Elizabeth Krouse, Jan. 4, 1816. J.B.T.
Clevinger, John and Nancy Stothard, April 27, 1799. A. B.
Cleavenger, James and Martha McGraw, July 17, 1786. C. S.
Clevenger, Maholan and Betsy Clark, June 29, 1803. L. C.
Cleavenger, William and Omeny Powers, Aug. 22, 1799. J.W.
Clevenger, William and Martha Gilham, April 29, 1817. A.S.
Clowser, Henry and Sarah Frye, Jan. 12, 1790. C.S.
Cline, Hiram and Elizabeth Green, April 15, 1812. J.W.
Cloud, Daniel and Elizabeth Hampton, Feb. 6, 1792. L.W.
Cloud, Isaac B. and Lettitia Buck, Jan. 5, 1826. T.B. Jr.
Cloud, Mordecai and Rebecca B. Hickman, Feb. 9, 1820. R.B.
Cloud, William and Mary Smith, Oct. 29, 1817. G.M.F.
Clows, Thomas and Fanny Hackley, Sept. 23, 1819. T.B.Jr.
Clowser, Benjamin and Eliza Shreck, Dec. 21, 1823. J.W.
Clowser, Henry and Regina Rozenburger, June 5, 1820. G.R.
Clowser, John and Magdalene Kackley, June 9, 1811. C. S.
Clutter, Jacob and _____ McIlways, March 12, 1792. E.P.
Clyne, John and Elizabeth Newcomb, Feb. 3, 1806. A. B.
Clyne, Philip and Elizabeth Switzer, March 31, 1791. C.S.
Coats, Aquilla and Rachel Pidgeon, May 15, 1823.
Cochran, James and Mary Hogan, Sept. 24, 1788. A. B.
Cochran, John and Jane Trig, Dec. 15, 1804. J. W.
Cochran, John and Helen Reed, Oct. 27, 1811. W. H.
Cochran, Landon and Susan Trisler, Jan. 7, 1815, J. W.
Cochran, William and Rachel Curlett, Sept. 27, 1789. C. S.
Cocks, John and Mary Baldwin, Aug. 8, 1790. A. B.
Coddington, Benjamin and Ann McVee, Oct. 28, 1788. A. B.
Coddy, John and Rebecca McDanial, April 19, 1792. B. S.
Coe, Daniel and Catherine Bogent, Feb. 28, 1822. J. D.
Coe, Henry and Sarah Anderson, Dec. 27, 1787. C. S.
Coe, John and Jane Bell, Aug. 3, 1784. J. M.
Cogill, Ralph and Mary Carter, July 3, 1796. A. B.
Coghill, George and Celia Jackson, Jan. 15, 1807. J.B.T.
Coghill, John and Margaret Steel, April 9, 1807. L. C.
Cohoon, John and Sarah Randolph, Jan. 21, 1794. E. P.
Cole, George and Mary Capper, April 10, 1799. J. P.
Cole, John and Elizabeth Persley, Nov. 10, 1803. A. B.
Cole, Joseph and Catherine Berry, July 10, 1810. S.O.H.
Cole, William and Mary McNelly, Sept. 3, 1808. A. B.
Coleby, James and Catherine Stonebrook, Oct. 16, 1801. J.B.
Coleman, Peter and Phebe Watson, May 10, 1792. C. S.
Collett, John and Elizabeth McDonald, Aug. 11, 1791. W. H.
Collins, Andrew and Margaret Mastin, July 24, 1825. T.B.Jr.
Collins, Beovan and Anna Long, June 8, 1797. A. B.
Collins, Jesse and Jenny Ewings, Sept. 1, 1785. J. M.
Collins, Thomas and Catherine Stein, June 14, 1801. A.B.
Collins, William and Ann Jones, Nov. 7, 1785. C.S.
Collins, William and Hephybeth Mason, Oct. 9, 1787. C. S.
Colville, John and Mary Jamason, Oct. 15, 1782. J. M.
Colville, Joseph and Mary Marquis, March 22, 1790. C. S.
Colville, Samuel and Sarah Barns, Oct. 1, 1811. A. S.
Colvin, Henderson James and Mary Russell, Aug. 28, 1787. A.B.
Compton, Alexander and Lucinda Ireland, March 30, 1809. J.B.T.
Compton, Levi and Rosanna Funk, Dec. 19, 1788. C. S.
Congore, William and Mary McMiller, June 3, 1782. . J. M.
Congrove, John and Tasia Goar, Feb. 16, 1796. A. B.

Conklin, Jacob and Sarah Williams, Feb. 7, 1792. C. S.
Conklin, Michael and Rachel Taylor, Dec. 2, 1789. A. B.
Conn, Hezekiah and Isabella Buck, Aug. 20, 1803. J. I.
Conner, John and Elizabeth Barns, Aug. 22, 1787. C. S.
Conner, Samuel and Sally Ball, Jan. 12, 1789. A. B.
Conner, Saveren and Hannah Hall, July 7, 1821. J. W.
Conner, Thomas and Elizabeth Holmes, Feb. 15, 1798. W.W.
Conrad, Frederick and Frances Thruston, April 25, 1793. A.B.
Conrad, Isaac and Mary Nowland, March 7, 1816. J.B.T.
Conrad, John and Elizabeth Rutherford, June 1, 1786. A. B.
Conrad, William and Elizabeth Doughty, April 11, 1802. W.W.
Cook, Samuel and Mary Hotzenspiller, March 1, 1812. J.B.T.
Cook, Thomas and Barbara Kemp, March 13, 1792. E. P.
Cook, Thomas and Rachel Ashby, Nov. 10, 1800. W.W.
Cook, William and Susannah Malo ?. Aug. 9, 1791. C. S.
Cooke, William and Elizabeth Baker, March 2, 1797. J. I.
Cooley, Peter and Elizabeth Crawford, Feb. 2, 1786. A.B.
Cooley, Peter and Eve Short, June 12, 1788. A. B.
Cooley, Peter and Sarah Adamson, April 11, 1793. C. S.
Cooley, Peter and Mary Powers, March 20, 1799. J. W.
Cooley, Samuel amd Fanny Barns, Sept. 19, 1815. J.W.
Coontz, Peter and Mary Grim, Oct. 11, 1801. A. B.
Coontzman, Daniel and Sarah Burton, Feb. 27, 1824. W. H.
Cooper, Cage and Mary Jack, June 11, 1791. C. S.
Cooper, George and Elizabeth Hampton, Sept. 20, 1792. C.S.
Cooper, John and Catherine Sunit, Sept. 23 1789. C.S.
Cooper, John W. and Rhoda O'Boyle, June 16, 1822. J. D.
Cooper,Martin and Anna Williams, Nov. 23, 1802. C. S.
Cooper, Spencer and Ann Bailey, May 8, 1787. A. B.
Cooper, Thomas and Sarah Livingston, Oct. 14, 1788. A. B.
Cope, John and Mary McCabe, May 3, 1804. A. B.
Cope, Joshua and Isabella McCrea, Feb. 4, 1807. W. H.
Copenhaver, John and Margaret Hoffman, Jan. 1, 1788. C.S.
Copenhaver, Michael and Margaret Price, March 9, 1786. C.S.
Copenhaver, Jacob and Nancy Pelter, March 23, 1819. G.M.F.
Copman, Andrew and Mary Balding, June 5, 1791. E. P.
Corbett, Henson? and Susannah Miller, May 23, 1787. C. S.
Corbett, John and Margaret Stanford, Dec. 7, 1797. A. B.
Corbin, John F. R. and Harriet T. Holm, Sept. 30, 1816. A.B.
Cordell, John and Rebecca Jennings, March 2, 1796. W. W.
Corder, James and Sarah Corder, Feb. 18, 1806. W. D.
Gorder, Jesse and Phoebe Corder, Feb.26, 1825. T. L.
Corder, John and Sarah Ramey, Sept. 2, 1823. T. B. Jr.
Cornwall, George and Sarah Fleming, Dec. 28, 1817. T. L.
Cornwall, John and Fanny Kline, Sept. 4, 1824. J. A.
Cornwell, Fielding and Milly Ashby, March 3, 1808. C. S.
Cornwell, William and Margaret Haynie, Feb. 18, 1804. A.B.
Cottrell, William and Isabella Chance, Dec. 10, 1800. W. H.
Courtney, John and Sarah Rice, Feb. 20, 1794. A. B.
Cowan, Nathaniel and Sarah Rice, Nov. 16, 1797. A. B.
Cowden, Walter and Mary Long, May 28, 1801. C. S.
Cox, John and Sarah Park, Nov. 29, 1785. C. S.
Cox, Moses and Lydia Remey, Aug. 24, 1792. W. H.
Crabb, James and Rhoda Garner, March 15, 1821. J. D.
Crabb, Vincent and Sally Jameson, Oct. 3, 1797. L. C.
Crafford, Reuben and Jane Jacobs, Aug. 17, 1795. J. H.

Crafford, William and Elizabeth Stonar, _____ 1809. J. W.
Crail, Charles and Mary Johnston, May 11, 1789. C. S.
Craig, Hugh and Elizabeth Thompson, Oct. 30, 1798. A. B.
Craig, Joseph and Elizabeth Martin, Jan. 8, 1795. C. S.
Craig, Robert and Mary McGonghen, April 10, 1814, J. W.
Craig, Samuel and Liddy Taylor, June 10, 1804. W. H.
Craig, Samuel and Elizabeth Tilley, Dec. 20, 1811. J. W.
Craig, William and Mary Sperry, March 27, 1817. J. B. T.
Crain, Lewis and Agy Smith, Oct. 22, 1806. G. R.
Crane, Lewis and Peggy Bowlin, Sept. 6, 1800. A. B.
Crawford, Aquilla and Elizabeth Beckley, Sept. 15, 1809. J.B.T
Crawford, James and Mary Stribling, Jan. 14, 1813. W. H.
Crawford, William and Juliana Slusher, March 1, 1790. C.S.
Creps, John and Hannah Wright, June 10, 1820. J. W.
Creswell, Abraham and Mary Chenowith, April 20. 1807. J. W.
Crispin, Silas and Mary Mason, May 8, 1791. E. P.
Crist, Henry and Ann Cartmell, Feb. 7, 1788. A. B.
Critsinger, Conrad and Mary Oliver, Dec. 30, 1790. E. P.
Crockwell, John and Catherine Messmere, Oct. 18, 1795. A.B.
Crofton, John Russell and Ann Mason (Wason) Jan. 31, 1799.A.B.
Crook, John and Rachel Murray, April 5, 1804. J. W.
Cross, Nicholas and Polly Turner, Dec. 20, 1810. C. S.
Crow, John and Martha Shepherd, March 1, 1808. W. Hill
Crozier, Arthur and Eliza Barton, Dec. 22, 1796. A. B.
Crum, Abraham and Rebecca McCord, April 17, 1823. J. W.
Crum, Anthony and Betsy Orey, Sept. 30, 1793. E. P.
Crum; Anthony and Freny Cyphret, Sept. 17, 1795. A. B.
Crum, Christian and Hannah Barr, Oct. 27, 1805. J. W.
Crum, John and Rachel McCartney, April 10, 1823. J. W.
Crum, Peter and Ann Conner, Nov. 21, 1811. C. S.
Crumley, Aaron and Jane Atherton, Feb. 4, 1796. A. B.
Crumley, John and Elizabeth Hancher, Jan. 21, 1812. J. W.
Crumley, Thomas and Elizabeth Gardner, Jan. 22, 1801. J.B.
Crummy, George and Winifred Kelly, July 31, 1800. A. B.
Cryder, John and Mary Johnston, June 20, 1793. C. S.
Cryder, John and Ann Gorley, Aug. 25, 1814. J. B. T.
Crysor, Jacob and Leah Jarret, Nov. 1, 1798. W. W.
Cullen, Lawrence and Martha Whittle, March 2, 1791. A. B.
Culver, John and Mary McCormick, Sept. 3, 1817. W. H.
Cunningham, Nicholas and Anna Lee, Sept. 16, 1795. A. B.
Cunningham, Thomas and Mary Keller, Sept. 25, 1793. C.S.
Cunningham, Thomas and Jenny Houston, Aug. 20, 1801. W.H.
Carlett, Thomas and Susannah Cochran, Sept. 21, 1790. C. S.
Curry, James and Eleanor Bryan, Sept. 26, 1791. A. B.
Cusick, David and Elizabeth Keeler, Oct. ____1806. J.B.T.
Cyders, Conrad and Margaret Thompson, June 2, 1803. A.B.
Cyphert, Andrew and Hannah Marrle, Aug. 20, 1801. J. B.
Cywood, Richard and Mima Everhoatt, Dec. 16, 1818. G.M.F.

Dailey, Dennis and Elizabeth Whitacre, Jan. 31, 1820. G.M.F.
Dailey, James and Comfort Wood, Dec. 14, 1815. A. B.
Dailey, John and Susannah Braithwaite, Nov. 20, 1817. E. G.
Dailey, Joseph and Leah Larrick, May 30, 1787. S. H.
Dailey, Joseph and Mary Shion, March 30, 1810. W. H.
Dailey, William and Elizabeth Kingore, April 3, 1804. J. W.
Daingerfield, Henry and Elizabeth M. Thruston, Aug. 10,1793.
                                                    A. B.

Dalbey, Aaron and Tacy Marple, Feb. 6, 1789. C. S.
Dalby, Joel and Elizabeth Smith, June 8, 1797. A. B.
Dalby, John and Jane Wiggington, March 29, 1821. J. D.
Dalby, Joseph and Hannah Stonebridge, Nov. 13, 1788. A. B.
Daniel, Benjamin and Sydney Fenton, Dec. 13, 1815. G.M.F.
Darlington, David and Anna McCoole, April 22, 1802. A.B.
Darlington, Gabriel and Barbara Rinker, April 19, 1792. C.S.
Darlington, Gabriel and Margaret Edwards, May 8, 1798. A.B.
Darlington, John and Polly Edwards, March 18, 1788. A. B.
Darlington, Meredith and Catherine McCoole, May 6, 1802. A.B.
Darlington, Meredith and Mary Doster, Aug. 10, 1809. A.B.
Darlington, William and Eleanor Cuthridge, July 22, 1792. A.B.
Daskins, Daniel and Sarah Daugherty, Feb. 25, 1783. J. M.
Daugherty, John and Jane Benegar, Nov. 1, 1796. A. B.
Davenport, Adrian and Olivia Clark, April 10, 1816. J. W.
Davenport, Benjamin and Margaret S. Cramer, Feb. 22, 1807. W.F
Davis, Enoc and Elizabeth Chamblyn, April 22, 1818. G.M.F.
Davis, Francis and Ann Calvert, Sept. 9, 1800. A. B.
Davis, Gabriel and Sarah Fenton, Aug. 19, 1799. A.B.
Davis, Gary, and Rosannah Peck, April 2, 1787. A. B.
Davis, George and Sarah McKnight, Dec. 3, 1795. A.B.
Davis, James and Mary Moore, June 5, 1787. J. M.
Davis, John and Elizabeth Marsh, Oct. 28, 1802. C. S.
Davis, John and Ann B. Scarff, Oct. 5, 1806. A. B.
Davis, John and Ann Milhorn, Oct. 12, 1809. C.S.
Davis, Stephen and Kitty Taylor,Pollard, Sept. 22, 1803. A.B.
Davis, Thomas and Ann McKee, Nov. 7, 1801. J. W.
Davis, William and Rachel Gawthrop, Feb. 1, 1812. J. W.
Davis, William and Margaret Davis, Jan. 22, 1811. S.O.H.
Davis, Samuel and Phebe Cornell, April 13, 1786. C. S.
Davis, Samuel and Nancy McGuinn, July 21, 1822. T. L.
Davis, Samuel and Jane Sturt, July 12, 1821. T. L.
Davis, Solomon and Elizabeth Hersha, Jan. 15, 1799. J. W.
Davis, Thomas and Lydia Wood, Sept. 26, 1792. E. P.
Davis, William and Nancy Wright, Aug. 18, 1787. C. S.
Davis, William and Mary Wickersham, Oct. 30, 1787. A. B.
Davidson, Alexander and Catherine Kline, Dec. 28, 1809. S.O.H
Davidson, James H. and Harriett B. Smith, July 8, 1802. C.S.
Davison, Daniel and Margaret Anderson, Sept. 13, 1803. J.W.
Davison, William and Martha Maria Smith, July 21, 1800. A. B.
Dawkins, John and Mary Ellis, May 13, 1790. W. H.
Dawkins, Thomas and Patty Loughland, June 29, 1786. C.S.
Dawson, John and Sarah Farmer, Jan. 29, 1803. J. W.
Dawson, William and Margaret Hull, Dec. 22, 1796. A. B.
Day, James and Mary Cline, Sept. 11, 1820. T.B. Jr.
Day, Samuel and Isabel Dunn, Dec. 15, 1789. C. S.
Deaderick, Thomas and Nancy Raworth, Aug. 18, 1789. A. B.
Deal, George and Catherine Hatt (Hott) Dec. 10, 1801. C.S.
Dean, Ely and Mary Murphy, June 8, 1820. G. R.
Dean, William and Martha Dixon, Jan. 10, 1802. J.B.
Dearmont, Michael and Lucinda Ferguson, Oct. 25, 1826. T.L.
Decker, Henry and Mary Clark, July 27, 1790. C. S.
Dehaven, Henry D. and Elizabeth Light, March 23, 1820. J.D.
DeHaven, William and Sarah Doster, Jan. 5, 1792. B. S.
Delaney, William and Frankey Jones Shackelford, Sept. 14, 1786
                                                         J. M.

Delong, John and Mary Toomy, May 20, 1794. C. S.
Demoss, Charles and Anna Lenox, Dec. 5, 1791. A. B.
Deneale, John E. and Matilda B. Earle, Nov. 17, 1825. T. K.
Denny, David and Catherine Nolan, Feb. 20, 1798. C. S.
Denny, John and Martha Hall, April 7, 1789. A. B.
Denny, John and Mary Jones, Jan. 3, 1816. J. W.
Denny, John and Margaret Swatz, Jan. 7, 1819. G.M.F.
Denny, William and Elizabeth Mytinger, Dec. 30, 1804. J.B.T.
Deus, Thomas and Elizabeth Stonestreet, Jan. 30, 1816. W.N.
Deselms, Jesse and Elizabeth Pickering, July 31, 1791. A.B.
Deshon, James and Peggy Craig, Sept. 17, 1817. G.M.F.
Devoe, David and Margaret Jewell, May 15, 1793. E. P.
Dicks, Alexander and Rachel Lewis, Dec. 10, 1808. J. W.
Dick, Benjamin J. E. and Catherine Ann Cornwell, Dec. 16,
                                                1824. T. K.
Dick, Charles and Patience Berry, May 12, 1789. C. S.
Dick, Hieronimus and Mary Ann Bruner, Dec. 30, 1819. J.D.
Dick, John and Catherine Ronimus, Oct. 30, 1787. C. S.
Dick, John and Elizabeth Caywood, Dec. 29, 1814. J. W.
Dick, John and Elizabeth Allmong, Jan. 14, 1819. J. D.
Dick, Peter and Nancy Garner, July 28, 1795. A.B.
Dick, Peter and Jane McWhorter, March 9, 1807. J.W.
Dick, Peter Jr. and Massy McKnut, Jan. 31, 1823. G.M.F.
Dick, Stephen and Sarah Jennings, May 4, 1805. A. B.
Dickey, Joseph and Elizabeth Fuller, Jan. 8, 1795. C.S.
Diggon, Samuel and Jane Sage, May 30, 1792. C. S.
Dillon, James and Sarah Ward, Sept. 21, 1810. J. W.
Dillon, Joel and Jane Butler, Aug. 31, 1820. G.M.F.
Dillon, John and Elizabeth Chapman, Nov. 1, 1792. W. H.
Dinges, George and Jane Temple, Oct. 20, 1808. A. B.
Dilworth, Amos and Rebecca Cabell, July 13, 1807. A. B.
Disponet, Abraham and Mary Seabert, March 25, 1794. C. S.
Dixon, Benjamin and Ann Mercer, May 16, 1823. J. W.
Dixon, William and Mary Cahoon, April 2, 1795. A. B.
Dodd, John and Sarah Clurk, Feb. 7, 1788. A. B.
Donaldson, John and Hannah Tice, Dec. 22, 1789. W. H.
Donner, Jacob and Hannah Senseny, Oct. 25, 1795. S. H.
Dooley, William and Nancy Martin, July 28, 1804. J. W.
Dorsey, John and Jean Loe, Jan. 21, 1786. A. B.
Dotts, Boston and Elizabeth Rice, Sept. 9, 1800. A.B.
Daugherty, Patrick and Mary Edmondson, July 19, 1790. A.B.
Doughty, Thomas and Elizabeth Komp, Jan. 10, 1800. J. I.
Doulman, Samuel and Anna Murphy, Feb. 16, 1794. C. S.
Doush, Christopher and Elizabeth Helm, April 11, 1787. C.S.
Dowell, Elijah and Dolley Shepherd, Nov. 21, 1812. J. W.
Dowell, Jesse and Jeny Conner, Dec. 17, 1799. W. N.
Dowell, Oliver and Chloe Horton, July 19, 1797. B. D.
Dowell, Richard and Sarah Figgins, April 6, 1825. J. W.
Dougherty, Enos and Jane Crampton, April 21, 1799. A. B.
Downing, Benjamin and Catherine Chamblin, Dec. 22, 1811. T.L.
Doyle, Peter H. and Betsy Marpole, June 6, 1822. J. D.
Drake, Edward and Catherine Lawyer, Oct. 5, 1795. A. B.
Drake, Francis and Eve Lawyer, Jan. 8, 1788. J. M.
Drake, Gersham and Phebe Coleman, Jan. 8, 1803. J. W.
Drake, John and Phebe Bosteyan, March 11, 1811. S. O. H.
Draper, Edward and Lucy Owins, March 10, 1800. J. I.
Draper, Thomas and Grace Antrim, Jan. 25, 1800. J. I.

Draper, Isaac and Ann McCord, Dec. 23, 1793. E. P.
Drew, Peres and Mary Richardson, Jan. 11, 1786. C. S.
Drum, John and Susannah Reding, Aug. 24, 1797. W. W.
Drury, William and Elizabeth Smith, May 22, 1820. J.B.T.
Ducker, John and Lydia Shepherd, Dec. 21, 1809. C. S.
Duff, Barney and Ann Shinn, June 11, 1787. A. B.
Duft, Anthony and Betsy Jones, Jan. 23, 1804. A. B.
Duke, Mark and Margaret McCarty, Feb. 25, 1818. W. H.
Duke, Thomas and Sidney Johnston, Aug. 7, 1817. T. L.
Duke, William and Elsea Lewis, March 19, 1805. J. W.
Dun, Robert and Hannah Shepherd, Nov. 17, 1810. J. W.
Dun, Thomas and Jane Moore, Nov. 15, 1820. J. W.
Dunbar, Robert and Hannah Cox Bryarly, Sept. 24, 1805. C.S.
Dunbar, William and Mary Royce, Feb. 25, 1790. A. B.
Duncan, Crosbury and Mary Smith, April 16, 1791. E. P.
Duncan, Patrick and Agnes White, May 17, 1803. C. S.
Duncan, Seth and Rhuamy Henshaw, Dec. 25, 1792. W. H.
Dunlap, Robert and Rebecca Jones, March 6, 1787. J. M.
Dunn, James and Rachel Pring, Aug. 22, 1786. C. S.
Dunovan, Isaac and Sarah Keeran, April 1, 1800. C. S.
Durham, James and Marian Emmons, Dec. 30, 1802. W. H.
Dutton, William and Ann Garnet, Nov. 22, 1804. J. W.
Duvall, William and Mary Williams, Nov. 27, 1794. C. S.
Dyer, Isaac and Susannah Ramey, March 14, 1793. N. L.
Dyer, James and Nancy Earheart, June 1, 1824. T. L.
Dyer, Zebulon and Rebecca Waggener, Nov. 19, 1801. A. B.
Dyson, John B. and Nancy Garrett, Sept. 23, 1810. J.B.T.

Eagle, Daniel and Maria Albert, Nov. 11, 1819. G.M.F.
Eagle, Daniel and Harriet Bean, Dec. 24, 1821. J. W.
Earhart, George and Polly Marks, Dec. 29, 1799. W. W.
Earle, (   ) as and Sarah Brownley, Dec. 15, 1785. J. M.
Eason, Samuel and Mary Striker, Oct. 14, 1800. J. B.
Easterwood, John and Peggy Mahony, Oct. 8, 1790. C. S.
Eaton, Henry and Catherine Britton, Aug. 29, 1822. J. D.
Eaton, Joseph and Susannah Fisher, May 30, 1805. J. W.
Eaton, Philip and Sarah Smith, Aug. 17, 1782. A. B.
Eaton, William and Rebecca McCann, Jan. 22, 1794. A. B.
Eberly, Jeremiah and Christiana Baker, Oct. 18, 1785. C. S.
Eddy, John and Jensy Sprout, Feb. 25, 1789. C. S.
Eddy, Samuel and Elizabeth Evans, March 20, 1815. J. W.
Edleman, Michael and Mary Mouser, Sept. 18, 1792. C. S.
Edmundson, Archibald and Nancy Wrenn, Oct. 29, 1789. A. B.
Edwards, Edward and Margaret Darlington, March 7, 1799. A.B.
Edmondson, John and Sarah Elkins, March 4, 1799. J. I.
Edmundson, Thomas and Ann Cambell, March 16, 1786. C. S.
Edwards, Gideon and Mary Dillon, Aug. 18, 1802. J. W.
Edwards, Hezekiah and Elizabeth Houseman, Oct. 4, 1804. W.H.
Edwards, Ignatius and Nancy Collins, April 5, 1804. J. W.
Edwards, John and Jenny Collins, Oct. 30, 1800. J. B.
Edwards, Joseph and Elizabeth Vance, May 23, 1787. C. S.
Edwards, Joseph B. and Mary D. Dicks, Jan. 1, 1824. T.K.
Edwards, Thomas and Martha Kesner, Dec. 13, 1785. C. S.
Edwards, William and Ann Albin, Aug. 23, 1796. A. B.

Elbon, Reuben and Margaret Nisewanger, Aug. 30, 1787. C.S.
Elkins, Stephen and Abigail Catterline, Dec. 28, 1796. J.I.
Elliot, Aquilla and Nancy Wright, Oct. 12, 1810. J. W.
Elliott, Benjamin and Maria R. Brown, July 26, 1821. T.B.Jr.
Elliott, John and Hannah Cather, April 17, 1813. J. W.
Ellis, Christopher and Elizabeth Carver, April 25, 1786. C. S
Ellis, Jonathan and Martha Owgan, July 19, 1799. J. W.
Ellis, Lewis and Mildred Ball, Dec. 26, 1816. A. S.
Ellis, Leonard and Mary Babb, April 21, 1808. C. S.
Ellis, Morris and Mary Smith, April 26, 1801. J. B.
Elsea, William and Polly Vouhire, Jan. 1, 1801. W.W.
Ellzea, Samuel and Fanny Self, Oct. 15, 1813. W. N.
Emmonds, Joel and Sarah Grubbs, June 28, 1787. C. S.
Emmons, Jonathan and Rebecca Vanort, June 5, 1787. A. B.
Emmons, Syrenius and Jane Frances, Sept. 26, 1805. L. C.
Emmons, Thomas and Polly Davis, March 9, 1803. L. C.
Emmons, Zerenius and Lydia Romine, Nov. 6, 1787. A. B.
Emory, Hezekiah and Ruth Hill, Oct. 5, 1790. W. H.
England, Titus and Sarah Freidley, June 25, 1788. A. B.
Eltz, John and Christian Keller, April 2, 1795. A. B.
Engle, Joseph and Eleanor Perkins, Aug. 7, 1795. A. B.
English, John and Jane Vance, Nov. 25, 1790. E. P.
Enlow, Jacob and Elizabeth Stephens, Oct. 31, 1793. E. P.
Ersman, Frederick and Mary Seidlemyer, March 2, 1788. C.S.
Ervin, William and Catherine Olleman, Sept. 16, 1790. W.H.
Esle, Ernest and Margaret Whipley, May 31, 1786. J. M.
Evans, Jesse and Elizabeth Winsel, Dec. 29, 1790. E. P.
Evans, Robert and Mary Ellis, July 19, 1792. C. S.
Evans, John and Elizabeth Evans, April 3, 1806. A. B.
Evans, Nathan and Mary Ann Haburn, March 1, 1812. J.B.T.
Evans, Robert and Catherine Richards, March 30, 1822. W.H.F
Everett, Elisha and Mary Light, April 13, 1791. A. B.
Everett, John and Susannah Null, Dec. 18, 1817. E. G.
Everhart, Jacob and Ruth Welsh, Sept. 7, 1815. G.M.F.
Everhart, Michael and Barbara Smith, Oct. 24, 1786. C. S.
Everly, John and Polly Shuler, May 30, 1789. C. S.
Eversole, John and Elizabeth Allemong, Dec. 10, 1789. C. S.
Ewen, John C. and Margaret Ritter, Aug, 8, 1825. J. A.
Ewins, Israel and Polly Anderson, Dec. 25, 1804. J.B.T.
Ewen, Thomas and Gereta Stephens, March 22, 1791. R. S.
Ewing, Samuel and Barbara Shipe, Nov. 10, 1789. E. P.
Ewing, Robert and Margaret Carr, March 5, 1790. E. P.

Fagan, Bernard and Ann Warden, March 31, 1795. C. S.
Fair, Thomas and Jane Sylvia, Nov. 25, 1793. C. S.
Fairfax, Thomas and Louisa Washington, Jan. 18, 1798. A. B.
Farroll, Patrick and Margaret Rycroft, Aug. 24, 1791. A. B.
Farrow, Jacob and Nancy Humphries, June 26, 1799. C. S.
Fallert, William and Jane McKee, Jan. 6, 1795. A. B.
Farmer, William and Hannah Fisher, May 8, 1798. J. W.
Faulkner, Henry and Martha Anderson, Sept. 6, 1787. A. B.
Fauntleroy, Joseph and Emily Fauntleroy, March 6, 1811. W.Hi
Fauntleroy, Moore and Frances W. Ball, April 12, 1809. W. H.
Fawcett, Elijah and Phoebe Holloway, Feb. 25, 1810. J.B.T.
Fawcett, Joseph and Milley Carpenter, Sept. 4, 1801. J. W.

Fawcett, Joshiah and Sarah Taylor, March 22, 1826.
Featherlin, John and Rebecca Bennett, Nov. 18, 1796. J.I.
Felton, Thomas and Mary McFerson, Oct. 1, 1793. C. S.
Fenton, Benjamin and Ann Jackson, Jan. 13, 1795. C. S.
Fenton, Benjamin and Mary Shepard, Jan. 17, 1807. J. W.
Fenton, Ephraim and Polly Ryan, Feb. 27, 1802. J. W.
Fenton, Joseph and Martha Gibson, June 6, 1803. W. H.
Ferguson, David and Joanna Clevenger, Sept. 9, 1802. L. C.
Ferguson, Samuel and Mildred Garrison, Jan. 7, 1800. W. H.
Ferser, Peter and Rachel Catterline, Jan. 1, 1793. N. L.
File, Jacob and Sarah Adams, June 4, 1801. J. B.
Fettee, Philip and Rachel Carter, Dec. 16, 1801. J. W.
Fetty, Thomas and Juliet Dyer, Feb. 10, 1824. T. L.
Figg, William and Mary Taylor, Jan. 15, 1791. W. H.
Files, Joseph and Sarah Hensell, Jan. 24, 1821. J. W.
Finlay, William and Rosanna Vise, Nov. 13, 1788. A. B.
Fish, Simon and Nancy Edwards, July 18, 1796. A. B.
Fisher, Barak and Martha Hoge, April 14, 1795. A. B.
Fisher, John and Mary Johnston, Sept. 1, 1791. C. S.
Fisher, Joseph and Elizabeth Lewis (widow), March 11, 1790.
       A. B.
Fisher, Thomas and Margaret Mackey, Dec. 4, 1789. A. B.
Fisher, William and Fanny Gaunt, Feb. 2, 1808. W. H.
Fitterlings, Jacob and Judy Good, Nov. 15, 1791. C. S.
Fitzpatrick, John and Phoebe Largent, Jan. 2, 1805. A. B.
Fitzsimmons, John and Ann Shipe, May 22, 1813. W. N.
Fleager, George and Margaret Goodekuntz, May 6, 1788. S. H.
Fleet, Lewis and Juliet Lowry, May 21, 1820. J. W.
Fleet, Littleton and Margaret Puller, March 6, 1791. A. B.
Fleming, John and Jane Short, March 9, 1788. C. S.
Fleming, Thomas and Hannah Marr, Sept. 24, 1795. J. I.
Fleming, Thornton and Grace Dunbar, April 11, 1802. H. J.
Fletcher, Johnston and Maria Lantz, March 10, 1796. A. B.
Flood, William and Eliza Goody, Feb. 16, 1791. W. H.
Flower, John and Elizabeth Gorden, Oct. 6, 1812. G. M. F.
Flower, Richard and Mary Fenton, Nov. 4, 1815; G. M. F.
Foglesong, Charles and Margaret Ewe, March 11, 1794. C. S.
Foley, Henry and Sarah Asbill, July 16, 1797. A. B.
Foley, James and Susannah Campbell, June 5, 1788. S. H.
Foley, Jacob and Catherine Swatz, Oct. 29, 1801. A. B.
Foley, William and Catherine Ball, March 10, 1798. A. B.
Folger, John and Susannah Sherrer, Oct. 9, 1812. G.M.F.
Folger, Robert and Martha Bailey, Jan. 20, 1801. J. B.
Folke, Charles and Jane Farmer, Nov. 18, 1797. A. B.
Ford, Alexander and Elizabeth Fegans, March 12, 1826. T.B.Jr.
Ford, James and Mary Bandil, May 2, 1786. A. B.
Ford, John C. and Margaret Leach, June 9, 1822. T. B. Jr.
Forreman, Amos and Hannah Goff, April 23, 1801. C. S.
Forster, James and Jane Helm Barnett, March 15, 1825. T. L.
Forsythe, Abraham and Jane Wright, June 18, 1819. J. B. T.
Foster, Nelson and Mary Roberts, Dec. 18, 1824. T.J.D.
Foster, William H. and Margaret Kingore, Nov. 4, 1824. T. K.
Foushee, William and Mildred I. Thacker, Oct. 31, 1821. R. B.
Frank, John and Ann Taylor, Jan. 1, 1788. C. S.
Frager, Michael and Peggy Shehan, Jan. 31, 1792. W. H.
Frank, Adam and Sarah Pugh, Nov. 28, 1815. G.M.F.
Franks, Edward and Nancy Franks, Sept. 1, 1825. T. L.

Franks, Henry and Ann Douglass, Nov. 23, 1826. T. L.
Franks, James and Malinda O'Rear, March 21, 1824. T. L.
Franklin, Richard and Elizabeth Stone, March 25, 1823. G.M.F.
Frazier, John and Rebecca Jenkins, Feb. 11, 1813. J.B.T.
Franklyn, Thomas and Betsy Parks, Oct. 3, 1791. W. H.
Frazer, Alexander and Mary Parker, March 4, 1801. A. B.
Frazier, Alexander and Mary Drake, Dec. 15, 1811. J. M.
Frederick, John and Lydia Earheart, Aug. 24, 1800. C. S.
Freeman, Benjamin and Catherine Frum, Jan. 20, 1800. J. W.
Freize, Michael and Rachel Ward, Sept. 7, 1802. J. W.
French, Chapleigh and Betty Kean Booth, March 18, 1787. A.B.
French, Henry and Abigail Anderson, May 11, 1790. C. S.
Friedley, Henry and Eliza Wilson, Oct. 19, 1786. J. M.
Friedly, Henry and Sarah Dyer, Dec. 5, 1803. W. D.
Frieze, Daniel and Catherine Tarflinger, Aug. 5, 1806. C. S.
Frieze, David and Mary Whollian, Jan. 26; 1802. C. S.
Frieze, Jacob and Jane Davison, March 10, 1814. J. W.
Frost, Amos and Betsy Taylor, May 29, 1788. J. M.
Frum, William and Catherine Spence, Sept. 23, 1799. J. W.
Fulkeson, John and Catherine Swier, Aug. 1, 1811. C. S.
Fulkerson, Lewis and Barbara Shipler, Aug. 26, 1810. C. S.
Fulton, Robert and Mary Ann Ranter, Sept. 11, 1786. C.S.
Fungoner, Conrad and Rebecca Scott, June 14, 1786. C. S.
Funk, John and Polly Reader, Oct. 23, 1792. E. P.
Furr, Jesse and Margaret Waggoner, June 5, 1822. T. L.
Furman, Augustus and Eleanor Stephens, Oct. 16, 1788. J. M.
Fry, Jacob and Catherine Fry, Sept. 21, 1790. C. S.
Fry, Jacob and Elizabeth Linn, Jan. 6, 1799. C. S.
Fry, John and Mary Linn, May 14, 1797. C. S.
Fry, Joseph and Elizabeth Hotsbeilar, March 25, 1794. C. S.
Fry, Joseph and Sarah Richard, Jan. 7, 1808. C. S.
Frye, Lodwich and Rachel Jenkins, Feb. 2, 1792. W. H.
Frye, Michael and Elizabeth Russell, Feb. 13, 1792. C. S.
Frye, Benjamin and Ann Jamison, Dec. 15, 1785. J. M.
Frye, George Michael and Mary Wolf, Dec. 22, 1803. J. W.
Frye, Isaac and Catherine Frye, April 19, 1791. C. S.
Frye, Isaac and Sarah Frye, March 19, 1815. J.B.T.
Frye, Jacob and Betsy Bean, Nov. 13, 1792. C. S.
Frye, Joseph and Catherine Kackley, Feb. 9, 1810. C. S.
Frye, William and Phebe Smith, March 17, 1789. J. M.

Gallino, Joseph and Nancy Harry, April 2, 1812. S. B.
Gamble, Joseph Jr. and Eliza Cook, Dec. 7, 1817. W. Hill
Gamble, Mathew and Mary Deaderick , Feb. 6, 1792. A. B.
Games, Zacariah and Sarah McCarty, June 19, 1821. J. W.
Gander, David and Rachel Shull, Dec. 26, 1822. J.B.T.
Gander, George and Catherine Smith, Sept. 27, 1814. W. N.
Gander, John and Catherine Shull, Dec. 27, 1821. J.B.T.
Gant, Edward and Mary Hite, May 25, 1797. A. B.
Gantz, Jacob and Elizabeth Fleming, Jan. 7, 1813. J.B.T.
Gantz, John and Eve Weaver, April 5, 1788. J. M.
Gard, Ephrim and Elizabeth Nixon, Dec. 5, 1794. A. B.
Gard, Henry and Margaret Shivarteere (acre), Feb. 24, 1784.J.M.
Gard, Jacob and Margaret Lemley, May 6, 1810. C. S.
Gardner, Adam and Elizabeth Mason, Jan. 6, 1789. J. M.

Gardner, George and Elizabeth Long, July 6, 1790. C. S.
Gardner, George and Jane Sharran, July 20, 1799. B. D.
Gardner, Isaac R. and Comfort M. Rust, Sept. 23, 1815. J.B.T.
Gardner, James John and Susannah Earheart, June 18, 1805. J.W.
Gardner, Zachariah and Elizabeth Holliday,   1794. E.P.
Garman, Jacob and Jane Griffin, Aug. 9, 1813. J. W.
Garn, William and Nancy Holt, April 20, 1788. C. S.
Garner, Absolom and Rosana Crum, July 23, 1806. J. W.
Garner, John and Elizabeth Grigsby, March 20, 1798. W. W.
Garner, William and Elizabeth Hurford, Nov. 28, 1802. L. C.
Garrecht, Jacob and Elizabeth Shaffner, Nov. 15, 1825. T. W.
Garret, Abraham and Phoebe Bly, March 30, 1820. J. W.
Garrett, George and E. Bond, Nov. 12, 1811. A. S.
Garrett, John and Ann Allensworth, June 17, 1793. E. P.
Garretson, Nehemiah and Rebecca Kennon, Jan. 19, 1803. W. H.
Garrison, Thomas and Jane Willington, Sept. 10, 1801. A. B.
Garrison, William and Sally McDonald, Jan. 12, 1826. T.B.Jr.
Gatewood, Wright and Louisiana Williams, Feb. 18, 1824. T.B.J
Gaunt, John and Jemima Jones, Jan. 14, 1801. W. H.
Gaunt, John and Tabitha Mott, Oct. 17, 1804. A. B.
Gay, Michael and Sarah Jones, May 12, 1789. C. S.
Gearling, Daniel and Sophia Lancaster, March 4, 1788. A. B.
George, Evan and Hannah Bond, Jan. 12, 1825.
George, James and Mary Barrett, April 13, 1825.
George, Lewis and Rebecca Barret, Oct. 2, 1823. J. F.
George, William and Margaret Flint, March 1, 1798. A. B.
Gibbons, Cornelius and Mary E. Aulick, Oct. 20, 1808. A.B.
Gibbons, Jacob and Mary Groves, May 26, 1804. J. W.
Gibbons, Jacob and Mary Ann Pierce, Nov. 21, 1811. J. W.
Gibbons, John and Elizabeth Thompson, May 25, 1802. W. H.
Gibbons, William and Elizabeth Whittington, Nov. 27, 1815. G.M
Gibson, Aaron and Esolth Chapel, April 5, 1810. T. L.
Gibson, Jacob and Sarah Kemp, Jan. 11, 1787. J. M.
Gibson, Jonathan and Elizabeth Leonard, July 11, 1813. J.B.T.
Gilbert, Edward and Elizabeth Dailey, June 25, 1816. W. H.
Gilbert, Youel and Sarah Southward, June 20, 1805. L. C.
Giltart, Francis and Ann Martin, (Daughter of Colonel T. B.
            Martin), November 7, 1785. A. B.
Gildhart, Francis and Sophia Starke, Jan. 8, 1792. A. B.
Gilham, Ezekiel and Isabelle McMillan, Sept. 23, 1813. A. S.
Gilham, Peter and Mary Marker, July 22, 1792. C. S.
Gilham, Peter and Elizabeth Jackson, Oct. 1, 1822. J.B.T.
Gilkeson, James D. and Sally D. Bell, Feb. 5, 1817. W. H.
Gilkeson, John and Lucy Davis, Jan. 23, 1810. A. S.
Gilkeson, William and Sally Gilkeson, May 18, 1815. A. S.
Gill, William F. and Mary Young, Nov. 17, 1819. G.M.F.
Gilpin, Edward and Nancy Featheringale, Jan. 31, 1802. R. F.
Gilpin, Samuel and Sarah Carpenter, Dec. 25, 1800. J. B.
Girtrell, Joseph and Mary Lupton, June 6, 1791. A. B.
Glass, Francis and Elizabeth Garnett, Dec. 20, 1804. W. H.
Glasscock, Gregory and Elizabeth White, Dec. 3, 1809. L. C.
Glasscock, Jesse and Dilley Lewis, May 19, 1798. A. B.
Glasscock, Silas and Phebe Temple, Jan. 29, 1798. A. B.
Glenn, Matthew and Ann Jinkins, Oct. 21, 1786. J. M.
Glenn, Matthew and Mary Miller, July 28, 1794. A. B.
Glenn, Samuel and Rachel Britton, May 22, 1796. A. B.
Glenholmes, James and Mary Rogers, July 14, 1792. A. B.

Glover, Asker M. and Nancy McFarland, July 23, 1815. J.B.T.
Golding, Michael and Jane Garner, April 4, 1798. A. B.
Good, Felix and Rachel Orndorff, Dec. 14, 1820. G. R.
Good, George and Judith Garrett, Aug. 20, 1812, J.B.T.
Goodwin, Gideon and Rachel Pierce, Aug. 16, 1797. A. B.
Goose, George and Florina Steele, Aug. 18, 1795. C. S.
Gordon, Amos and Elizabeth Carter, June 10, 1788. C. S.
Gordon, Arthur and Mary Littlejohn, Jan. 1, 1795. C. S.
Gordon, Francis and Mary Barger, June 10, 1793. C. S.
Gordon, John Willisom and Sarah Bryarly, May 31, 1814. A.B.
Gordon, Joseph and Rachel Follis, Dec. 18, 1792. W. M.
Gore, Joshua and Elizabeth Lindsay, May 27, 1788. J. M.
Gorman, John and Fanny Masterson, July 30, 1782. J. M.
Goss, Martin and Lydia Simpson, March 8, 1816. J. W.
Gossett, William and Nancy Smith.
Gough, William and Christiana Wisecarver, Dec. 29, 1814. G.M.F.
Gourley, Thomas and Nancy Hughs, Jan. 30, 1821. T. L.
Gowen, John and Mary Boling, Dec. 26, 1805. A. B.
Graham, Arthur and Martha Withers, June 27, 1806. W. H.
Graham, James and Becky Robinson, April 1, 1801. J. B.
Graham, Philip and Nelly Beasley, Nov. 29, 1787. C. S.
Grammer, John and Juliana S. P. Barton, Dec. 14, 1819. W.H.
Grant, Jacob and Nancy King, March 20, 1810. W. H.
Grant, Stewart and Elizabeth Fridley, Aug. 20, 1818. A.B.
Grantham, James and Elizabeth Claspill, May 13, 1822. J. W.
Grantham, James and Phoebe Larue, Jan. 4, 1825. W. Hill
Granton, John and Margaret Gooden, May 25, 1788. J. M.
Grapes, Abraham and Barbara Clyne, May 19, 1792. C. S.
Grapes, David and Hannah Lemon, April 19, 1795. C. S.
Grapes, Henry and Rachel White, Feb. 16, 1786. J. M.
Graves, Charles and Elizabeth Barney, June 5, 1783. A. B.
Gray, John and Susannah Jenkins, Dec. 24, 1789. C. S.
Graves, Joseph and Susannah Dyer, Jan. 15, 1793. N. L.
Gray, Cyrus and Mary Magdalene Bougher, Aug. 14, 1795. A.B.
Gray, Hannans and Mary Craig, Oct. 30, 1798. A. B.
Gray, John and Elizabeth Taylor, March 29, 1787. A. B.
Gray, William and Nancy Leizure, Aug. 30, 1821. J. D.
Grayson, Robert Osborne and Margaret Susannah Peyton, Feb. 28,
              1811. A. B.
Green, George and Charlotte Babb, April 26, 1798. J. W.
Green, Henry and Mary Pringle, Feb. 16, 1796. A. B.
Green, James and Elizabeth Stage, July 23, 1804. A. B.
Green, Thomas and Ann Miller, March 5, 1801. A. B.
Green, Samuel Ball and Elizabeth Blair, May 23, 1799. A. B.
Green, William and Ann Taylor, Feb. 7, 1799. A. B.
Green, William and Elizabeth Brent, April 2, 1804. W. H.
Greenfield, Thomas and Alice Benham, Nov. 11, 1790. W. H.
Greenins, William and Winifred Wolfe, Jan. 11, 1790. E. P.
Gregory, John and Sarah Wheatley, Dec. 28, 1814. G.M.F.
Grice, George and Mary Farmer, Dec. 25, 1806. W. H.
Grice, John and Deborah Sumption, Jan. 19, 1792. W. H.
Griffen, John and Rosanna Johnston, May 15, 1799. J. W.
Griffick, Richard and Catherine Glass, Feb. 2, 1797. A. B.
Griffin, George and Nancy Johnston, Oct. 10, 1799. J. W.
Griffin, John and Sarah McKee, March 25, 1803. J. W.
Griffin, Levi and Elizabeth Bedinger, Feb. 20, 1822. R. F.
Griffis, William and Milly Sandberry, March 17, 1796. A.B.

37.

Griffith, David and Priscilla Griffith, Nov. 28, 1798. J.W.
Griffith, Samuel and Eleanor Ruble, Dec. 15, 1801. JB
Griffith , Samuel and Rebecca Myers, April 24, 1822. J. S.
Griffy, Jonas and Catherine Grim, Nov. 2, 1790. C. S.
Grigg, Mahlon S. and Emily Anderson, Jan. 6, 1825. T. L.
Griggs, James and Frances H. Timberlake, Nov. 1, 1826. T.K.
Grigsby, Jesse and Betsy Northern, May 17, 1798. W.W.
Grigsby, John and Rebecca Juell, April 9, 1789. A. B.
Grim, Christopher and Ann Davey, Jan. 15, 1801. C. S.
Grim, George and Mary Curlett, Feb. 12, 1790. C. S.
Grim, George and Mary Kelly, Nov. 13, 1800. C. S.
Grim, Daniel and Rebecca Miller, May 9, 1822. J.B.T.
Grimes, Charles and Mary Stephens, July 30, 1810. J.B.T.
Grimes, James and Elizabeth Strickling, Aug. 4, 1791. W.H.
Grimes, Robert and Polly French, Jan. 1, 1804. J.W.
Grimes, Thomas and Rachel Brady, Oct. 25, 1790. W. H.
Grimes, William and Ann McGann, May 3, 1786. J. M.
Grimes, William and Nancy Johnston, April 17, 1807. J. W.
Grimes, William and Lydia Minser, Feb. 12, 1823. J. W.
Grist, Grovenor and Ruth Gray, Dec. 26, 1793. A. B.
Grotz, Jacob and Margaret Rebecca Altrit, Nov. 17, 1793. C.S.
Grove, Abraham and Sidney Mercer, Sept. 26, 1819. J. D.
Grove, Adam and Eve Shiner, Aug. 6, 1795. A. B.
Grove, Daniel and Eve Samsel, Nov. 14, 1792. C. S.
Grove, Daniel Jr. and Catherine Shipe, May 19, 1814. J.B.T.
Grove, Jacob and Catherine Lonas, Oct. 13, 1795. A. B.
Grove, Jacob and Mary Sharer, Oct. 5, 1810. A. S.
Grove, John W. and Jane Young, Jan. 31, 1813. J.B.T.
Grove, Peter and Phebe Arnold, June 21, 1798. J.W.
Grove, Philip and Anna Maria Shull, June 12, 1805. C. S.
Groverman, William and Catherine Conrad, Dec. 17, 1790. C. S.
Groves, Henry and Susannah Kline, Sept. 27, 1795. C. S.
Groves, Henry and Mary Lawyer, Nov. 22, 1799. J. W.
Groves, Jacob and Elizabeth Kaile, Feb. 28, 1797. A. B.
Groves, Michael and Elizabeth Bucher, May 14, 1793. C. S.
Groves, Solomon and Fanny Marquis, May 10, 1798. C. S.
Groves, William and Mary Ann Thompson, Dec. 30, 1802. J.B.
Grub, William and Rachel Smith, June 17, 1800. J. I.
Grubbs, Daniel and Sally Grubbs, March 7, 1792. L. C.
Grubbs, David and Hannah Rodgers, Nov. 28, 1816. J.B.T.
Grubbs, Darias and Elizabeth Greeding, June 11, 1789. A.B.
Grubbs, Samuel and Margaret Windsor, Feb. 13, 1823. T.B.Jr.
Grubbs, Thomas and Elizabeth Scott, Jan. 21, 1793. A. B.
Grubbs, Thornburg H. and Mary Beatty, Aug. 1, 1822. T.B.Jr.
Gruber, Adam and Barbara Baughman, Nov. 17, 1816. W. Hill.
Grymes, Thomas and Jane Ryley, Nov. 15, 1797. A. B.
Guard, John and Isabella Cornelius, April 27, 1809. J.B.T.
Guy, Hezekiah and Mary Sigler, Sept. 28, 1806. L. C.
Gwathmey, John and Ann Buchanan Booth, July 22, 1800. A. B.
Gwynn, William and Sarah Grace, Oct. 26, 1809. A. B.

Haas, John and Catherine Mumma, April 20, 1813. J.B.T.
Hacker, John and Anna Sperry, Oct. 23, 1787. S. H.
Hacley, Joseph and Lucy Ranes, July 26, 1792. E. P.
Hackley, Jefferson and Lucy M. Berry, Dec. 23, 1823. J.B.Jr.

Hackley, John and Elizabeth Vaughan, Sept. 23, 1819. T.B.Jr.
Hackney, James and Jane Boyd, June 17, 1806. W. H.
Haddox, William and Caty Myers, Dec. __ 1805. J. B. T.
Hagger, Joan and Catherine Amiss, March 8, 1807. J. W.
Haines, Henry and Elizabeth Huntsacre, Jan. 29, 1792. C. S.
Haines, Josiah and Sarah Buill, March 22, 1790. A. B.
Haines, Nathan and Rachel McKay, March 4, 1813. J.B.T.
Haines, Thornton and Sarah Barr, Sept. 1, 1823. G. R.
Hair, Jacob and Lydia Squibb, Nov. 19, 1789. W. H.
Hair, Joseph and Elizabeth Kortze, Dec. 3, 1789. W. H.
Hais, Mark and Nancy Malone, May 1, 1805, G. R.
Halbert, Thomas and Mary Beevers, Dec. 24, 1801. A. B.
Hale, Christian and Elizabeth Ewens, Oct. 27, 1805. J.B.T.
Hale, Michael and Rosamond Ralph, Jan. 6, 1807. J.B.T.
Hale, Thomas and Alice McDonald, Oct. 6, 1788. A. B.
Hatfield, Edward and Elizabeth Hoover,Feb. -- 1794. C. S.
Hall, Edward and Elizabeth Briant, Feb. -- 1807. J. B. T.
Hall, Elisha I. Esq. and Catherine Smith, Sept. 25, 1800. C. S.
Hall, Henry and Hannah Messer, Nov. 20, 1817. E. G.
Hall, James and Maza McDonald, April 10, 1800. C. S.
Hall, James B. and Margaret Rozenburger, Aug. 7, 1822. G.R.
Hall, John and Ann Garner? Nov. 17, 1785. A. B.
Hambaugh, Adam and Matilda Catlett, Feb. 3, 1813. W. N.
Hamilton, Archibald and Mary Richards, Aug. 23, 1787. S. H.
Hamilton, Henry and Catherine Keckley, Jan. 1, 1811. J.B.T.
Hamilton, Robert W. and Betsy Earle, Feb. 26, 1811. S.O.H.
Hamilton, Thomas and Elizabeth Windsor, Sept. 21, 1823. T.B. Jr
Hamilton, William and Nancy Demoss, Feb. 17, 1822. T. L.
Hammock, Samuel S. and Louisa Mauk, Nov. 23, 1824. J.B.T.
Hammock, Daniel S. (?) and Elizabeth Ann Taylor, Sept. 22, 1826. J. A.
Hammock, Jacob and Catherine Delong, Oct. -- 1807. J.B.T.
Hammock, John and Catherine Cline, April 8, 1788. J. M.
Hammond, James and Polly Rankin, Jan. 21, 1790. A. B.
Hammond, James and Margaret Skilling, Nov. 28, 1797. J. W.
Hammond, James and Milly Buckley, April 24, 1800. A. B.
Hammond, Thomas Rankin and Maria Ellen Conrad, Jan. 13, 1814. A.
Hampton, George and Winney Howell, Aug. 5, 1787. A. B.
Hampton, James and Delphy Lee, Nov. 20, 1789. E. P.
Hampton, Joseph and Ann Tate, April 7, 1796. W. W.
Hamrick, James and Catherine Stigler, March 24, 1803. R. F.
Hancher, John and Sally Cooper, Nov. 16, 1819. G.M.F.
Hancher, Smith and Mary Steward, March 13, 1822. G. R.
Hand, Robert and Sarah Cordell, June 6, 1809. C. S.
Handle, Nicolas and Sidney Ann Crawford, April 19, 1826. T.L.
Hanes, William and Margaret Northern, , Feb. 6, 1787. C. S.
Haney, Charles and Sarah Kanara, Dec. 23, 1817. J.B.T.
Haney, John and Ann Reynolds, April 8, 1810. T. L.
Hankins, John and Sarah Gill, Oct. 30, 1783. A. B.
Hannum, James and Sarah Clowser, July 31, 1813. J. W.
Hannum, Thomas and Jane Nawcett, Jan. 20, 1789. J. M.
Hansberry, John and Mary Kirk, Feb. 13, 1787. C. S.
Hansbrough, John and Sarah Grubbs, July 19, 1814. W. N.
Hansell, John and Hannah Adams, Oct. 31, 1811. J. W.
Hansell, Joseph and Sally Lemley, Sept. 26, 1822. J.B.T.
Hanshaw, Benjamin and Susannah Symson, Dec. 29, 1811. J.W.
Hahsicker, Thomas and Ruth Rusk, Jan. 20, 1804. W. H.

Harska, James and Margaret Taylor,Sept. 1, 1799. A.B.
Hanway, Patrick and Polly Brown, June 24, 1801. W. W.
Harbough, Adam and Nancy Wolfe, Dec. -- 1806. J.B.T.
Harbough, Jacob and Margaret Garret, March 12, 1805. C. S.
Hardacre, Benjamin and Nancy McFadden, Dec. 11, 1806. L.C.
Hardaire, Aquilla and Nancy Oglesby, Aug. 10, 1809. J.B.T.
Hardesty, George and Mary Chipley, Aug. 14, 1788. J. M.
Hardesty, George and Cordelia Dooley, June 6, 1809. C. S.
Hardesty, Richard and Sarah Smith, May 19, 1791. W. H.
Hardin, Richard and Abigail Rubel, Dec. 25, 1820. J. D.
Hardwick, Robert and Elizabeth Cross, Jan. 6, 1791. A. B.
Hardy, Martin and Hannah Robinson, Oct. 30, 1806. J. W.
Harkins, John and Nancy Osborn, Oct. 26, 1822. J. W.
Harman, Jacob and Christian Mock, Oct. 29, 1797. C. S.
Harman, Michael and Elizabeth Fridley, April 4, 1790. A. B.
Harmer, William and Catherine Burns, Nov. 7, 1806. J. R.
Harper, John and Mary Cuningham, Nov. 25, 1782. J. M.
Harper, John and Hannah Gilham, Jan. 30, 1822. G. R.
Harrell, Nathan and Nancy Willey, March 10, 1787. S. H.
Harrell, Nathan and Ann Betty, Jan. 19, 1790. S. H.
Harris, Gabriel and Susannah Cooper, Feb. 15, 1821. J. W.
Harris, John and Mary Rhomine, Feb. 24, 1789. C. S.
Harris, Samuel and Ann Griggs, Jan. 20, 1791. W. H.
Harris, John and Alice Seybold, Oct. 30, 1794. A. B.
Harris, John and Nancy Binnegar, Aug. 20, 1801. J. B.
Harris, John and Elizabeth Northern, Oct. 31, 1822. W. M.
Harrison, Isaac and Mary Hughes, June 18, 1818. J.B.T.
Harrison, John and Phoebe Milburn, Nov. 12, 1810. J. W.
Harrison, Robert and Eliza Bruce, Oct. 11, 1822. J. W.
Harrison, Samuel and Lydia Allen, Sept. 7, 1794. C. S.
Harry, David and Margaret Wholtham, Nov. 30, 1812. J. W.
Harry, James and Polly Ciner, April 30, 1799. J. W.
Harry, James and Lydia Brown, Oct. 4, 1813. G. M. F.
Harry, John and Mary Ranolds, --- - 1794. E. P.
Harry, Jonathan and Louisa Walls, Feb. 2, 1814. J. F.
Harshey, Joseph and Mary Rutter, Feb. 24, 1796. A. B.
Hart, Adam and Sarah Arnold, Dec. 9, 1793. C. S.
Hart, David and Eve March, March 13, 1790. C. S.
Hart, James, and Peggy Poyles, June 14, 1806. W. H.
Hart, Samuel and Mary Farmer, Sept. 10, 1789. C. S.
Harter, Adam and Margaret McDonald, Nov. 23, 1786. C. S.
Hartman,.Peter and Louisa O'Rear, June 16, 1825. T. L.
Harvey, Thomas and Ann Griffith, June 24, 1809. J. W.
Harvey, Thomas B. and Jane S.Trussler,Oct.3, 1821. J. W.
Hastings, Joel and Ann Cancer, June 22, 1797. A. B.
Hastings, John and Sarah Pugh, Nov. 15, 1792. C. S.
Hasfeldt, John and Elizabeth Kennan, June 16, 1812. W. H.
Hass, George and Barbara Price, Aug. 31, 1809. C. S.
Hathaway, Frances and Sally Bourn, March 2, 1806. W. H.
Hathaway, James and Henrietta Baylis, Jan. 2, 1812. A. S.
Hatt, Adam S. and Catherine Hatt, March 12, 1801. C. S.
Hatt, Peter and Catherine Deal, Nov. 5, 1799. C. S.
Hathaway, James and Mary Gibbs Helm, Sept. 20, 1795. J. I.
Hawkins, Abel and Deborah Cook, Jan. 4, 1787. A. B.
Hawkins, Amos and Nancy Chipley, Aug. 3, 1800. J. B.
Hawkins, John and Eliza Talbott, May 4, 1813. G.M.F.
Hay, James and Eliza G. Burwell, June 17, 1817. A. B.
Hayes, David and Mary Horseman, Oct. 23, 1803. J. W.

Hayes, Electius and Keziah Marquis, Jan 29, 1789. A. B.
Haymaker, Adam Jr. and Sally Grim, Dec. 25, 1811. C. S.
Haymaker, John and Margaret Chapman, Nov. 15, 1787. A. B.
Haymaker, John and Christina Bostion, Jan. 5, 1790. C. S.
Haymaker, Thomas and Sarah Ferrell, Feb. 27, 1810. G.M.F.
Haynie, Edward and Elizabeth Anderson, Jan. 2, 1802. J. W.
Headly, Newton and Mary E. Northorn, June 10, 1823. T. K.
Heafer, John and Priscilla Ryan, Jan. 22, 1800. J. W.
Heard, James and Betsy Morgan, Oct. 17, 1785. C. S.
Hearkin, Daniel and Christiana Bulliner, Feb. 23, 1798. A.B.
Heath, Jonah and Catherine Teal, Dec. 28, 1791. C. S.
Heavely, William and Hannah DeHaven, Jan. 29, 1803. J. W.
Hedges, Edward and Mary Dalby, March 25, 1819. J. D.
Hefferin, William and Margaret Murphy, April 12, 1790. C. S.
Heironimus, Jacob and Elizabeth Brown, Oct. 24, 1808. J.W.
Heiskell, John and Ann Sowers, June 17, 1802. C. S.
Heiskell, John and Sarah White, March 16, 1824. R.H.C.
Heiskell, Peter and Susanah Wetzell, May 13, 1783. J. M.
Heiston, Joseph and Sarah Farmer, May 19, 1796. A. B.
Helling, Nathanial and Polly Riley, Dec. 2, 1799. B. D.
Helm, Thomas and Elizabeth Mott, Jan. 8, 1806. W. H.
Helm, William T. and Mary Page Brooke, April 4, 1822. W. F.
Helphinstene, Peter and Susannah Catherine Lantz, Jan. 26,
                                                 1790. C. S.
Helphenstine, Peter and Elizabeth Watson, Oct. 21, 1805. J.W.
Heltzell, Charles and Kitty Hover, Feb. 12, 1788. C. S.
Helviston, William and Sarah Cordell, Jan. 18, 1795. C. S.
Hemilwright, Henry and Elizabeth Fisher, Nov. 25, 1824. J.D.
Hemilwright, John and Catherine Brill, May 15, 1792. C. S.
Hench, Charles Fred and Elizabeth Toomy, Oct. 28, 1797. C.S.
Henckel, Solomon and Rebecca Miller, Sept. 9, 1800. C. S.
Hendrin, William D. and Sally Allensworth, Jan. 12, 1802. W.W.
Hendron, Robert and Sarah Hand, Aug. 1, 1811. W. N.
Hening, James and Sarah Williams, Jan. 10, 1797. A. B.
Hening, William and Mary Irvin Beatty, Aug. 16, 1818. W. H.
Henning, David and Leticia Rust, May 22, 1808. JB.T.
Henry, Aaron and Ann Aires, Oct. 5, 1798. W. W.
Henry, Isaac and Elizabeth Lowry, June 12, 1789. A. B.
Henry, John and Susannah Weaver, June 27, 1788. A. B.
Henry, John and Clarkey Riley, Aug. 9, 1798. W. W.
Henry, John and Polly Lloyd, May 28, 1816. S. O. H.
Henry, John and Mary Swarts, Dec. 2, 1826. J. W.
Henshaw, Thomas and Margaret Baldwin, July 15, 1814. W. H.
Henshaw, William D. and Charlotte Cooper, Oct. 20, 1825. T.W.
Hensher, Thomas and Sarah Pierce, April 20, 1794. S. R.
Henson, Thomas and Nancy Dick, -- -- 1809. J. W.
Herbert, George and Charlotte McCoole, March 16, 1812. G.M.F.
Hersulf, Charles Andrew and Catherine Keyes, Jan. 22, 1798. A.
Hess, Abraham and Nancy Puller, Dec. 16, 1824. T. L.
Hess, Conrad and Elizabeth Barton, Aug. 8, 1822. J.B.T.
Heskett, Zedekiah and Jane Yats, May 21, 1820. T. L.
Hessart, George and Mary Sommerville, Oct. 18, 1791. C. S.
Heterick, Robert and Mary Reid Carey, June 2, 1805. A. B.
Hickey, David and Ann Richardson, March 20, 1800. A. B.
Hickle, Henry and Rebecca Reed, Dec. 26, 1806. A. L.
Hickman, Abraham and Mary Nelson, May 30, 1816. A. S.
Hickman, Jacob and Alice Way, Jan. 11, 1800. C. S.
Hicks, Jeremiah and Catherine Anderson, April 21, 1791. A. B.

Hicks, John and Elizabeth Stewart, Jan. 17, 1786. A. B.
Hicks, John and Sarah Shores, Sept. 27, 1811. T. L.
Hicky, David and Catherine Cohagen, June 4, 1793. A. B.
Hickey, James and Phebe Gibbons, March 18, 1799. J. W.
Hickman, Adam and Massey Pickering, April 9, 1792. A. B.
Hiett, John and Mary Locke, Jan. 2, 1792. W. H.
Hiett, John and Sarah Locke, Dec. 9, 1799. W. H.
Hiett, John and Elizabeth Rinker, May 3, 1820. G. M. F.
Higgins, Charles and Elizabeth Weaver, Dec. 6, 1814. J. W.
Higgins, James and Elizabeth Welsh, April 4, 1814. J. W.
Higgins, Robert and Mary Jolliffe, March 7, 1797. A. B.
Higgins, William and Margaret Powers, March 10, 1811. C. S.
Hill, Adam and Ann Likens, Feb. 25, 1802. H. J.
Hill, George and Susan Balees (?), Feb. 14, 1818. T. L.
Hill, John and Barbara Buller, Aug. 13, 1782. J. M.
Hilliard, Jacob and Elizabeth Taylor, Sept. 29, 1803. A. B.
Hilling, William and Miriam Ramey, May 21, 1789. A. B.
Hinds, William and Mary Haymaker, June 4, 1795. A. B.
Hindson, Thomas and Hester Dewell, March 27, 1792. C. S.
Hines, William and Ann Halfpenny, Dec. 1, 1792. A. B.
Hinton, Solomon and Nancy Andle, Dec. 20, 1787. C. S.
Histone, Jacob and Catherine Fisher, Feb. 8, 1791. C. S.
Hite, Jacob and Catherine Sheiner, April 4, 1786. C. S.
Hite, John and Cordelia Ragan, Jan. 31, 1793. S.R.
Hite, John and Rachel Grubbs, Jan. 29, 1818. J. B. T.
Hite, Matthias and Catherine Grove, Oct. 29, 1792. S. H.
Hobson, William and Sarah Milburn, July 22, 1788. C. S.
Hockman, Benjamin and Elizabeth Purkhiser, Aug. 10, 1802. W.W
Hodge, James and Elizabeth Cooper, Aug. 9, 1822. J. W.
Hodgson, Abner and Rebecca Johnson, Dec. 31, 1797. J. B.
Hodgson, David and Rebecca McBean, March 28, 1789. J. M.
Hodgson, John and Rebecca Johnston, May 27, 1794. A. B.
Hodgson, John and Elizabeth Lewis Brooks, Nov. 17, 1788. J. M
Hodgson, Robert and Susannah Long, March 10, 1795. C. S.
Hodson, Robert and Susannah Watson, Dec. 31, 1799. J. B.
Hodson, William and Christianna Rife, Feb. 6, 1792. A. B.
Hodgson, William and Sarah Albert, April 18, 1811. J. W.
Hoff, Lewis and Margaret Sowers, Oct. 23, 1806. C. S.
Hoffman, Conrad and Elizabeth Keeler, March 2 , 1784. J. M.
Hoffman, Jacob and Mary Gilham, March 28, 1802. C. S.
Hoffman, John and Phoebe Clayton, Jan. 31 , 1811. A. B.
Hogan, Samuel and Jane Murphy, Nov. 21, 1797. A. B.
Hog, Solomon and Mary Glass, Feb. 15, 1787. J. M.
Hogan, William and Mary Lewis, Aug. 24, 1802. C. S.
Hoge, William and Rachel Steele, July 16, 1795. A. B.
Holdbrook, Ezra and Judith Breedlove, Jan. 2, 1791. A. B.
Holker, Joseph and Hannah Hay Cooper, Feb. 10, 1806. A. B.
Holland, Archibald and Mary McGuire, Sept. 18, 1812. W. H.
Holland, John and Hannah Newman, Feb. 10, 1813. W. H.
Holland, Zachariah and Sarah Simpson, May 27, 1794. A. B.
Holliday, Elsworth and Ann Bennett, April 24, 1789. C. S.
Holliday, Richard and Nancy McDonald, Feb. 7, 1793. E. P.
Holliday, Richard J. McKim and Mary Catherine Taylor, April
                        30, 1823. J. R.
Holliday, William and Margaret Blair, Jan. 16, 1791. R. S.
Holliday, William M. and Helen Billmyer, Feb. 9, 1806. W. H.
Hollingsworth, George & Mary Gaunt, April 7, 1799. W. H.

Hollingsworth, Samuel and Susan Richardson, Dec. 22, 1811. C.S.
Hollingsworth, Solomon and Sarah Brown, Feb. 7, 1810. J. W.
Hollingshead, James and Mary Scarf, Nov. 28, 1811. J. W.
Hollis, John and Ruth Hall, Feb. 28, 1792. W. H.
Holloway, Thomas and Mary Gardiner, Aug. 21, 1806. J. W.
Holmes, Alexander and Priscilla Roberts, Sept. 9, 1801. A. B.
Holmes, Hugh and Elizabeth Briscoe, Dec. 20, 1791. A. B.
Honecker, Jacob and Mary Foley, Jan. 23, 1787. S. H.
Honnold, Jacob and Abigail Shipman, Oct. 5, 1799. J. H.
Hooe, Thomas and Susan Cpie, Sept. 27, 1807. A. B.
Hook, William and Elizabeth Johnson, March 6, 1813. G.M.F.
Hooman, Mathias and Mahala Davis, Jan. 22, 1794. C. S.
Hooper, Emnor and Elizabeth Way, Feb. 14, 1793. C. S.
Hooper, Frederick and Hannah Richards, Dec. 22, 1789. C. S.
Hooper, John and Polly Bailey, April 12, 1798. J. W.
Hooper, Walter and Lydia Litter, June 12, 1787. A. B.
Hoover, David and Mary Martin, March 28, 1799. C. S.
Hoover, Henry and Nancy Rutter, Dec. 21, 1808. J. W.
Hoover, James and Leah Cooper, Aug. 9, 1821. W. F.
Hoover, John and Nancy McKeever, Feb. 5; 1800. A. B.
Hoover, Samuel and Nancy Weaver, June 8; 1806. W. H.
Hope, James T. and Phebe White, Jan. 13, 1825. T. B. Jr.
Hopewell, Benjamin and Sarah Wilson, Jan. 13, 1788. C. S.
Hopewell, William and Catherine Padgett, July 23, 1822. W. M.
Hopper, John and Elizabeth Timberlake, May 16, 1822. W. M.
Hopper, Joshua and Phebe Moore, Dec. 29, 1788. C. S.
Horrocks, Edward and Margaret Lentz, Sept. 21, 1801. A. B
Horse, Conrad and Susannah Slusher, Dec. 28, 1790. C. S.
Horsman, William and Rachel Pickering, July 21, 1791. L. C.
Horton, Henry and Catherine Hamel Shaw, Dec. 23, 1792. A. B.
Hotsebieler, Joseph and Margaret Wilson, May 12, 1793. C.S.
Hott, Conrad and Mary Stipe, April 11, 1805. C. S.
Hott, George and Kitty Hott, March 10, 1801. A. B.
Hott, Henry and Mary Loy, March 23, 1809. C. S.
Hott, Jacob and Anna Freeze, March 28, 1811. C. S.
Hott, John and Margaret Frees,, Dec. 13, 1804. C. S.
Hotzenpiller, Jacob and Milly Seagle, Sept. 16, 1793. S. H.
Hotzenpiller, Jacob and Mary Spurr, Jan. 6, 1804. J. W.
Houseley, John and Villemencher Davis, Oct. 16, 1786. A. B.
Houser, Frederick and Mary Myars, Sept. 22, 1806. J. W.
Howard, Charles and Sarah Drake, Dec. 24, 1811. J. M.
Howard, James and Mary Myers, Jan. 7, 1813. A. S.
Howe, George and Polly Dean, May 27, 1817. W. N.
Howe, James and Peggy Dean, Jan. 6, 1803. L. C.
Howe, John and Sarah Methany, Aug. 21, 1814. W. H.
Howell, Reuben and Hannah Harper, Nov. 22, 1810. A. B.
Howell, William and Rachel Bonham, March 10, 1806. W. D.
Howsman, William and Abigail Britton, May 27, 1803. J. W.
Hubbard, Robert and Nancy Waln, Sept. 21, 1816. G.M.F.
Huddle, George and Barbara Wilfong, May 16, 1801. A. B.
Huff, Charles and Lydia Copass, Nov. 17, 1803. A. B.
Huff, Cornelius and Elizabeth Ronimus, April 25, 1786. C. S.
Huffman, Anthony and Elizabeth Mytinger, May 26, 1814. J.B.T.
Huggins, William and Hannah Rogers, Oct. 13, 1818. J.B.T.
Hughs, Aaron and Lucy Stewart, Feb. 8, 1794. B. S.
Hughs, Jonathan and Ruth Patterson, March 4, 1790. W. H.
Hughes, Samuel and Catherine Cooper Holker, Jan. 29, 1798. A.B.

Hughes, William and Amelia Crockwell, June 21, 1807. J. W.
Hulet, Charles and Catherine Miller, Jan. 16, 1787. A. B.
Hull, Christian and Mary Weaver, March 1, 1812. E. H.
Hume, Robert and Lydia Ross, Feb. 20, 1811. W. H.
Hummell, Henry and Eleanor McKaughton, Jan. 3, 1799. A. B.
Hunsicker, Jacob and Alce Cooper, March 23, 1820. J. McC.
Hunt, Eli and Catherine Shepherd, Dec. 28, 1792. N. L.
Hunter, John and Mary Derrough, Oct. 27, 1791. A. B.
Hunter, Moses Theodoric and Mary Snickers, Nov. 27, 1812. A.B
Huntsberry, Conrad and Sally Day, April 30, 1791. W. H.
Huntsberry, Conrad and Margaret Holden, Nov. 2, 1804. A. B.
Huntsberry, Isaac and Eliza Wright, Jan. 19, 1820. J. W.
Huntsberry, John and Mary Marks, Jan. 26, 1826. T. W.
Hurford, Isaac and Penelope Johnston, Nov. 16, 1815. J.B.T.
Hurford, Jesse and Eve Ann Hass, Dec. 18, 1817. J. B. T.
Hurst, James G. and Catherine A. Gemmell, Aug. 16, 1825. J.B.
Hutchins, Francis and Elizabeth Marquis, Dec. 18, 1738. A. B.
Hutchings, Francis and Betsy Turner, March 7, 1811. T. L.
Hutton, William and Elizabeth Redman, Oct. 13, 1811. J. W.
Hutzlar, Jacob and Nelly Davis, March 16, 1809. J. W.
Hutzlar, John and Sarah Griffy, November 15, 1813. J. W.
Hydenrick, Gregory and Jane Chapman, Dec. 29, 1814. J. W.
Hye (Frye), Henry and Susannah Myers, Feb. 17, 1803. A. B.
Hynkinnis, Peter and Catherine Shriver, March 3, 1789. J. M.

Iden, Johithan and Catherine Jolly, March 19, 1811. J. W.
Idonis, William and Mary Spillman, Oct. 10, 1814, W. N.
Ingle, Philip and Margaret Steele, Sept. 21, 1786. S. H.
Ireland, James and Isabella Newell, Oct. 4, 1810. A. S.
Isler, Abraham and Susan Cloud, Jan. 14, 1818. W. H.

Jack, Samuel and Catherine Knight, June 13, 1782. J. M.
Jackson, Samuel and Cynthia McVeigh, Dec. 2, 1824. J. D.
Jackson, James and Elizabeth Roland, June 28, 1795. A. B.
Jackson, James and Mary Hastings, Aug. 15, 1812. A. B.
Jackson, Nathaniel and Elizabeth Vincent, March 13, 1791. A. B.
Jackson, Richard and Elizabeth Spencer, Aug. 12, 1813. J. B.
Jackson, Solomon R. and Nancy Cleveland, Jan. 10, 1816. J. W.
Jackson, Thomas and Nancy Smith, April 23, 1789. A. B.
Jackson, Thomas and Mary Bostian, April 25, 1808. A. B.
Jackson, William and Elizabeth Carter, Aug. 21, 1816. W. H.
Jackson, William and Hannah Shepherd, Feb. 20, 1818. T. L.
Jacobs, Baylor and Mary Kendrick, Jan. 7, 1813. W. N.
Jacobs, John and Edy Grubbs, Dec. 29, 1790. E. P.
Jacobs, John and Mary Thatcher, Dec. 13, 1821. R. B.
Jacobs, John and Elizabeth Taylor, Aug. 25, 1825. R. F.
Jacobs, Moses and Linney Collins, Sept. 6, 1799. A. B.
Jacobs, William and Lyddy Luttle (?) April 3, 1787. C. S.
Jacobs, William and Jemima Mullican, June 14, 1792. E. P.
James, David and Margaret Cumins, June 13, 1799. A. B.
Jamison, Alexander and Polly Jones, June 23, 1805. L. C.
Janney, Asa M. and Lydia N. Haines, Oct. 12, 1826.
Jarrett, Asbury and Eliza Lafever, Oct. 30, 1822. T. K.

Jenkins, Alexander and Mary Boliver, Sept. 30, 1794. C. S.
Jenkins, John and Jane Taylor, Oct. 15, 1789. A. B.
Jenkins, Stephen and Barbara Buckley, Jan. -- 1806. J.B.T.
Jenkins, William and Elizabeth McKoy, Feb. 7, 1799. B. D.
Jennings, Angus and Susannah Smith, Sept. 8, 1788. J. M.
Jennings, Daniel and Polly Parker, Dec. 12, 1787. C. S.
Jennings, Joseph and Evelina Withers, May 8, 1822. J. W.
Jewell, Samuel and Rachel Painter, Dec. 31; 1798. J. I.
Jewell, William and Sarah Devore, Sept. 12, 1792. E. P.
Jewell, William and Ruth Rea, Nov. 22, 1796. W. W.
Jinkins, Esrael and Elizabeth Horseman, Sept. 20, 1802. J. W.
Job, John and Hannah Cooper, Dec. 30 1813. J. W.
Johnes, David and Sarah Ewings, June 29, 1790. E. P.
Johnson, Adam and Margaret Ashahurst, Jan. 7, 1796. A. B.
Johnson, Joseph and Anna McGinnis, Feb. 28, 1805. C. S.
Johnson; Stephen and Elizabeth White, Nov. 2, 1817. J. B. T.
Johnson, Thomas and Susannah Hons, Dec. 31, 1801. J. B.
Johnson, William and Susannah Johnson, Jan. 13, 1801. J. B.
Johnston, Amos and Mary Grosman, Oct. 24, 1799. A. B.
Johnston, Amos and Rachel Williams, Feb. 22, 1825. J. D.
Johnston, Armstrong and Catherine Rigle, Sept. 14, 1809. L.C.
Johnston, Baldwin and Catherine Drish, Oct. 28, 1811. T. L.
Johnston, David and Catherine Bruner, Jan. 15, 1806. C. S.
Johnston, Dennis and Judy Jones, May 3, 1810. G.M.F.
Johnstone, George and Sarah Betting, July 5, 1792. C. S.
Johnston, George and Susannah Johnston, Sept. 16, 1816. A. B.
Johnston, George and Mary Day, April 24, 1822. J. W.
Johnston, John and Becky Riley, Aug. 12, 1790. C. S.
Johnston, John I. and Emily Brownley, Sept. 13, 1821. J.B.Jr.
Johnston, Joseph and Sarah Bonard, Nov. 29, 1792. A. B.
Johnston, Samuel and Sarah Carr, Dec. 28, 1809. J. W.
Johnston, Tunis and Margaret Martin, Sept. 3, 1790. C. S.
Johnston, William and Rose Mitchell, April 1, 1790. E. P.
Johnston, William and Frances Reynolds, June 28, 1789. A. B.
Johnston, William and Elizabeth Miller, April 15, 1813. J.B.T.
Johnston, William and Nancy Johnston, Feb. 7, 1811. J. W.
Joliffe, Amos and Margaret Perry, Oct. 16, 1794. A. B.
Joliffe, John and Frances Helm, March 19, 1807. A. B.
Jones, Benjamin and Susannah Murphy, Dec. 11, 1792. W. H.
Jones, Charles and Peggy Farmer, Oct. 18, 1796. A. B.
Jones, Elias and Jane Smith, Nov. 26, 1792. A. B.
Jones, Elias and Nancy Bishop, June 7, 1811. W. H.
Jones, Hubbard and Rachel Conway, Aug. 8, 1799. W. W.
Jones, John and Mary Schackelford, Oct. 24, 1783. A. B.
Jones, John and Dorothy Helpbringer, July 4, 1805. C. S.
Jones, John and Catherine Richards, Oct. 18, 1812. J.B.T.
Jones, John and Susan Usher, Aug. 1, 1812. G.M.F.
Jones, Joseph Harnet and Mariah Smith, Nov. 5, 1788. A. B.
Jones, Joseph H. and Lucy Young, Aug. 16, 1795. A. B.
Jones, Lewis and Arabella Pepper, Dec. 24, 1807. A. B.
Jones, Richard and Polly Lowry, March 19, 1816. G.M.F.
Jones, Robert and Celia Ann Myers, Jan. 3, 1820. G. R.
Jones, Steven and Catherine Bonhams, March 23, 1783. A. B.
Jones, Thomas and Elizabeth Peroint, Aug. 10, 1810. S.O.H.
Jordan, Thomas and Elizabeth Frost, June 11, 1816. W. H.

Kackley, Elias and Jane B. Dyson, Feb. 16, 1809. J.B.T.
Kackley, George and Elizabeth Johnston, June 7, 1808. C. S.
Kackley, Isaac and Catherine Milhorn, April 10, 1800. C. S.
Kackley, Jacob and Sarah Snapp, April 8, 1806. C. S.
Kain, Henry and Winny Jones, May 3, 1802. A. B.
Kain, James R. and Susan Kline, Nov. 5, 1822. J.B.T.
Karns, Elisha and Rachel Whitacre, Dec. 14, 1820. J. D.
Karns, Nathan and Elizabeth Noll, Jan. 11, 1821. J. D.
Karns, Nicholas and Ann Groves, Sept. 23, 1788. J. M.
Karr, David L. and Eleanor Pope, May 19, 1823. J. W.
Kean, Hugh and Margaret Thompson, Nov. 17, 1790. W. H.
Kean, William and Molly Brim, Dec. 16, 1798. A. B.
Kearnes,Edward and Rachel Barnett, Sept. 17, 1793. A. B.
Kearns, George and Elizabeth.Griffin, March 22, 1821. J. D.
Keeler, David and Louisa Uncowiter, May 30, 1811. JBT.
Keeler, John and Margaret Thompson, Nov. 27, 1817. J.B.T.
Keenan, Thomas and Margaret Lindsay, Dec. 28, 1794. A. B.
Kehoe, Michael and Jane McAll, July·14, 1792. A. B.
Kehoe, Peter and Ann Keary, Nov. 15, 1788. J. M.
Keller, Jacob and Elizabeth Cyfret, Aug. 20, 1801. A. B.
Keller, James and Christiana Hickman, Oct. 26, 1790. C. S.
Keller, John and Elizabeth Hickman, March 21, 1793. C. S.
Keller, Peter and Elizabeth Beaty, Nov. 18, 1804. J.B.T.
Kelly, Andrew and Mary Thomas, Dec. 2, 1790. A. B.
Kelly, John and Winnifred Boxwell, July 15, 1782. A. B.
Kelly, William and _____ McCab, March 7, 1799. J. W.
Kemble, John and Catherine Clemin, Dec. 23, 1786. A. B.
Kemp, John and Elizabeth Hooper, Dec. 24, 1792. N. L.
Kemp; John and Tabitha Love, Dec. 12, 1799. W. W.
Kemp, William and Sarah Headly, Jan. 8, 1800. J. I.
Kendall, Ranson and Lucy King, March 16, 1804. W. D.
Kendrick, Abraham and Hannah Harrell, Feb. 9, 1790. S. H.
Kendrick, Benjamin and Ann Funk, Oct. 18, 1785. S. H.
Kendrick, Jacob and Rebecca Headly, Dec. 5, 1816. W. N.
Kendrick, John and Lucinda Headley, Dec. 28, 1815. W. N.
Keneaster, John and Catherine Philips, Nov. 10, 1808. C. S.
Keneaster, John and Rebecca Boucher, Dec. 23, 1813. J.B.T.
Kennedy, John and Isabella Gray, April 2, 1797. A. B.
Kenner, Rhodam and Eleanor Roe, Dec. 29, 1790. E. P.
Kenner, Winder H. and Rachel McKay, June 10, 1817. J.B.T.
Kennerly, Thomas and Ann S. Carnegy, May 30, 1822. J.B.T.
Kenny, Joseph and Ann Windle, Nov. 14, 1822. W. H.
Kerby, John Jr. and Rebecca Farrell, Feb. 2, 1797. A. B.
Kerfoot, George L. and Catherine D. Sowers, Dec. 4, 1824. D.D
Kerfott, John B. and Elizabeth Taylor, Feb. 12, 1822. T.B.Jr.
Kerfott, Samuel and Elizabeth Chipley, Dec. 11, 1787. J. M.
Kerlin, Robert and Hannah Brooks, Sept. 23, 1799. J. W.
Kern, Adam and Christianna Andrews, Oct. 25, 1791. A. B.
Kern, Jacob and Rachel Cowgill, Feb. 15, 1791. B. S.
Kerns, Adam and Ruth Snyder, April 18, 1788. J. M.
Kerns, Daniel and Hannah Audedell, April 13, 1803. L. C.
Kerns, Jacob and Margaret Dawson, March 1, 1810. W. H.
Kerns, Nathan and Rachel Reed, Jan. 5, 1804. J. W.
Keyes, George and Anna Sands, Dec. 17, 1808. A. L.
Kieser, George and Mary Clinch, Oct. 13, 1787. C. S.
Kiger, George and Milly King, Jan. 20, 1790. C. S.
Kiger, George W. and Rebecca Rice, Jan. 5, 1809. C. S.

Kiger, Isaac and Lydia Rutter, Jan. 31, 1814. J. W.
Kiger, Jacob and Kitty Burkett, March 5, 1801. C. S.
Kiger, Joseph W. and Sally Townsend, Feb; 8, 1821. T. L.
Kile, Francis and Nancy Marpole, Feb. 13, 1817. G.M.F.
Kile, Isaac and Catherine Huntsberry, Dec. 4, 1822. J. W.
Kile, James and Sarah Freefar, Dec. 23, 1802. J. W.
Kindall, John and Velinde Sansbury, Oct. 19, 1797. W. W.
King, Elias and Lettice Norris, Jan. 13, 1806. W. D.
King, Henry and Jemimah Johnston, Feb. 5, 1816. G.M.F.
King, William H. and Alice Duff, Sept. 28, 1800. A. B.
Kinghan, John and Frances Walker, Oct. 24, 1793. C. S.
Kinlin, William and Lydia Littler, Oct. 18, 1798. J. P.
Kinner, Rodham and Betsy Haddox, Nov. 11, 1800. W. W.
Kiter, Jacob and Mary Lewis, Dec. 31, 1816. G.M.F.
Kizer, Philip and Elizabeth Gebhaart, Dec. 2, 1783. J. M.
Kline, Adam and Catherine Magdaline Boucher, April 4, 1786. C.S.
Kline, Caspar and Catherine Samsell, Nov. 12, 1795. E. P.
Kline, Philip and Polly Featherling, Oct. 24, 1799. C. S.
Klotz, Jacob and Eve Cryder, Sept. 30, 1794. S. H.
Klyne, Michael and Margaret Jones, Nov. 29, 1791. C. S.
Knabenshue, John and Elizabeth Sample, Aug. 8, 1797. A. B.
Knife, Jacob and Margaret Leonard, Jan. 4, 1816. J.B.T.
Knight, James Jr. and Elizabeth Williams, Oct. 23, 1783. J. M.
Knight, James and Martha Orr, Dec. 21, 1826. T. L.
Knox, Thomas F. and Mary Riely, April 5, 1803. W. H.
Koeler, John and Elizabeth Matthias, Jan. 23, 1814. J. W.
Koons, Philip and Abigail Baker, June 25, 1787. C. S.
Krim, Simon and Sarah Drake, July 31, 1826. J. A.
Kurtz, Adam and Elizabeth Bennett, Dec. 30, 1813. J. W.
Kyle, Frederick and Ann Mauck, July 23, 1803. J. W.

Lacey, Johnston and Ruth Clevenger, July 31, 1805. L. C.
Lafever, Thomas and Margaret Kearfoot, Dec. 16, 1818. G.M.F.
Lafler, John and Jemima Kendall, Dec. 10, 1793. C. S.
Lafolett, George and Sarah Stansbury, June 29, 1797. A. B.
Lafolett, George and Hannah Moore, March 1, 1803. J. W.
Lafolet, Isaac and Mary Kail, April 7, 1795. A. B.
Laidley, Thomas and Susannah Gray, Aug. 25, 1791. C. S.
Lambert, Frederick and Suannah Snodgrass, Aug. 1, 1809. C. S.
Lambert, Thomas and Cecelia Bennett, Dec. 4, 1792. A. B.
Lambert, Thomas and Dianna Harkins, Sept. 15, 1801. A. B.
Lamp, Mr. and Miss Ridgway, Feb. 11, 1813. A. S.
Lamp, George and Christianna Seecrist, July 2, 1811. C. S.
Lamp, John and Sarah Morrison, Feb. 11, 1813. A. S.
Landrom, Thomas and Margaret Ann Cryder, Aug. 10, 1816. J.B. T.
Lane, George Steptoe and Elizabeth T. Stribling, June 14, 1810. W
Lane, William and Catherine Vanmetre, Dec. 25, 1812. W. H.
Lang, Job and Nancy Griffen, June 27, 1798. J. W.
Lang, John and Mary Bealle, Jan. 1, 1807. A. B.
Lang, William Simpson and Elizabeth Smith, Nov. 11, 1798. W. W.
Langley, Benjamin and Martha Cochran, Sept. 21, 1790. C. S.
Langley, David and Mary Dore, Nov. 21, 1791. L. C.
Langley, Isaac and Rachel Barns, Aug. 14, 1788. J. M.
Langley, Jeremiah and Elizabeth Wilson, Feb. 22, 1791. C. S.
Langley, Joseph and Agnes Cochran, Dec. 3, 1795. E. P.

Lanham, Enos and Hannah Furr, March 5, 1813. G. M. F.
Lanham, George B. and Nancy Urton, Dec. 25, 1824. T. L.
Lanham, John and Matilda Fish, Aug. 19, 1823. T. L.
Lantz, Henry and Mary Tespers, Sept. 1, 1805. C. S.
Largent, Lewis and Betsy Hull, May 5, 1806. A. B.
Largent, Moses and Nancy Sevail, Nov. 8, 1804. A. B.
Larrick, Frederick and Elizabeth Seecrist, Dec. 18, 1806. C.
Larrick, Isaac and Mary Hodson, Feb. 1, 1807. C. S.
Larrick, Jacob and Catherine Snap, Sept. 6, 1804. C. S.
Larrick, John and Catherine Yoe, March 14, 1799. C. S.
Larrick, Joseph and Nancy Mauck, March 30, 1816. J. B.T.
Larue, Jacob and _____ Hatgen, Feb. 21, 1796. W. H.
Larue, John and Hannah Jackson, Aug. 16, 1798. J. H.
Latham, George and Lucy Drake, Dec. 19, 1786. C. S.
Lauck, Abraham and Anna Maria Sperry, Dec. 21, 1794. C. S.
Lauck, Simon and Mary Senseney, Oct. 26, 1803. J. W.
Lauck, William and Ann Cochran, Oct. 6, 1815. J. W.
Laugheed, John and Hannah Hanley, Oct. 11, 1792. W. H.
Law, John and Sarah Windsor, April 10, 1823. G. R.
Lawrence, James and Margaret Cumins, Nov. 26, 1785. C. S.
Lawson, William and Rebecca Grigsby, Oct. 17, 1809. W. N.
Lawyer, John and Catherine Carper, Aug. 2, 1792. C. S.
Lay, George and Una Martin, Feb. 9, 1817. T. L.
Leach, Benjamin and Mary Hooper, Jan. 5, 1804. J. W.
Leach, Collin and Dorcas Grasman, March 26, 1808. G. R.
Leach, William and Sarah Davis, April 23, 1812. J. W.
Lease, John and Magdalene Haymaker, June 24, 1792. C. S.
Ledig, Benedick and Catherine Martin, Feb. 7, 1792. C. S.
Lefever, John and Elizabeth Knight, June 2, 1786. J. M.
Lee, Asa and Elizabeth Higgins, March 15, 1816. J. W.
Lee, Barnet and Elizabeth Eltin, Nov. 5, 1789. E. P.
Lee, George and Mary Ridgeway Dec. 1, 1788. C. S.
Lee, John and Mary Riggles, Jan. 14, 1790. C. S.
Lee, Richard and Ann Green, Oct. 28, 1788. A. B.
Lee, Richard and Susan Abernathy, July 21, 1812. W. H.
Lee, Richard D. and Hannah Bryarly, Nov. 20, 1821. J.R.
Lee, Squire and Alcinda Alexander, Sept. 7, 1826. T. L.
Lee, Theodrica and Katherine Kite, April 20, 1793. A. B.
Lee, William and Matilda Ryan, March 12, 1826. T. L.
Leech, James and Elizabeth Cartmell, March 5, 1805. C. S.
Legrand, Nash and Peggy Holmes, March 7, 1793. M. H.
Lehu, Moses and Hannah Branson, April 15, 1800. J. I.
Lehue, William and Delphia McLeod, April 19, 17?2. E. P.
Leighton, James and Ann Burrell, Oct. 25, 1786. J. M.
Leisure, Zephaniah and Elizabeth Atchison, May 27, 1802. A.B.
Leitch, Joshua and Margaret Gobens, Aug. 6, 1812. J. C.
Leizure, John and Ann Hardin, Oct. 9, 1823. G. R.
Lemley, Jacob and Elizabeth Hotzenpiller, Dec. 24, 1818.JB.T.
Lemley, John and Susa Tay, Oct. 29, 1811. J.B. T.
Leonard, Peter and Jane Hammond, Dec. 27, 1791. C. S.
Lepscomb, John and Sarah Smith, Oct. 30, 1806. C. S.
Lester, John and Mary Grove, Jan. 29, 1797. A. B.
Lett, Benjamin and Mary Callaman, Jan. 5, 1809. J. W.
Lewis, Abraham and Dinah Fair, March 12, 1810. J. W.
Lewis, Edward and Nancy Clark, March 18, 1806. J. W.
Lewis, Evan and Margaret Fleet, Nov. 9, 1813. J. W.
Lewis, Henry and Susanna Hoge, Aug. 26, 1786. C. S.
Lewis, John and Rebecca Hott, Nov. 21, 1793. A. B.

Lewis, John and Elizabeth Trowbridge, Aug. 3, 1821. J. W.
Lewis, Samuel and Sarah Bailey, Nov. 15, 1735. A. B.
Lewis, Samuel and Sarah Sullivan, Oct. 8, 1800. J. W.
Lewis, Thomas and Diana Neff, March 11, 1817. G. M. F.
Light, Adam and Hannah Martin, Dec. 29, 1796. A. B.
Light, Frederick and Mary Oubry, April 9; 1801. J. B.
Likins, Jonas and Mary Eskstine, Aug. 22, 1786. C. S.
Likins, Joseph and Elizabeth Fawcett, March 11, 1819. J.B.T.
Likins, Leonard and Ruth Carter, Nov. 16, 1819. G.M.F.
Likins, Williams and Ruth Hays, Feb. 6, 1804. W. H.
Lilly, John and Eve Horn, Feb. 28, 1792. C. S.
Lindsey, Jacob and Mary Ewin, Nov. 12,1797. W. H.
Lindsay, James and Sarah Beiry, Jan. 28, 1807. W. H.
Lindsay, James B. and Sarah Shraack, Jan. 9, 1819. G.M. F
Lindsay, Thomas and Mary Ragan, Aug. 14, 1786. C. S.
Lindsey, Thomas and Keziah Jones, Oct. 16, 1806. C. S.
Lindsay, Thomas and Susan Stubblefield, Feb. 5, 1811. W. H.
Linkens,Belfield and Elizabeth Stokes, Sept. 28. 1815. J.B.T.
Linkheart, Thomas and Ellen Fisher, April 19, 1823. G. R.
Linn, John and Polly Mooney, Dec. 6, 1792. W. H.
Linn, William and Deborah Morgan, Oct. 4, 1792. W. H.
Linton, George and Elizabeth Adiddle, May 14, 1791. E. P.
Linvill, John and Elizabeth Shivertaker, Oct. 23, 1792. E. P.
Lipscomb, William and Nancy Marcus, Aug. 4, 1791. A. B.
Lister, William and Juliet Dawson, Dec. 23, 1809. J. W.
Little, Adam and Martha Patton, Sept. 1, 1808. J. B. T.
Little, David and Nancy Riggle, Sept. 4, 1814. J.B.T.
Littler, Joseph B. and Mary E. Savage, Apr. 4, 1809. S.O.H.
Littler, Samuel and Nancy Williams, Oct. 18, 1792. W. H.
Littler, Thomas and Mary Ridgway, Sept. 12, 1822.
Livingston, John and Pleasants Waters, Jan. 22, 1793.C.S.
Lloyd, Henry and Nelly Warren, June 5, 1821. T. L.
Lloyd, Shadrack and Elizabeth Shrock, Sept. 29, 1796. A. B.
Lloyd, William and Ann Tilman, June 28, 1787. A. B.
Lloyd, William and Elizabeth Blake, March 23, 1817. T. L.
Lloyd, William and Sarah Skaggs, Jan. 2, 1812. J.B.T.
Lobb, Charles and Sarah Ross, Nov. 23, 1801. A. B.
Lockhart, David and Rachel Lewis, Aug. 21, 1789. C. S.
Lock, William and Catherine Moody, Feb. 28, 1799. C. S.
Lockhard, William and Joanna Train, (widow) Nov. 22, 1787. S.
Lockry, Philip and Margaret Harmun, Oct. 2, 1797. A. B.
Long, John and Henrietta Chrisman, Dec. 4, 1806. C. S.
Long, Nimrod and Eleanor E. Williams, Sept. 26, 1793. A. B.
Long, Thomas and Mary Hodson, April 17, 1792. C. S.
Long, Thomas and Elizabeth Elliott, Feb. 10, 1817. T. L.
Longacre, Joseph M. and Elizabeth Sexsmith, Dec. 12, 1820. J.B.T
Louchery, Daniel and Mary Wickam, March 15, 1791. R. S.
Louchry, Patrick and Caty Hickman, Nov. 15, 1791. R. S.
Louder, Henry and Mary Henderson, May 27, 1788. J. M.
Lovell, Charles U. and Mary E. Long, Sept. 22, 1814. A. B.
Low, William and Mary Peterson, Oct. 5, 1785. C. S.
Lowry, Moses and Mary Snapp, Nov. 14, 1799. C. S.
Lowery, William and Rachel Bell, June 24, 1825. W. H.
Lowndes, Charles and Frances Whiting, Nov. 23, 1809. A. B.
Lowry, Frederick and Elizabeth Shell, Sept. 9, 1809. J. W.
Lowry, George and Nancy Boyce, Dec. 4, 1814. J. W.
Lowry, James and Mary Dutton, Aug. 14, 1811. J. W.
Lowry, John and Jane Thompson, Nov. 16, 1805. W. H.

Lowry, Robert and Rachel Crum, Nov. 4, 1813. W. A.
Lowry, William and Margaret Bellert, June 1, 1815. A. B.
Loy, Andrew and Mary Smith, Aug. 24, 1820. G. R.
Loy, Conrad and Catherine Hannon, Dec. 29, 1791. C. S.
Loy, Michael and Thesby Anderson, Jan. 24, 1788. S. H.
Loy, Peter and Elizabeth Lewis, Sept. 5, 1807. W. H.
Loyd, Stephen and Sally Pingstaff, Sept. 15, 1791. C. S.
Ludwick, John and Elizabeth Cooley, Sept. 3, 1790. C. S.
Luke, John and Susannah Johnston, April 21, 1787. C. S.
Lukins, Peter and Hannah Thompson, March 10, 1819.
Lupton, David and Ruth Adams, Jan. 3, 1816. G.M.F.
Lupton, John and Elizabeth Cartmell, July 20, 1790. E. P.
Lupton, John and Mary Ann Williams, May 31, 1811. J. W.
Lupton, Nathaniel C. and Elizabeth Hodgson, March 13, 1822. J
Lupton, Thomas C. and Sarah Hamilton, -- -- 1813. J. W.
Luttrel, Robert and Barbara Buzzard, Nov. 1, 1796. A. B.
Luttrell, Robert and Fanny Grove, March 8, 1821. J. D.
Lyle, James and Mary Horseman, May 3, 1811. J. W.
Lynn, John and Catherine Cook, Nov. 21, 1798. C. S.
Lyons, Levi and Rachel Kackley, Feb. 18, 1810. C. S.
Lytle, Charles and Lydia Parkins, April 24, 1822.

McAllester, John and Alice Wilson, June 25, 1818. W. Hill.
McAllister, John and Elizabeth Joliffe, Oct, 5, 1797. A. B.
McAnulty, William and Elizabeth Jenkins, May 30, 1792. C. S.
McArter, Eli and Rebecca Grum, Nov. 16, 1801. Jas. W.
McAtee, Thomas and Sarah Paine, Nov. 15, 1796. A. B.
McBride, James and Catherine Frister, Oct. 8, 1798. A. B.
McBride, John and Ann Maloy, Aug. 11, 1803. C. S.
McBride, Thomas and Mary McVicker, March 9, 1797. A. B.
McCabe, William and Mary Kelley, Oct. 26, 1799. Jas. W.
McCallum, Samuel and Nancy Spears, July 31, 1806. A. B.
McCally, Barnebas and Anna Doughty, Oct. 9, 1800. W. W.
McCally, Joshua and Jane Rusk, Sept. 10, 1799. C. S.
McCann, William and Jane McLaughlin, Oct. 16, 1794. C. S.
McCandless, Robert and Rachel Perry, Sept. 22, 1796. A. B.
McCarty, Joseph and Rebecca Curlett, Dec. 10, 1795. E. P.
McCaully, William and Nancy Templeman, Oct. 17, 1799. Jas. W.
McCausland, John and Mary Hamilton, July 2, 1791. C. S.
McChestney, William and Rebecca Shadacre, March 28, 1786. C.S.
McClue, Jesse and Elizabeth Whitacre, June 11, 1795. E. P.
McClunn, Jonathan and Sarah Cryder, Dec. -- 1807. J.B.T.
McClun, Thomas and Elizabeth Bailey, April 16, 1793. E. P.
McClure, John and Sarah Burke, Jan. 19, 1821. W. Hill.
McCoole, John and Cassandra Dent, Oct. 3, 1822. J. D.
McCoole, Lewis and Nancy Weaver, Sept. 22, 1808. A. B.
McCord, George and Elizabeth Hendrick, Aug. 2, 1792. C. S.
McCormick, Chapline E. and Lydia Gorden, May 22, 1822. Jas. W
McCormick, Dawson and Florinda L. Milton, Jan. 8, 1824. W. Hi.
McCormick, James and Jemimah Violet, Feb. 26, 1792. W. H.
McCormick, Michael and Mary Ann Cooke, April 6, 1786. J. M.
McCormick, Obur (?) and Mary Easten, March 7, 1786. A. B.

McCormick, William and Eliza Rice, Jan. 10, 1795. W. Hill.
McConnel, James and Elizabeth Luckey, May 3, 1808. W. Hill.
McConnell, Abraham and Margaret Touchstone, June 15, 1809. A.B
McCoy, John and Lydia Sugand, Aug. 7, 1798. Jas. W.
McCoy, Otho and Nancy Rockerbaugh, Dec. 29, 1825. T. L.
McCracken, Thomas and Margaret Smith, March 5, 1795. A. B.
McCrea, Charles and Phebe Lindsay, Jan. 13, 1807. W. Hill.
McDaniel, Shelton and Mary Lyons, Aug. 8, 1822. T. L.
McDaniel, Stephen and Margaret Peacock, Oct. 19, 1799. Jas. W.
McDaniel, William and Hannah Phillips, May 15, 1794. C. S.
McDonald, Benjamin and Mercy Reed, Dec. 31, 1788. C. S.
McDonald, Charles and Jemimah Carter, Dec. 14, 1797. A. B.
McDonald, Daniel and Susannah Nicklen, Apr. 14, 1796. A. B.
McDonald, Enoch and Peggy Evans, Oct. 23, 1799. W. W.
McDonald, James and Jane McCormack, Apr. 14, 1791. W. H.
McDonald, James and Eleanor Bulger, Aug. 21, 1794. C. S.
McDonald, James and Mary Cather, March 12, 1795. A. B.
McDonald, Jared and Elizabeth McDonald, Feb. 2, 1825. T. L.
McDonald, Jesse and Nelly Leach, Jan. 15, 1799. W. W.
McDonnall, Moses and Catherine Light, Nov. 1, 1806. Jas. W.
McDonald, Samuel and Elizabeth Graves, July 4, 1822. T. L.
McDonald, Thomas and Susannah Corder, Dec. 19, 1803. W. D.
McDonald, Thomas and Mary Magruder, Dec. 20, 1826. T. L.
McDonald, William and Lucinda Ferguson, March 26, 1823. T. L.
McEndree, Nimrod and Mary Ramey, April 1, 1824. T. L.
McFadden, John and Susannah McIlwaine, May 7, 1801. J. Wells
McFarland, Joseph and Hannah Speers, Dec. 28, 1798. J. I.
McFarling, James and Eleanor Dowling, Nov. 22, 1818. T. L.
McFarling, John and Judith Snyder, Feb. 21, 1807. Jas. W.
McGhahay, Jeremiah Oxley and Elizabeth Murray, Feb. 1, 1801. J
McGairy, Edward and Elizabeth Potter, Oct. 25, 1790. A. B.
McGrath, Charles C. and Ann McLaughlin, July 15, 1798. A. B.
McGruder, Aquilla and Mary Anne McGruder, March 26, 1799. A. B
McGuin, Philip and Ann Moulding, June 25, 1818. T. L.
McGuinn, William and Elizabeth Hall, Dec. 3, 1815. A. B.
McGuire, Andrew and Molly Smith, April 16, 1801. A. B.
McGuire, William and Mary Little, April 11, 1792. A. B.
McIlhenny, John and Harriet Milton, March 13, 1806. A. B.
McIntire, Daniel and Lydia Hittle, July 7, 1816. J. B. T.
McIntosh, John and Sarah Wilkenson, Jan. 16, 1783. J. M.
McIntosh, Joseph and Rachel Bruce, July 8, 1817. J. F.
McIntyre, William and Elizabeth Conner, Oct. 28, 1790. A. B.
McKay, Abraham and Harriet Stephens, Jan. 8, 1823. W. M.
McKay, George and Mary Ferguson, Feb. 6, 1823. T.B. Jr.
McKay, Jacob Jr. and Elizabeth Antrim, Dec. 24, 1807. L. C.
McKay, Joseph and Sally E. Garrison, Nov. 24, 1825. T.B. Jr.
McKee, John and Rebecca Wickersham, Aug. 7, 1792. A. B.
McKee, John Ferguson and Jane Marple, Jan. 31, 1799. C. S.
McKee, Joseph and Elizabeth Reed, Feb. 5, 1799. J. W.
McKee, Joseph and Sidney Capper, March 24, 1825. J. D.
McKee, Robert and Jane Cather, Sept. 5, 1793. C. S.
McKee, Robert and Susannah Dalby, Jan. 23, 1793. A. B.
McKee, William and Martha Hammond, May 4, 1791. A. B.
McKee, William and Ann LaFollett, Sept. 16, 1819. J. D.
McKeever, Paul and Margaret Swisher, Feb. 12, 1794. B. S.
McKenny, Oliver and Catherine Barton, April 27, 1817. J.B.T.

McKeewan, Michael and Mary Sedwick, Dec. 29, 1785. A. B.
McKeewan, Thomas and Rachel Harry, Oct. 19, 1797. A. B.
McKinsay, James and Susannah Bruin, April 26, 1798. C. S.
McLaughlin, Joseph and Polly Berlyn, Sept. 15, 1811. Jas. W.
McLaughlin, Thomas and Frances A. Taylor, July 1, 1824. R.F.F
McLeod, Henry and Parthenia Shackelford, July -- 1804. J.B.T.
McLeod, Martin and Elsey Self, March 21, 1797. J. I.
McLury, Thomas and Polly Linn, Dec. 18, 1792. W. H.
McMakir, John and Mary Miers, Jan. 2, 1790. E. P.
McMan, Timothy and Mary Gold, Aug. 6, 1822. D. D.
McMichael, Nathaniel and _____ Fossett, Nov. 8, 1792. E. P.
McMillan, John and Celia Davis, Dec. 10, 1789. C. S.
McMillon, Hugh and Mary Love, April 9, 1801. W. W.
McMorris, David and Sarah White, March 3, 1811: T. L.
McMullen, Alex. and Elizabeth Murphy, April 12, 1789. C. S.
McMullen, Alexander and Frances Richards, March 14, 1807. G.
McMullen, Hugh and Patty Stewart, May 21, 1806. A. B.
McMullen, Robert and Mary Ann Rust, Nov. 6, 1787. A. B.
McMunn, George and Elizabeth Litler, Dec. 12, 1793. C. S.
McMurray, John W. and Elizabeth Kerfott, Jan. 26, 1815. A.A.S.
McNeilly, Hugh and Mary Kiger, April 1, 1790. C. S.
McPherson, Jesse and Ann Ash, Sept. 4, 1788. C. S.
McPherson, John and Jemimah Murdock, July 6, 1789. A. B.
McPherson, Samuel and Sally Douglass, July 27, 1815. A. B.
McPherson, Stephen and Sarah Kibbs, July 2, 1791. C. S.
McPherson, Stephen and Phoebe Murdick, Dec. 11, 1794. A. B.
McReedy, William and Hester Scoggen, Nov. 17, 1788. C. S.
McWade, Edward and Sarah Lewis, Feb. 24, 1803. Jas. W.
McWheat, James and Elizabeth King Shaw, May 15, 1796. A. B.
McWhorter, Alexander and Jane Alban, July 7, 1803. Jas. W.
McWhorter, Robert and Mary Linn, May 4, 1818. G.M.F.
McWilliams, Robert and Martha Lindsey, Feb. 6, 1806. C. S.
Mackall, Frederick and Elizabeth Mires, Sept. 11, 1783. A. B.
Macky, John and Hannah Smith, Feb. 26, 1811. C. S.
Macky, John and Rebecca Holmes McGuire, May 25, 1815. A. B.
Madden, Maba (?) and Sarah Bonham, March 29, 1791. W. H.
Madden, Peter and Susan Wheelin, Jan. 31, 1799. B. D.
Madden, George and Phebe Farmer?, Jan. 17, 1786. C. S.
Madden, William and Jenny Hainey, May 12, 1800. J. I.
Madden, William and Sarah Risler, Jan. 8, 1816. J. W.
Madison, James Jr.(Pres. of U.S.) & Dolly Payne Todd, Sept. 15,
Magill, Charles & Mary Thruston, May 24, 1792. A. B.
Mahany, Lewis and Julia Cartwright, Dec. 8, 1811. J.B.T.
Maheny, Thomas and Mary McDonald, June 4, 1804. J. W.
Mahew, Lloyd and Sarah Thompson, Jan. 27, 1825. J.D.
Mahew, Nathan and Betsy Ruble, Jan. 27, 1825. J.B.
Mahu, Benjamin and Sarah Reed, Jan. 10, 1794. A. B.
Mahoney, James and Betsy McLunn, Dec. 28, 1792. A.B.
Mainer, Benjamin and Catherine Marsh, Dec. 21, 1814. W. H.
Mainey, James and Rachel Burns, Oct. 8, 1782. J. M.
Malin, Job and Ann March, May 16, 1793. C. S.
Malloy, Thomas and Sary Brown, May 21, 1801. C. S.
Malone, George and Sarah Davis, May 31, 1818. T. L.
Maloney, John and Elizabeth Keys, April 12, 1793. N. L.
Mann, James and Sarah Schofield, Oct. 4, 1786. J. M.
Mann, Rorak and Ann Perkeson, Sept. 25, 1784. J. M.
Mann, William and Sarah Rinker, Aug. 28, 1822. J. W.
Mara? Francis and Ann Hulett, April 22, 1789. A. B.
Mariner, Benjamin and Catherine Roach, Jan. 19, 1823. J.J.R.

Mark, Harry and Caty Stone, April 19, 1798. A. B.
Mark, John and Martha Smiley, Oct. 11, 1796. W. W.
Marks, John and Rebecca Elzey, Oct. 25, 1800. W. W.
Marks, Zachariah and Jane Craig, Oct. 30, 1794. A. B.
Markwood, David and Elizabeth Ensley, May 24, 1821. J. W.
Marlow, John and Rebecca Nisewanger, Aug. 16, 1792. C. S.
Marple, Benjamin and Barbara Purtlebaugh, March 16, 1805. J.D.
Marple, Enoch and Elizabeth Johnston, June 17, 1819. J. B.
Marple, Joseph and Mary Purtlebaugh, Sept. 17, 1805. J. W.
Marple, Thomas and Abigail Smith, Oct. 12, 1790. C. S.
Marpole, Thomas and Ann Fuller, April 20, 1807. J. W.
Marple, Uriah and Rachel Wright, Feb. 8, 1821. J. D.
Marney, John and Jane Vance, Oct. -- 1806. J. B. T.
Marquis, Isaac and Elizabeth Beavers, Feb. 16, 1795. C. S.
Marquis, James and Rebecca Smith, Sept. 6, 1787. A. B.
Marquis, Levi and Sarah Davis, Dec. 29, 1824. T. L.
Marquis, Zacariah and Hettalom Lowry, March 31, 1816. A. B.
Marricke, George and Elizabeth Kerns, July 3, 1786. C. S.
Marsh, Edward and Anna Maria Linn, May 30, 1805. C. S.
Marsh, John and Mary Maloney, Dec. 21, 1814. W. H.
Marshall, Thomas and Jennett Gilkeson, March 8, 1787. J. M.
Marshall, Thomas and Catherine G. Taylor, March 24, 1819. W. H.
Marshall, William and Betsy Coale, Dec. 27, 1792. W. H.
Marshall, William and Nancy Rust, Nov. 7, 1815. J.B.T.
Martain, Hugh and Rebecca Baldwin, Sept. 30, 1790. W. H.
Marthena? Daniel ? and Sarah Curry, Oct. 14, 1788. A. B.
Martin, Conrad and Eva Yanders, Dec. 29, 1804. W. H.
Martin, Jacob and Hannah Henshaw, March 31, 1808. A. B.
Martin, Joel and Rachel Ellis, March 23, 1805. J. W.
Martin, James Lee and Mary Frye, May 21, 1793. C. S.
Martin, Robert and Caty Hickman, Aug. 10, 1791. C. S.
Martin, Silas and Polly Thompson, Sept. 12, 1792. A. B.
Martin, Snowden and Elizabeth Thornborough, April 14, 1801. C. S
Martin, Thomas and Mary T (L)avender, Aug. 21, 1794. A. B.
Martin, Vincent and Rhody Williams, Dec. 3, 1788. C. S.
Martin, William and Mary Johnston, Nov. 26, 1817. T. L.
Mash, Henry and Betsy Likins, Dec. 29, 1792. W. H.
Mason, Abraham and Elizabeth Grove, Dec. 11, 1786. C. S.
Mason, Andrew and Mary Everett, Dec. 27, 1796. A. B.
Mason, Armistead T. and Eliza Parker, May 24, 1809. A. B.
Mason, Jacob and Hannah Cogill, Feb. 24, 1803. W. D.
Mason, Jonathan and Helen Braithwaite, March 20, 1822. J. D.
Mason, William and Sarah Shackelford, Dec. 17, 1792. C. S.
Massie, Duncan T. and Louzetta Tuly, Feb. 4, 1623. W. M.
Massie, Thomas B. and Sidney Ashby, June 2, 1825. T. K.
Massie, Welford P. and Patsy D. Kiger, June 20, 1817. T. L.
Mathias, Francis and Airy Brown, May 3, 1789. A. B.
Matlock, Thomas and Martha Reese, Nov. 1, 1792. A. B.
Matson, Aaron and Polly Hollingshead, --'-- 1809. J. W.
Matson, John and Parthena Cooper, May 15, 1811. J. W.
Mattox, Robert and Eleanor Anderson, Nov. 12, 1811. A. S.
Mauck, George and Elizabeth Mauck, July 25, 1811. J.B.T.
Mauck, Jacob and Rebecca Weaver, Jan. 28, 1817. J.B.T.
Mauck, Michael and Barbara Keiser, Oct. 21, 1788. A. B.
Mauk, Anthony and Sarah Price, Feb. 9, 1804. C. S.
Mauzey, Peter and Elizabeth Buzzard, July 12, 1790. A. B.
Maxell, John and Parthenia Cartmell, June -- 1807. J.B.T.
May, John and Elizabeth Campbell, July 27; 1801. J. B.
Mayhew, Tilghman and Ruth Parscel, May 15, 1819. J.B.T.
Marker, George and Mary Strosnyder, Jan. 17, 1811. A. S.

Marker, Jacob and Mary Kline, Jan. 17, 1786. C. S.
Marker, John and Sarah Sibert, Nov. 15, 1810. A. S.
Majors, Joseph and Polly Pollock, May 2, 1802. C. S.
Mayhugh, William andMary Ducker, Feb. 28, 1812. J. W.
Mayhew, William and Kitty Winn, Aug. 8, 1805. A. B.
Meade, William and Mary Nelson, Jan. 31, 1810. A. B.
Maldrum, Robert and Elizabeth Bell, Jan. 13, 1816. J. W.
Mellon, William and Esther Berry, Oct. 25, 1792. W. H.
Melton, Thomas and Mary Pickett, Dec. 14, 1790. W. H.
Mendenhall, Samuel and Martha Reed, Aug. 29, 1817. W. H.
Mercer, Edward and Mary Dinah Steere, April 29, 1793. C. S.
Mercer, Edward and Mary Ellis, Sept. 9, 1794. C. S.
Mercer, John and Lysia Barrett, April 21, 1789. C. S.
Mercer, John and Ann Babb, Sept. 12, 1792. A. B.
Mercer, Jonathan and Sampson Babb, Aug. 9, 1790. A. B.
Mercer, Joseph and Comfort Nottingham, Sept. 9, 1790. A. B.
Mercer, Joseph and Nancy Young ?, Oct. 10, 1799. J. W.
Mercer, Moses and Eleanor Ellis, Sept. 19, 1792. C. S.
Mercer, Robert and Hannah Mercer, Nov. 18, 1797. A. B.
Mercer, William and Ann Webb, Aug. 1, 1786. C. S.
Merchant, John and Sarah Bishop, Nov. 16, 1790. W. H.
Merly, John and Elizabeth Shepherd, June 14, 1792. C. S.
Messmore, Peter and Susannah Chisel, June 19, 1800. A. B.
Metheny, Archibald and Jean Curry, Dec. 13, 1786. A. B.
Metz, Henry and Polly Kingan, Jan. -- 1810. J. W.
Miars, George and Mary Windel, Aug. 12, 1808. J. W.
Michan, William and Mary Lindsey, June 9, 1783. A. B.
Middleton, John and Eleanor Hardy, March 28, 1797. A. B.
Middleton, William and Milley McPherson, Oct. 12, 1797. A. B.
Miers, Jacob and Lydia Snyder, March 3, 1814. J.B.T.
Miers, Jacob and Jane Brown, Nov. 15, 1792. C. S.
Miers, Martin and Christiana Somers, Feb. 14, 1792. C. S.
Milburn, Everet and Rachel Clark, March 11, 1812. J. W.
Milburn, John Sr. and Mary Bryant, Nov. 24, 1791. C. S.
Milburn, John and Eleanor Glen, Nov. 9, 1790. W. H.
Milburn, John and Rebecca Likins, March 24, 1807. J. W.
Milburn, Joseph and Mary Long, Sept. 18, 1820. J. W.
Milbourne, Robert and Sebely Enghan, Feb. 26, 1783. A. B.
Miles? George and Hannah Parker, May 4, 1786. C. S.
Miley, Jacob and Fannie Glasscock, Dec. 5, 1798. C. S.
Milhorn, Henry and Catherine Ewe, Sept. 22, 1789. C. S.
Milhorn, Henry and Polly Williams, Jan. 31, 1793. E. P.
Milhorn, John and Elizabeth Hackly, Dec. 25, 1797. C. S.
Milhorn, John and Mary Shull, Jan. 21, 1823. G.M.F.
Milhorn, Peter and Catherine Lamp, July 21, 1789. C. S.
Millar, Isaac and Rachel Anderson, Dec. 1, 1793. A. B.
Millar, John W. and Polly Headly, Sept. 17, 1803. J. I.
Millar, Robert and Margaret Nelson, Jan. 14, 1798. A. B.
Miller, Adam and Nancy Cheek, June 7, 1798. W. W.
Miller, Abraham and Ann Stickley, March 16, 1822. J.B.T.
Miller, Alexander and Elizabeth Barton, April 27, 1797. J.B.
Miller, Benjamin and Susannah Bush, Dec. 4, 1799. J. W.
Miller, Casper and Barbara Weaver, Oct. 9, 1787. C. S.
Miller, Christopher and Mary Weaver, Dec. 11, 1793. C. S.
Miller, George and Eve Gilbert, June 28, 1788. C. S.
Miller, Henry and Actstiah Warner(?), May 14, 1782. J. M.
Miller, Henry and Catherine Barr, Oct. 6, 1803. C. S.
Miller, Jacob and Lucy Hicks, Sept. 14, 1798. A. B.
Miller, Jacob and Martha Miller, April 27, 1801. C. S.
Miller, James and Kitty Allensworth, March 8, 1816. W. N.

Miller, John and Margaret Sperry, April 14, 1803. C. S.
Miller, John and Julianna Shaver, Jan. 19, 1812. J.B.T.
Miller, John and Hannah Bell, Jan. 25, 1820. G.M.F.
Miller, Joseph and Elizabeth Parkins, April 9, 1795. C. S.
Miller, Joseph and Mary Rust, Dec. 10, 1800. L. C.
Miller, Peter and Priscilla Watson, April 29, 1806. A. B.
Mills, Robert and Eliza B. Smith, Oct. 15, 1808. A. B.
Miller, Robert F. and Martha W. Williams, June 3, 1824. T.B.Jr.
Miller, Samuel and Mariah Bedinger, March 27, 1816. A. B.
Miller, William and Rebecca Powell, April 5, 1787. C. S.
Milton, Alexander and Sarah Stribling, July 1, 1802. C. S.
Milton, Alexander Ross and Harriet McCormick, April 20, 1819.
                                                       W. Hill
Milton, Elijah and Catherine Taylor, Jan. 28, 1794. A. B.
Milton, John and Ann Stribling, July 21, 1782. A. B.
Milton, John and Catherine Nelson, Feb. 20, 1812. A. B.
Milton, John and Louisa T. Taylor, Sept. 7, 1826. W. H.
Mills, Isaac D. and Charlotte Simpson, Oct. 16, 1825. J. W.
Mimm, Gilbert and Frances Simrall, Aug. 1, 1793. A. B.
Minein?, Jacob and Rebecca Hancher, June 28, 1787. A. B.
Minick, Jasper and Caty Kain, Aug. 19, 1790. C. S.
Minshall, Isaac and Catherine Allison, April 23, 1801. J. W.
Minson, John and Tamson Butler, July 2, 1811. J. W.
Mitchell, Henry and Mary Tuly, Nov. 20, 1811. W. H.
Mitchell, Joseph and Winifred Jones, April 23, 1803. J. W.
Mitchell, Thomas and Deborah Parkins, Dec. 4, 1794. C. S.
Mock, Frederick and Barbara Cryser, Aug. 16, 1783. A. B.
Moloy, Hugh and Margaret Davis, Jan. 25, 1786. C. S.
Monroe, John and Sarah Craig, Jan. 6, 1805. A. B.
Monroe, John and Lucy Louthan, April 21, 1812. W. H.
Monroe, John and Ethalinda Wilkerson, March 31, 1822. W. M.
Monroe, Robert M. and Sidney Grubbs, May 13, 1824. T.B.Jr.
Montgomery, Benjamin and Ann Nottingham, Dec. 24, 1789. C. S.
Moore, Elijah and Frances Weedon, Oct. 3, 1825. J.B.T.
Moore, James and Catherine Elizabeth Sperry, Dec. 9, 1792. C.-i
Moore, John and Mary Brown, April 29, 1783. J. M.
Moore, John and Deliah Taylor, June 22, 1790. W. H.
Moore, John and Kitty Siders, Jan. 14, 1808. L. C.
Moore, Solomon and Rebecca Barrow, June 11, 1818. J.B.T.
Moore, William and Maria Chloe Grim, Jan. 28, 1790. C. S.
More, Elisha and Jane Ross, Oct. 9, 1792. W. H.
More, John and Catherine Larick, April 1, 1794. C. S.
Morehead, Joel and Kitty Ashby, Feb. 13, 1804. W. D
Morford, James and Jane Kennedy, Oct. 12, 1790. C. S.
Moreland, John B. and Galazy Lloye, April 18, 1822. T. L.
Morgan, Abel and Rachel Bennett, Nov. 27, 1800. A. B.
Morgan, Daniel and Elizabeth Lindsay, Oct. 16, 1794. A. B.
Morgan, George and Clara Coates, Sept. 10, 1801. A. B.
Morgan, John and Elizabeth Gaunt, Dec. 25, 1804. W. H.
Morgan, Noah and Sarah Wilson, Sept. 11, 1806. A. B.
Morgan, William and Phebe Ball, March 2, 1795. C. S.
Morgan, Zacquill and Rachel Marple, May 29, 1798. A. B.
Morison, Patt and Eleanor Lines, May 30, 1797. A. B.
Morris, Enoch and Susannah Wilson, June 10, 1788. J. M.
Morris, Frisby and Betsy Ann Cooley, March 16, 1817. A. B.
Morris, Manly and Elizabeth Dowell, Dec. 4, 1811. J. W.
Morris, Samuel and Rebecca McDonald, Nov. 2, 1797. A. B.
Morris, Thomas and Elizabeth Hall, -- 25, 1813. J. W.

Morrison, James and Arisby McGinnis, July 15, 1789. A. B.
Morrison, James and Mary Spender, Aug. 19, 1800. J. I.
Morrison, Jesse and Sarah Taylor, Dec. 22, 1796. A. B.
Moseley, Jesse and Mary Kortze, Dec. 21, 1790. W. H.
Moseley, William and Elizabeth Smith, Jan. 14, 1795. E. P.
Mott, John and Elizabeth Helm, March 8, 1806. W. H.
Mouser, Jacob and Eve Banner, Nov. 10, 1789. C. S.
Mouser, Jacob and Christiana Andries, Oct. 18, 1790. C. S.
Mowry, Frederick and Jane Wilson, Oct. 22, 1811. J. B. T.
Mowser, John and Catherine Hunsicker, April 9, 1787. C. S.
Mowry, Hiram and Rebecca Frye, Sept. 26, 1824. R. F.
Muckay, John and Catherine Pangler, March 17, 1822. J.B.T.
Mulini, Jonathan and Elizabeth Chapman, Nov. 21, 1799. A. B.
Mullinix, Jacob and Elizabeth Hays, March 23, 1820. G.M.F.
Mullinix, Nathan and Catherine Pulse, June 14, 1816. G.M.F.
Mumma, George and Nancy Garmong, Dec. 22, 1814. J.B.T.
Mumma, John and Peggy Hass, April 5, 1822. W. M.
Murdock, George W. and Jacqueline H. Smith, Nov. 10, 1815. J.W.
Murdock, William and Elizabeth Read, June 9, 1796. A. B.
Murphy, Daniel and Ann Davis, Sept. 13, 1810. T. L.
Murphy, Josiah and Mary Ramey, April 1, 1824. T. L.
Murphy, Samuel and Polly Thruston, March 27, 1817. A. B.
Murphy, Zachariah and Catherine Hoyle, Dec. 6, 1795. A. B.
Murray, Cyrus W. and Elizabeth Baker, Oct. 26, 1809. W. H.
Murray, George and Mary Christian, March 21, 1786. A. B.
Murray, John and Elizabeth Williamson, Oct. 10, 1797. A. B.
Murray, John and Cynthia Johnston, Aug. 26, 1804. J. W.
Muse, Elisha and Charity Boyd, Oct. 30, 1787. A. B.
Muse, John and Susannah Johnston, Oct. 1, 1811. W. H.
Musgrove, John and Elizabeth Shown, July 25, 1786. A. B.
Musgrove, Thomas and Mary Newton, Feb. 7, 1786. C. S.
Mussleman, Michael and Sophia Gier, March 15, 1820. J.B.T.
Myers, Daniel and Ann French, Aug. 4, 1824. J. A.
Myers, George and Polly Showalter, Nov. 4, 1819. J.B.T.
Myer, John and Mary Delong, Sept. 28, 1800. C. S.
Myers, John and Margaret Bost, Nov. 23, 1802. J. W.
Myers, John and Sarah Love, April 5, 1808. J.B.T.
Myers, John and Rachel Rosebrock, Oct. 3, 1811. J.B.T.
Myers, Joshua and Tibetha Stephens, July 2, 1793. E. P.
Myers, Joseph and Mary Mumma, July 13, 1816. J.B.T.
Myers, Leonard and Emily C.Poland Feb. 15, 1826. J. A.
Myers, Michael and Jane Peterson, Sept. 4, 1786. C. S.
Myers, Samuel and Mary Trout, Dec. 21, 1818. T. K.
Myers, Stephen and Rachel Griffin, Nov. 6, 1802. J. W.
Mytinger, Isaac and Elizabeth Pitman, July 16, 1807. J.B.T.
Mytinger, Daniel and Catherine Campfield, Nov. 25, 1782. J. M.

Nagle, John and Elizabeth Pickler, July 3, 1798. W. F.
Neff, Francis and Elizabeth Hollingshead, Aug. 7, 1815. G.M.F.
Neff, Jacob and Elizabeth Nutt, March 18, 1816. G.M.F.
Neff, James and Catherine Singhorse, Nov. 13, 1808. A. B.
Neff, John and Elizabeth Hicky, Oct. 5, 1801. J. W.
Neill, Lewis and Ann Stribling, Sept. 20, 1815. W. H.
Neill, Thomas and Phebe Larue, Aug. 20, 1795. W. H.
Neill, William and Hannah Mahoney, May 26, 1811. W. H.
Neilson, William and Arianna J. Wormeley, March 2, 1813. W. H.

Nelson, Abraham and Mary Conner, Sept. 15, 1803. C. S.
Nelson, Matthias and Catherine Reynolds, Dec. 20, 1793. C. S.
Nelson, Robert and Mary Oats, Feb. 27, 1820. J. D.
Neville, Hiram and Harriet Babb, July 22, 1818. G.M.F.
Nevill, John and Elizabeth Carper, May 14, 1823. J. W.
Newell, William and Rebecca Cooper, April 27, 1809. J. B. T.
Newbrough, William and Ann Ridgeway, Jan. 13, 1825. J. D.
Newgent, John and Mary Ann Davis, March 4, 1791. W. H.
Newland, Abraham and Helen Brumback, April 18, 1802. H. B.
Newland, Jacob and Martha Maloney, Dec. 25, 1806. A. B.
Newland, John and Margaret Ware, Sept. 20, 1788. A. B.
Newland, John and Elizabeth Gaunt, Sept. 2, 1807. W. H.
Newland, Marcus and Catherine Weir, Dec. 1, 1788. J. M.
Newland, Powell and Polly Brumback, Aug. 23, 1795. A. B.
Newland, Thornton and Sarah Lewis, Aug. 30, 1818. E. G.
Newman, Alexander R. and Ellen Ash, Dec. 20, 1825. J.B.T.
Newman, Andrew and Sarah Halbert, June 23, 1800. J. B.
Nichodemus, Philip and Nancy Supinger, Sept. 26, 1811. A. S.
Nicholas, John and Jane Glassgow, April 29, 1798. A. B.
Nichols, Nathaniel and Rebecca Frye, Nov. 25, 1789. A. B.
Nichols, Nathan and Hannah Hodgson, Sept. 21, 1784. J. M.
Nichols, Samuel and Ann Edmondson, April 28, 1795. A. B.
Nicklyn, Jacob and Clarissa Marsh, Jan. 1, 1812. G.M.F.
Nighswanger, Abraham and Lydia Nighswanger, June 23, 1793. S.H.
Nighswanger, Solomon and Elizabeth Kern, May 10, 1787. S.H.
Nisewander, David and Mary Danner, Nov. 28; 1819. J.B.T.
Nisewander, William and Mary Wood, June 12, 1823. T. K.
Nison, George and Catherine Poston, Jan. 17, 1793. A. B.
Noaks, Thomas and Margaret Bush, July 18, 1808. J. W.
Noble, Mr. and Miss Spence, Nov. 28, 1812. A. S.
Noble, Charles and Judith Gall, Jan. 17, 1788. A. B.
Noland, Henry and Milley Thompson, April 23, 1815. J.B.T.
Noland, John Baptist and Elizabeth Moore, Sept. 25, 1788. A.B.
Noland, Philip and Martha Gibson, May 4, 1798. J. W.
Noland, Thomas and Nancy Chapman, May 10, 1791. W. H.
Noland, William and Rosina Bitman, Jan. 21, 1787. C. S.
Nolen, John and Elizabeth Groves, Sept. 30, 1819. J.B.T.
Nolen, Obed and Priscilla Bailey, Sept. 28, 1798. J.W.
Nolls, Carter Bailey and Sarah Vanhorn, Aug. 17, 1826. T. L.
Nonan? James and Sarah Smith, Dec. 5, 1791. A. B.
Norfolt, Thomas and Leah Patch, Dec. 29, 1808. J. W.
Norman, Joseph and Nancy Jennings, June 24, 1800. W. W.
Norman, Wilson and Charity Jacobs, Jan. 25, 1800. A. B.
Norris, George Horton and Jane Bowles Wormley, Nov. 10, 1804.
                                                        A. B.

Norris, Thaddeus and Nancy Calbert, Jan. 5, 1802. H. J.
Norton, John Hatley, and Catherine Bush, March 27, 1790. C. S.
Northern, Emery and Elizabeth Finley, Oct. 9, 1787. J. M.
Northern; Reuben and Lydia Loyd, July 27, 1786. A. B.
Northern, William and Dorcas Haddox, April 26, 1792. E. P.
Nosset, Joseph and Eva Myers, March 6, 1808. J.B.T.
Nuel, Samuel and Leah Adams, Oct. 1, 1811. A. S.
Null, Jacob and Susannah Puffinberger, Dec. 18, 1817. E.G.
Nutt, James and Rachel Cartmell, Sept. 21, 1800. J. W.
Nutt, John and Polly Cochran, April 15, 1806. W. H.

Oar, John and Susannah Luke, Dec. 1, 1785.   A. B.
O'Bannon, Presley N. and Matilda Heard, Jan. 24, 1809.   A. B.
Ober, Benjamin and Sarah Gilhan, Dec. 11, 1794.   C. S.
O'Conner, Dennis and Elizabeth Hesser, July 1, 1812.   W. Hill.
O'Conner, Jeremiah and Elizabeth Finchman, June 11, 1808.   A. B
Ogden, Thomas L. and Anna Robinson, April 4, 1819.   J.B.T.
Oglesby, Aaron and Susannah Emmons, Sept. 9, 1788.   C. S.
Oglesby, Elias and Mary Stump, Aug. 30, 1817.   J.B.T.
Oglesby, Isaac and Sarah Devoe, Sept. 13, 1817.   J.B.T.
Oglesby, Isiah and Phebe Painter, Aug. 16, 1785.   A. B .
Oglesby, Mr. and Miss Barr, Aug. 24, 1813.   A. A. S.
Oglesby, Robert and Honor Holding, Jan. 12, 1786.   C. S.
Oister, Christian and Elizabeth Sensening, Oct. 25, 1788.   S. J
Olby, Dennis and Rebecca Vannort, Dec. 26, 1791.   E. P.
Oldacre, Henry and Susannah Groves, Jan. 13, 1803.   Jas. W.
Olive, David and Celia Starrett, Sept. 16, 1792.   W. H.
Oliver, Elie and Lucy Corder, May 8, 1817.   W. N.
Olleman, Christian and Ruth Rhoads, Oct. 26, 1790.   W. H.
Oredorf, Philip and Eleanor Williams, Sept. 29, 1795.   C. S.
O'Rear, Benjamin and Catherine Jones, Sept. 3, 1818.   T. L.
Orem, William and Mary Ann Martin, March 15, 1825.   T. L.
Orndorff, John and Margaret Renner, June 5, 1792.   A. B.
Orndorf, John and Elizabeth Pitcock, March 19, 1812.   Jas. W.
Orndorf, Philip and Elizabeth Seabert, Oct. 15, 1782.   J. Mont.
Orndorf, Philip and Catherine Eo, Dec. 10, 1812.   J.B.T.
Orndorf, Henry and Martha Lawrence, May 19, 1796.   A. B.
Orndorf, William and Elizabeth Cooper, Sept. 26, 1801.   C. S.
O'Roark, Jesse and Kitty Kennedy, Feb. 7, 1819.   J.B.T.
Orr, Robert and Mary Douglass, Nov. 17, 1796.   A. B.
Orr, William and Mary Kemp, Jan. 28, 1783.   J. Mont.
Orrick, George and Mary Phelps, April 11, 1810.   Jas. W.
Osborn, Enos and Sarah Castleman, Jan. 8, 1823.   E.G.S.
Osborn, Richard and Patsy Shepherd, June 13, 1822.   T. L.
Osburn, James and Lydia Anderson, July 16, 1795.   A. B.
Osburne, Joseph and Rhody Romine, Sept. 22, 1796.   A. B.
Overakre, Daniel and Susannah Friedley, June 5, 1788.   A. B.
Overacre, Isaac and Rebecca Thorn, Nov. 30, 1790.   A. B.
Owens, John and Elizabeth Weaver, Dec. 19, 1805.   C. S.

Page, Abednigo and Elizabeth Shehen, Nov. 20, 1817.   E. G.
Page, Matthew and Anne R. Meade, March 23, 1799.   A. B.
Paggett, Edward and Jane Wroe, June 21, 1792.   E. P.
Pain, William and Frances Powers, Aug. 30, 1804.   L. C.
Painter, Abraham and Sarah Branson, Sept. 2, 1807.   L. C.
Painter, John and Rachel Redd, June 2, 1808.   L. C.
Painter, John and Lucy Elkins, Aug. 24, 1814.   A. B.
Painter, Mahlon and Clarisse Prat, Nov. 25, 1810.   A. S.
Palm, John and Mary McDonald, April 2, 1789.   C. S.
Palmer, Daniel and Sarah Lloyd, Feb. 8, 1825.   T. L.
Palmer, John and Ann Bonham, Oct. 26, 1785.   C. S.
Palmer, John and Elizabeth Orr, Sept. 14, 1790.   C. S.
Pangle, David and Nancy Johnston, June 18, 1812.   J.B.T.
Parent, Samuel and Jane Lynn, Oct. 16, 1806.   L. C.
Park, Samuel and Ann McKeever, Nov. 7, 1785.   C. S.
Park, John and Margaret Millslagle, March 28, 1786.   C. S.

Park, Uriah and Susannah Sample, June 9, 1821. Jas. W.
Parker, John and Amy Cheshire, Sept. 30, 1802. A. B.
Parker, William and Mary Bedinger, Aug. 16, 1824. J. A.
Parr, Henry and Mary Perry, Nov. 18, 1815. G.M.F.
Parrell, George and Henny Callin, May 21, 1817. G. M.F.
Parrell, John and Christiana Bumgardiner, Oct. 11, 1786. A. B.
Parscale, John and Elizabeth Crupper, Feb. 18, 1816. J.B.T.
Passmore, Joseph and Sarah Fenton, March 12, 1795. C. S.
Pasmore, Joseph and Eleanor Edmondson, May 4, 1814. G.M.F.
Patch, Isaac and Polly Anderson, Aug. 21, 1799. Jas. W.
Patterson, Abner and Rebecca Miley, Nov. 29, 1792. W. H.
Patterson, Samuel and Nancy Anderson, Aug. 26, 1790. A. B.
Patty, George and Martha White, Dec. 27, 1787. J. Mont.
Paul, Henry and Sarah Ann Taylor, Dec. 16, 1819. J.B.T.
Payne, Isaac and Elizabeth Bruce, April 20, 1808. W. Hill
Payne, James and Elizabeth Overton, Dec. 12, 1797. A. B.
Payne, John and Nancy C. Miller, Nov. 6, 1820. W. Hill
Payne, William and Catherine Bolton, Dec. 20, 1810. J.B.T.
Peake, W. Oscar and Mary Ellen Sydnor, April 9, 1822. J.B.T.
Pearce, James and Lavina Carter, Feb. 11, 1819. G.M.F.
Pearce, John and Martha McMurray, March 25, 1817. W. Hill.
Peake, Henry and Isabella Sydnor, Jan. 4, 1812. A. S.
Peck, William and Peggy Craig, Aug. 30, 1790. A. B.
Pecke, Samuel C. and Mary Craig, Jan. 21, 1816. T. L.
Pearce, James and Margaret Sperry, Oct. 11, 1787. A, B.
Pearson, James and Jemimah Stanbury, Aug. 26, 1789. A. B.
Pearson, William and Mary Barns, March 19, 1789. J. M.
Peirce, John and Mary Louthan, Nov. 15, 1825. J. B.
Peeling, John and Sarah Brooks, June 14, 1786. A. B.
Perrell, Joseph and Sarah Smith, March 23, 1801. Jas, W.
Perry, John and Nancy Anderson, Aug. 3, 1793. A, B.
Perry, Nicholas and Abigail Hodgson, March 17, 1818. G, M. F.
Peters, Abner and Mary Stepens, Nov, 7, 1822. W. M.
Peters, Isaac and Margaret Moore, June 24, 1788. A. B.
Petit, Isaac H. and Malinda Walter, Aug. 3, 1822. C.P.P.
Peyton, Evan and Mary Ann Jenkins, Nov. 11, 1821. T, L.
Peyton, Henry James and Ann Morgan, Heard, Jan. 22, 1807. A. B.
Peyton, Valentine and Elizabeth Morgan, Jan. 4, 1812. Jas. W.
Pharis, Thomas and Margaret Martin, May 4, 1801. A. B.
Phelps, Elisha and Elizabeth Hughes, April 21, 1789. W. Harvey
Philips, Jacob and Phebe Simons, March 29, 1792. S. H.
Philips, James and Ann Graves, Jan. 23, 1812. A. B.
Philips, Joshua and Susannah Harden, Jan. 18, 1821. J. D.
Phillips, Alexander and Mary Howard, April 28, 1791. W. H.
Phillips, Jacob and Susannah Henry, Jan. 14, 1800. J. I.
Phillips, Philip and Betsy Soover, May 14, 1789. C. S.
Phillips, William and Mary Bogan, April 24, 1782. J. Mont.
Phillips, William and Mary Thrasher, Sept. 22, 1799. A. B.
Phleager, Abraham and Margaret Goodekunts, Dec. 12, 1797. C. S.
Pickenee, John Henson and Catherine Yoe, Feb, 8, 1817. A. S.
Pickens, David and Mary Raworth, Oct. 2, 1800. A. B.
Pickering, John and Sarah Likins, Sept. 5, 1786. C. S.
Pickering, John and Mary Carpenter, Nov, 10, 1795. A. B.
Pickering, John and Ann Garrett, Oct. 27, 1809. W, Hill
Pickering, William and Susannah Speck, March 13, 1799. Jos, W.
Pickering, William and Ruth Fenton, July 22, 1815. G.M.F.
Pidgeon, Isaac and Mary Saunders, April 10, 1816. Jas. W.

Pidgeon, Isaac and Sarah Hollingsworth, Aug. 17, 1826.
Pierce, Joseph and Mary Suter, Nov. 15, 1806. Jas. W.
Pierce, Michael and Elizabeth Groves, Aug. 30, 1790. C. S.
Pilcher, Joshua and Mary Ann Davison, Sept. 24, 1808. Jas. W.
Pine, Jacob and Catherine Williams, Oct. 24, 1813. J. F.
Pine, James and Mary Swhier, Dec. 17, 1817. G.M.F.
Pine, Lazarus and Mary Putney, March 1, 1804. Jas. W.
Pinkley, David and Rachel Fry, Dec. 30, 1810. J.B.T.
Piper, Henry and Elizabeth Samsell, Nov. 12, 1801. C. S.
Piper, Jacob and Catherine Snapp, June 1, 1802. C. S.
Piper, John and Margaret Snapp, March 10, 1807. C. S.
Pitcock, John and Magdalene Renner, Dec. 13, 1804. C. S.
Pitman, John and Elizabeth Nicewanger, --- -- 1794. E. P.
Poe, John and Catherine Borders, Nov. 26, 1804. G. R.
Poe, Jacob and Jane Kidd, Dec. 16, 1792. A. B.
Polk, Robert and Penelope I. Maury, April 16, 1811. A. B.
Pollard, John and Mary Duff, Nov. 19, 1793. C. S.
Pollard, William and Franc·s Hampton, Feb. 21, 1790. A. B.
Pollock, Thomas and Elizabeth Disponet, Oct. 18, 1787. C. S.
Poling, William and Mary Britton, July 21, 1796. A. B.
Pomphrey, John and Mary Hamilton, Feb. 20, 1821. T.B.Jr.
Poole, John C. and Elizabeth Williamson, Dec. 25, 1796. A. B.
Pool, William and Sarah Marpole, Dec. 29, 1803. Jas. W.
Pore, __os and Susannah Miller, Dec. 10, 1795. E. P.
Porter, Eli and Margaret Sly, Feb. 28, 1786. A. B.
Porter, Elias and Nancy Davis, Oct. 9, 1800. A. B.
Porter, Philip and Sarah Sargent, Feb. 28, 1786. A. B.
Potts, John and Phebe Grantham, July 27, 1790. W. Harvey.
Potty, Jonathan and Mary Mason, Dec. 26, 1792. N. L.
Potts, Joshua and Milly Suvilly, Aug. 3, 1797. A. B.
Potts, Nathan and Mary Chamblain, Dec. 25, 1792. N. L.
Potts, Nathaniel and Mary Hamson, Oct. 13, 1803. A. B.
Potts, William and Isabella Dowling, Nov. 26, 1807. G. R.
Powell, Alfred Henry and Sidney Ann Thruston, Nov. 19, 1801. A.
Powell, Alfred H. and Ann Kean, May 16, 1816. W. Hill.
Powell, Stephen and Lydia Leister, Dec. 23, 1809. Jas. W.
Powell, William Alexander and Lucy Peachy Lee, Dec. 20, 1820. A.
Powers, Daniel and Mary Ann Carnegy, Jan. 27, 1825. T. K.
Preist, Lewis and Mary Baker, Oct. 18, 1808. S.O.H.
Price, Andrew and Sarah Nebitt, Dec. 25, 1787. J. M.
Price, Benjamin and Rebecca Fisher, Aug. 7, 1798. Jas. W.
Price, George and Catherine Krebs, April 10, 1787. C. S.
Price, Michael and Susannah Burke, April 12, 1804. A. B.
Price, Michael and Mary Cochran, Oct. 3, 1826. W. Hill.
Price, Richard and Sarah Starks, Dec. 6, 1787. C. S.
Prichard, Elijah and Mary Norris, Feb. 21, 1804. W. D.
Pritchard, John and Rebecca Phalen, Jan. 10,1822. G. R.
Printz, Henry and Elizabeth Barr, March 23, 1805. 'I. Hill
Printz, John and Elizabeth Egar, Sept. 17, 1797. A. B.
Printz, Michael and Katy Price (widow), Feb. 28, 1799. C. S.
Printz, Peter and Sarah Barr, March 12, 1805. C. S.
Pritchett, Jesse and Sarah G. Norris, Jan. 15, 1799. Wm. W.
Probasco, George and Elizabeth Carter, Feb. 25, 1802. J. B.
Profater, Christian and Eleanor Hall, May 7, 1798. W. Hill.
Pugh, Azariah and Elizabeth Rigle, Dec. 31, 1809. J.B.T.
Pugh, Eli and Catherine Fisher, April 27, 1795. A. B.
Pugh, Hanamiah and Sarah Darlington, Dec. 23, 1804. A. B.

Pugh, Jesse and Elizabeth Gray, July 24, 1786. C. S.
Pugh, John and Deborah Day, April 3, 1804. W. Hill.
Pugh, Michael and Margaret Reese, Nov. 16, 1796. A. B.
Puller, Lusty and Nancy Bailes, Aug. 30, 1789. A. B.
Pulley, Jonathan and Elizabeth Bleake, March 24, 1791. A. B.
Pulse, George and Elizabeth Harper, Sept. 14, 1815. G.M.F.
Pumaraw,(Pomeroy), Richard and Mary Lehew, Nov. 5, 1792. L. C.
Purcell, George and Priscilla Noke, Oct. 8, 1798. A. B.
Purcell, Hansford and Rebecca Wood, Jan. 29, 1817. A. B.
Purtlebaugh, Daniel and Eliza Mayhugh, March 8, 1822. Jas. W.

Racy, John and Rebecca Orndorff, June 20, 1808. Jas. W.
Racey, William and Mary Myers, June 16, 1808. A. L.
Ragan, Jonathan H. and Selina W. Jacobs, Sept. 8, 1824. T.J.D.
Raines, George and Elizabeth Brown, Sept. 14, 1809. L. C.
Raines, Thomas and Mary Brown, Feb. 13, 1817. A. B.
Rairden, Richard and Margaret Kirk, Aug. 8, 1790. A. B.
Ralph, Joseph and Sarah Beddinger, March 6, 1817. J.B.T.
Ralston, John and Sarah Cockran, Feb. 2, 1800. J. B.
Ramey, Asa and Dorcas Elzey, Sept. 19, 1803. J. I.
Ramey, Caleb and Elizabeth Hankins, Nov. 14, 1792. E. P.
Ramey, Daniel and Catherine Graves, Dec. 23, 1821. J. L.
Ramey, Levi and Margaret Petty, March 4, 1806. W. D.
Ramey, Samuel and Hannah Fetheringale, Feb. 21, 1800. J. I.
Ramsey, Abraham and Susannah Thompson, March 20, 1822. J. W.
Randolph, Archibald and Lucy Burwell, April 6, 1797. A. B .
Randolph, John and Jenny Owen, Oct. 10, 1799. A. B.
Randolph, William B. and Lydia Lupton, June 3, 1805. J.B.T.
Rankin, William and Ann Ridgeway, Feb. 20 1797. A. B.
Raynolds, George and Sallie Haynie, Feb. 15, 1798. W. W.
Raynolds, Thomas and Elizabeth P. Wigginton, Jan. 19, 1817. W.H.
Rea, Allen and Eleanor Fisher, April 25, 1793. C. S.
Rea, John and Frances Williams, Jan. 6, 1789. A. B.
Read, Michael and Delila Ann Hodgson, Jan. 13, 1823. Jas. W.
Read, Samuel and Jane Dowell, Jan. 26, 1802. W. Hill.
Reading, William and Amy Jacobs, March 7, 1787. C. S.
Reager, Michael and Nancy Roper, April 12, 1804. L, C.
Reagle, George and Mary Shipley, Aug. 26, 1788. J. Mont.
Reagle, Michael and Hannah McLaughlin, Aug. 31, 1790. C. S.
Redd, Abner and Elizabeth Lawrence, March. 31, 1814. J.B.T.
Redmon , Thomas and Winny Taylor, Jan. 10, 1793. N. L.
Reed, James and Ann Bell, April 15, 1802. L. C.
Redd; James and Elizabeth Myers, Feb. 21, 1822. J.B.T.
Reed, Jacob and Nancy Stipe, April 16, 1818. J.B.T.
Reed, Jeremiah and Elizabeth Hickle, March 3, 1807. A. L.
Reed, Jeremiah and Nancy Cowgill, Dec. 19, 1815. J.B.T.
Reed, John and Eliza Ann Babb, Feb. 5, 1812. G.M.F.
Reed, John B. and Maria Benn, Jan. 11, 1817. S.O.H.
Reed, John and Lamaria R. Rinker, Feb. 8; 1825. W. Hill.
Reed, Philip and Mary Richards, Sept. 11, 1794. C. S.
Reed, Thomas and Catherine White, May 7, 1801. A. B.
Rees, Isaac and Agnes Bryant, Jan. 3, 1793. C. S.
Reese, Joseph and Maria Stillions, Jan. 4, 1821. T. L.
Reeser, Frederick and Celia Cooper, Nov. 27, 1787. C. S.
Regan, Michael and Jenny Craig, June 29, 1786. C. S.

Regart, Lewis and Elizabeth Settlemiers, Dec. 3, 1789. C. S.
Reiley, Thomas and Sarah Savage, June 3, 1803. Jas. W.
Reiley, Samuel and Mary Lister, Aug. 2, 1790. C. S.
Reilly, John and Polly Aldridge, Dec. 23, 1798. A. B.
Relsford, Bernard and Ann Simpson, Sept. 11, 1808. A. L.
Renner, Daniel and Mary Gustine, Sept. 22, 1810. A. B.
Renner, Jacob and Barbara Wisecarver, Nov. 4, 1790. C. S.
Renner, Peter and Magdaline Shultz, Dec. 12, 1811. J.B.T.
Respess, Machen Curtis and Fanny Hickman, Jan. 4, 1798. A. B.
Reveal, Joseph and Catherine Morgan, Oct. 30, 1794. A. B.
Roveale, William and Mary Ashby, Jan. 14, 1796. A. B.
Reynolds, George H. Jr. and Frances C. Williams, Sept. 27, 1821
                                                    T.B.Jr.
Reynolds, Hugh and Mary Lockridge, Nov. 10, 1795. A. B.
Reynolds, Jeremiah and Patsy Jenkins, Jan. 14, 1810. S.O.H.
Reynolds, John and Sarah Thompson, Oct. 11, 1782. J. Mont.
Reynolds, William and Rebecca Harris, March 10, 1795. C. S.
Rhodes, David and Elizabeth Clyne, Sept. 16, 1819. J.B.T.
Rhodes, Henry and Lydia Winfield, Oct. -- 1814. J.B.T.
Rhodes, Jacob and Martha Shipler, April 5, 1801 . C. S.
Rhodes, William and Eliza Baldwin, Dec. 13, 1821. J. W.
Rhy, Jacob and Julianna Willey, Feb. 16, 1786. S. H.
Rice, Andrew and Rosanna Burkhammer, Aug. 14, 1800. A. B.
Rice, Frederick William and Katherine McKillop, April 2, 1790.
Rice, Moses and Rebecca Stonebridge, May 20, 1788. J. Mont.
Richards, Benjamin and Mary Bowers, June 24, 1809. Jas. W.
Richard, Benjamin and Mary Gilham, Aug. 28, 1811. J.B.T.
Richards, Gersham and Harriet Malcolm, April 24, 1823. T. L.
Richards, John and Mary Bean, June 5, 1798. C. S.
Richards, John and Ann Christey, Dec. 12, 1805. G. R.
Richards, John Jr. and Elizabeth Garrett, March 10, 1824. J.B.
Richards, Thomas and Susannah Hall, Oct. 16, 1783. A. B.
Richardson, John and Elizabeth Vice, Dec. 8, 1790. A. B.
Richardson, John and Heany Reed, March 21, 1794. A. B.
Richardson, Marquis and Henrietta Catlett, Feb. 19, 1789. A. B
Ricketts, John and Eliza Robinson, May 15, 1823. G.H.R.
Riddle, Jeremiah and Mary Berry, Dec. 23, 1803. J. I.
Ridgeway, Edward and Martha Brownfield, June 24, 1798. C. S.
Ridgeway, Josiah and Ann Likins, April 20, 1789. A. B.
Ridgway, John and Abigail Bower, Sept. 12, 1811. C. S.
Ridings, Edwin and Lydia Rodes, Feb. 12, 1824. J.B.T.
Riggle, Joseph and Rachel Gray, Dec. 26, 1802. L. C.
Rigsby, Thomas and Margaret Williams, May 9, 1787. A. B.
Right, William and Mary Clevenger, Dec. 25, 1792. N. L.
Riley, George and Sarah Brown, Nov. 2, 1797. W. W.
Riley, Elisha and Sarah Smith, Aug. 10, 1820. J. Paynter.
Riley, James and Martha Lane, April 20, 1824. T. B. Jr.
Riley, John and Tereza Benn, Jan. 11, 1817. S.O.H.
Riley, John and Elizabeth Conrad, Aug. 1, 1799. W. W.
Rinedell, John and Margaret Anderson, Nov. 8, 1785. C. S.
Rinker, Caspar and Betsy Pugh, Feb. 28, 1811. S.O.H.
Rinker, William and Catherine Yakeley, April 5,1814. Jas. W.
Risler, John and Kitty Madden, Dec. 12, 1815. G.M.F.
Risler, Thomas and Louisa Clark, March 16, 1816. J. W.
Ritter, James and Mary Likens, Dec. 31, 1821. Jas. W.
Ritter, Stephen and Polly Ritter, Jan. 7, 1811. Jas. W.
Ritenour, John and Elizabeth Martin, Aug. 16, 1791. C. S.

Roads, Jacob and Catherine Aire, Jan. 8, 1788. A. B.
Rober?, Thomas and Rebecca Burnside, Sept. 22, 1785. A. B.
Roberts, Enos and Mary Kendrick, Jan. 22, 1790. E. P.
Roberts, Philagalhus and Peggy Helm, March 26, 1801. A. B.
Robertson, James E. and Eveline Allensworth, Dec. 7, 1826. T.B.Jr.
Robertson, William M. and Elizabeth Henry, July 12, 1821. R.B.
Robinson, Alexander and Priscilla Booth, June 5, 1788. A.B.
Robinson, Andrew and Peggy Jackson, Oct. 24, 1808. Jas. W.
Robinson, Archibald G. and Drusilla Dehaven, Sept. 13, 1818. E.G.
Robinson, Braxton and Ann Hood, Aug. 29, 1790. E. P.
Robinson, Charles and Ann Kendrick, Dec. 31, 1785. A. B.
Robinson, Henry and Mary Clevenger, March 29, 1792. S. H.
Roe, Benjamin W. and Elizabeth Pagett, April 10, 1816. S.O.H.
Rodgers, Ralph and Frances Kelly, April 28, 1810. J.B.T.
Rodgers, Robert and Mary Venable, March 3, 1818. J.B.T.
Rogers, Isaac and Maria Jane Pugh, Oct. 1, 1822. J.B.T.
Rogers, James and Ann Short, March 25, 1800. J. H.
Rogers, James and Mary Dinges, Dec. 26, 1811. J.B.T.
Rogers, James and Elizabeth Carper, Sept. 9, 1812. W. H.
Rogers, John and Mary Olleman, Oct. 30, 1787. C. S.
Rogers, John and Margaret Harbert, April 26, 1817. G.M.F.
Rogers, John and Elizabeth Hammock, Sept. 10, 1818. J.B.T.
Rogers, John and Mary Allemong, June 11, 1820. J. D.
Rogers, Levi and Martha McCleave, July 1, 1824. J. B. Jr.
Rogers, Owen and Eleanor Nelson, Sept. 10, 1798. Jas. W.
Rogers, Robert and Marcey Beall, April 15, 1798. Jas. W.
Rogers, Samuel and Margaret Smith, Jan. 6, 1795. E. P.
Rogers, Thomas and Hannah Moore, March 12, 1811. Jas. W.
Rogers, William and Mary Leonard, Dec. 19, 1811. J.B.T.
Rogers, Zedick and Mary Joice, Jan. 29, 1804. W. Hill.
Rolls, Henry and Winifred Milver, Sept.23, 1787. A. B.
Roman, Thomas and Nancy Stephenson, Dec. 23, 1800. A. B.
Romine, Abraham and Hannah Romine, Jan. 2, 1800. W. W.
Romine, Andrew and Lyna Ellsey, Dec. 18, 1793. S. H.
Romine, Christopher and Sarah Pratt, March 29, 1798. W. W.
Romine, Cornelius and Hannah Smith, Dec. 1, 1788. C. S.
Romine, Joseph and Catherine Davis, Jan. 4, 1798. C. S.
Romine, Peter and Peggy Northern, Feb. 20, 1787. C. S.
Rhomine, Reuben and Liddy Smallwood, March 31, 1789. C. S.
Ronamus, Andrew and Catherine Allemong, Dec. 24, 1801. Jas. W.
Ronimus, Henry and Catherine Anderson, April 25, 1786. C. S.
Rootes, Philip and Sarah Miller, Aug. 28, 1800. A. B.
Roper, John and Ann Jones, Feb. 9, 1806. L. C.
Rose, Thomas and Polly Murphy, April 7, 1805. J.B.T.
Rosebraugh, John and Mary Winterton, March 27, 1787. J. M.
Rosinberry, Asa and Mary Carnes, Aug. 26, 1794. C. S.
Ross, John and Agnes Miller, July 8, 1785. J. Mont.
Roszell, Stephen G. and Mary Calvert, April 12, 1808. Jas. W.
Rowland, Martin and Margaret Campbell, March 13, 1822. G. R.
Rowles, William and Dolly Leach, Dec.8, 1816. W. N.
Rozenburger, Isaac and Eliza McClung, Nov. 15, 1825. J.B.T.
Ruble, George and Jane T (G) obin, April 12, 1805. Jas. W.
Rudolph, George and Christianna Hotsebeiler, May 28, 1793. C.S.
Rumgen, John and Elizabeth Carr, Nov. 21, 1788. N. C.
Russell, Bennett and Mary Blue, June 26, 1824. T. L.
Russell, David and Hannah Greenway, Feb. 2, 1789. C. S.
Russell, James and Esther Vale, Dec. 24, 1788. J. Mont.

Russell, James and Ann Throckmorton, Nov. 25, 1795. W. Hill.
Russell, John and Uris Darkes, May 9, 1824. T. L.
Rust, George and Hannah Larue, March 9, 1788. J. I.
Rust, George and Martha Marshall, Aug. 29, 1815. J.B.T.
Rust, Marshall and Augusta Redman, Dec. 24, 1822. G.H.R.
Rust, Matthew and Margaret Rust, Aug. 28, 1822. Jas. W.
Rust, Thomas and Hannah M. Lamkin, April 2, 1812. J.B.T.
Rust, Peter and Elizabeth Rust, Jan. 9, 1816. J.B.T.
Rutherford, Elliott and Ruth Wilkins, June 17, 1787. C. S.
Rutherford, John and Mary Carter, Jan. 21, 1818. W. Hill.
Rutter, Henry and Eleanor Cole, April 22, 1783. J. Mont.
Rutter, Henry Jr. and Mary Beatty, April 29, 1818. G.M.F.
Rutter, Henry and Elizabeth Lowry, Feb. 19, 1811. J. W.
Rutter, Jacob and Kitty White, Nov. 10, 1815. J. W.
Rutter, John and Susannah Hoover, Aug. 25, 1809. Jas. W.
Ryan, James and Mary Harden, April 6, 1790. A. B.
Ryan, Jesse and Dolly Redman, Sept. 6, 1810. T. L.
Ryan, Samuel and Ann Collings, Sept. 3, 1820. A. B.
Ryan, William and Mary Seemer, April 7, 1798. Jas. W.

Sadler, Samuel and Mary Ronemus, Oct. 26, 1803. Jas. W.
Saffer, George and Rebecca Griffin, Dec. 24, 1789. A. B.
Salyards, Reuben and Margaret DeLong, June 12, 1817. J.B.T.
Sample, Joseph and Catherine Pearce, Nov. 30, 1799. Jas. W.
Sample, Joseph and Mary Hoge, Jan. 29, 1810. Jas. W.
Sample, Samuel and Jane Moyers, Nov. 5, 1797. A. B.
Sample, Samuel and Nancy Ridenour, March 29, 1804. C. S.
Sample, William and Elizabeth Hamilton, Jan. 7, 1790. A. B.
Samsell, Henry G. and Susannah Williams, April 2, 1823. W.M.
Samsell, John and Anna Groves, Sept. 28, 1797. C. S.
Santmire, George and Elizabeth Dun, March 14, 1797. A. B.
Santmire, Jacob and Jane Knaps, July 20, 1794. L. C.
Sappington, John B. and Sarah Carter, March 27, 1822. D. D.
Sargent, Amos and Henrietta M. Clark, Sept. 9, 1818. J. D.
Sargent, Joseph and Mary Williams, April 22, 1818. J. D.
Sarratt, George and Ann Cooke, March 24, 1791. A. B.
Saunders, John and Charity Cole, Oct. 31, 1788. A. B.
Saunders, John and Susannah Taylor, Jan. 14, 1819. J.B.T.
Saunders, John and Winifred Kingore, March 21, 1826. T. K.
Sanders, Joseph and Hannah Eyre, April 19, 1792. W. H.
Saunders, William B. and Mary B. Gwynn, Sept. 15, 1808. A. B.
Savage, George and Mary Mires, Aug. 14, 1799. L. C.
Savage, Joseph and Jane Murray, Aug. 18, 1788. J. I.
S (L)aveall, Thomas and Sarah Hagerty, Feb. 20, 1787. A. B.
Scaggs, James and Mary Brinker, Feb. 20, 1798. A. B.
Scarf, James and Polly Foley, Oct. 30, 1814. J.B.T.
Scarf, John and Rachel Curl, Nov. 28, 1810. Jas. W.
Scarf, William and Elizabeth Likins, Jan. 4, 1818. G.M.F.
Schofield, Henry and Judith Taylor, Dec. 12, 1793. A. B.
Schofield, Henry and Nancy Carpenter, Feb. 12, 1789. A. B.
Schooley, Enoc and Sarah Brown. April 14, 1824.
Schrack, Henry and Rosanna Suverly, March 9, 1797. A. B.
Schreckingast, Daniel and Mary Snyder, Feb. 1, 1795. S. H.
Scriviner, Vincent and Mary Russell, Jan. 14, 1793. N. L.
Schultz, Henry and Rachel Pitcock, March 27, 1810. C. S.

Schultz, John and Catherine Harr, March 8, 1791. C. S.
Scoffield, Harcom and Elizabeth Long, March 6, 1804. J.B.T.
Scoggins, Solomon and Jane Taylor, Oct. 9, 1792. C. S.
Scoggins,, Turner and Elizabeth Archey, May 30, 1793. E. P.
Scoggins, William and Elizabeth Tomlyn, Nov. 28, 1793. E. P.
Scott, Isaac and Elizabeth Thompson, Dec. 17, 1801. A. B.
Scott, James and Hannah Johnston, March 10, 1796. A. B.
Scott, John and Lydia Mercer, March 10, 1825. J. D.
Scott, Moses and Lacy Craig, Sept. 12, 1805. Jas. Wells.
Scribiner, Benjamin and Barbara Bruner, July 2, 1820. J. D.
Scribiner, Edward and Elizabeth Bucher, July 26, 1812. J.B.T.
Scribiner, William and Elizabeth Coe, April 27, 1816. G.M.F.
Scroggin, James and Elizabeth Jackson, Dec. 23, 1787. A. B.
Scroggin; Turner and Mary Vaughn, March 30, 1820. T. B. Jr.
Scroggin, William and Sarah Clark, Nov. 28, 1797. W. W.
Seale, Hugh and Ann Lewis, Sept. 17, 1789. S. H.
Seal, Caleb and Ann Smith, Dec. 24, 1799. C. S.
Seaton, Harrison and Sarah Pritchard, Jan. 5, 1789. C. S.
Seecrist, George and Ann Fry, Aug. 13, 1793. C. S.
Secrist, Henry and Catherine Clowser, May 25, 1815. A. B.
Seecrist, Jacob and Mary Moore, Oct. 14, 1794. A. B.
Seecrist, Philip and Elizabeth Milhorn, July 28, 1811. C. S.
Seever, Caspar and Rosannah Streit, July 16, 1795. C. S.
Seever, Henry and Hannah Grapes, Dec. 14, 1790. C. S.
Seevers, Henry Jr. and Elizabeth Shumate, June 19, 1823. T.K.
Seevers, James and Rebecca Wilkins, July 28, 1820. W. H.
Seidelmyer, Casper and Amey Willcox, Oct. 4, 1787. C. S.
Seill, James and Nancy Alsup, July 30, 1807. C. S.
Self, Harris and Eliza Grubbs, Sept. 22, 1814. W. N.
Self, William and Deborah Freestone, Oct. 19, 1796. A. B.
Senseney, John and Margaret Young, Oct. 20, 1820. J.B.T.
Senseney, Peter and Louisa Catlett, Nov. 22, 1808. S.O.H.
Senseney, John and Catherine Groober, Nov. 1, 1788. S. H.
Sensing, John and Nancy Garber?. July 9, 1790. S. H.
Senright, Robert and Elizabeth Price, Dec. 22, 1792. N. L.
Settle, Daniel and Jane Wroe, Nov. 5, 1801. L. C.
Settle, Hugh and Delilah Redding, Aug. 12, 1814. W. N.
Sexton, Jareb and Lettitia Williams, April 9, 1807. J.B.T.
Sexton, Joseph and Dorcas Lindsay, Jan. 11, 1801. A. B.
Sexton, William and Mary Ann Williams, July 16, 1815. A. S.
Seybold, Jesse and Margaret Dodson, Oct. 8, 1795. A. B.
Shade, Jacob and Gertrant Huft, April 27, 1790. G. S.
Shadley, John and Docia Oglesvie, Jan. 7, 1795. E. P.
Shafer, John and Winney Lloyd, March 31, 1817. A. B.
Shambaugh, Abraham and Rebecca Carter, Feb. 23, 1815. J.B.T.
Shambaugh, Isaac and Nancy Barrow, Sept. 12, 1816. S.O. H.
Shambaugh, Joseph and Anna Duffey, Dec. 14, 1816. S.O.H.
Shane, John and Catherine Mason, Dec. 20, 1821. J. D.
Shank, Abraham and Polly Cochran, May 15, 1806. W. Hill.
Sharp, George and Elizabeth Brown, Oct. 4, 1820.
Sharp, Moses and Rebecca Hankins, Sept. 28, 1790. A. B.
Sharp, William and Deborah Allen, Nov. 9, 1785. C. S.
Shaw, Henry and Keziah Summers, April 3, 1790. A. B.
Shaw, Richard and Deborah Jones, July 12, 1789. A. B.
Shearman, William and Frances Wilkey, Nov. 28, 1822. W. H.
Shearer, Jacob and Mary Raby, May 3, 1812. Jas. W.
Shearer, Philip and Susannah Helpenstein, March 16, 1784. J. M.

Shearer, Robert and Sarah Edmonds, Jan. 18, 1810. W. N.
Sheffner, George and Susannah Curtis, Jan. 10, 1822. G. R.
Sheehan, William and Hannah Light, Sept. 16, 1800. J. B.
Sheetz, John and Susan Chinn, March 10, 1793. A. B.
Shell. John and Betsy Stype, Nov. 13, 1810. A. B.
Shell, Samuel and Mary Ralph, Dec. 29, 1809. J.B.T.
Shener, George and Elizabeth Moore, Dec. 14, 1786. C. S.
Shepherd, Adam and Elizabeth Mercer, Jan. 4, 1791. C. S.
Shepherd, Humphrey and Catherine Crigler, Feb. 14, 1822. T.L.
Shepherd, Presley and Hannah Alexander, Aug. 5, 1790. A. W.
Shepherd, Richard and Sally Webb, Feb. 12, 1789. A. B.
Shepherd Robert and Catherine Earheart, Oct. 7, 1824. T.L.
Shepherd, Thomas and Elizabeth Buff, Dec. 23, 1823. T. K.
Sherley, Robert and Rachel Gilbert, Jan. 28, 1791. W. H.
Sherran, James and Fanney Moore, Jan. 8, 1811. C. S.
Sherrard, Henry and Martha Glass, June 2, 1785. J. M.
Shiner, John and Margaret Rutter, May 15, 1806. C. S.
Shinholtzer, Jacob and Hannah Loy, Nov. 13, 1822. Jas. W.
Shipe. Adam and Betsy Jennings, April 23, 1799. W. W.
Shipe, Daniel and Lizza Jones, May 31, 1792. E. P.
Shipe, Isaac and Clarissa Turner, June 27, 1822. W. M.
Shipe, Jacob and Nancy Hannans, Feb. 23, 1792. E. P.
Shipler, George and Elizabeth Shull, Dec. 23, 1810. A. S.
Shipler. John and Henrietta Scroggin, Feb. 28, 1819. J.B.T.
Shipman, Benjamin and Margaret Stipe, Sept. 20 1786. C. S.
Shiveley, Jacob and Elizabeth Castleman, March 15, 1810. T. L.
Shiwertaker, Michael and Ann Gaunt?, Dec. 13, 1787. J. M.
Shaffer, Godfrey and Elizabeth Derflinger, March 23, 1788. C.S.
Shore, Thomas and Jemima Reed, Oct. 28, 1792. A. B.
Shotton, Christopher and Dorothea Hutchinson, Jan. 2, 1806. A.I
Showalter, Andrew and Dorothy Snyder, Dec. 22, 1811. J.B.T.
Showalter, Andrew and Polly McFarland, March 25, 1821. T.B.Jr.
Showalter, John and Elizabeth Estes, Aug. 23, 1810, J.B.T.
Shrack, Christian and Mary Barr, Nov. 7, 1793. C. S.
Shrack, John and Margaret Thompson, Dec. 22, 1793. E. P.
Shriver, Abraham and Mary Cackley, May 31, 1791. C. S.
Shriver, Jacob and Elizabeth Shull, Dec. 2, 1783. J. M.
Shriver, John and Alice Richards, Feb. 21, 1786. J. Mont.
Shull, Abraham and Rachel Likans, May 16, 1822. J.B.
Shull, Jonathan and Margaret Wissent, March 11, 1794. C. S.
Shull, Tobias and Sarah Frye, Sept. 26, 1811. A. A. S.
Shultz, Benjamin and Nancy Perrill, Nov. 16, 1824. J.B.T.
Shultz, Frederick and Mary Loy, May 24, 1787. C. S.
Shultz, John and Catherine Otto, Aug. 12, 1788. A. B.
Stump?, John and Rachel DeHaven, April 11, 1811. Jas. W.
Shutt, George and Catherine Light, March 22, 1821. J. D.
Shutz, William and Fanny Strickling, Dec. 11, 1823. J. W.
Sickfritz, George and Elizabeth Williams, Aug. 26, 1824. T.B.Jr
Sidebottom, Isaac and Mary Ann Ryan, April 20, 1823. G. R.
Sidner, John and Catherine Mouser, Aug. 30, 1791. C. S.
Siebert, Jacob and Catherine Fry, May 12, 1792. C. S.
Sigafuse, Jacob and Elizabeth Brill, Aug. 31, 1808. C. S.
Siggerfough, John and Mary Beese, April 2, 1801. J. B.
Silkwood, Solomon and Elizabeth Jinkins, Aug. 16, 1791. L. C.
Silkwood, Solomon and Hannah Reed, June 20, 1803. Jas. W.
Silver, Gersham and Mary Elkins, Jan. 2, 1823. T. B. Jr.
Silver, James and Nancy Hand, Dec. 25, 1795. W. W.

Simmons, James B. and Elizabeth Weaver, June 9, 1818. J.B.T.
Simmons, Thomas and Hannah Emmons, Sept. 7, 1809. J.B.T.
Simpson, James and Mary Newcomb, March 24, 1789. C. S.
Simpson, John and Anna Anderson, Feb. 10, 1807. A. B.
Simpson, John and Nancy Lang, Feb. 12, 1823. J. W.
Simpson, Samuel and Mary Carson Williams, Oct. 17, 1820. T.B. Jr.
Simpson, Thomas and Mildred Savage, Feb. 26, 1801. A. B.
Simrall, Alexander and Sally Donaldson, Dec. 4, 1797. A. B .
Simrall, James and Rebecca Graham, Dec. 30, 1804. W. Hill.
Simson, John and Betsy Patton, March 8, 1814. Jas. W.
Singhass, Michael and Charlotte Barley, Dec. 22, 1811. C. S.
Singhorse, Christian and Barbara Smith, Jan. 7, 1786. A. B.
Singleton, Conrad and Nancy Gray, Nov. 28, 1792. W. H.
Singleton, James and Judith Ball, Oct. 26, 1797. A. B.
Singleton, Washington G. and Maria A. Waite, April 7, 1823. J.J.R.
S(L)int, Conrad and Elizabeth Helphenstine, May 1, 1787. C.S.
Sirbaugh, Jacob and Molly Anderson, Sept. 8, 1789. C. S.
Sitzer, John and Mary Verner, Aug. 23, 1783. J. Mont.
Skelton, Isaac and Rebecca Lehew, Nov. 7, 1816. W. N.
Slain, James and Margaret Sargent, Feb. 19, 1786. A. B.
Slain, John and Phebe Hyatt, Feb. 19, 1786. A. B.
Slappington, Thomas and Rachel Lane, Jan. 3, 1805. A. B.
Slone, Thomas and Margaret Neilson, Aug. 7, 1792. A. B.
Slonaker, Christopher and Mary Stephens, Dec. 1, 1825. C. S.
Slosher, Christopher and Christianna Gardner, Dec. 12, 1787. C.S.
Slusher, Elisha and Matilda Riley, March 25, 1824. T. L.
Smallwood, David and Catherine Noland, March 11, 1789. C. S.
Smallwood, Elijah and Nancy Beckham, Jan. 14, 1793. N. L.
Smallwood, Israel and Elizabeth Hargrave, Oct. 14, 1822. G.R.
Smallwood, James and Pattey Graham, Oct. 19, 1801. Jas. W.
Smallwood, James and Sarah Lloyd, May 27, 1807. A. B.
Smilie, Alexander and Katy Robinson, Sept. 20, 1810. J.B.T.
Smith, Andrew and Margaret Moore, Feb. 13, 1810. Jas. W.
Smith, Augustine Charles and Elizabeth Dangerfield Magill,
                Oct. 30, 1811. A. B.
Smith, Bartholomew and Margaret Haymaker, Nov. 6, 1792. C.S.
Smith, Benjamin and Amelia Hotzenpiller, Sept. 14, 1815. J.B.T.
Smith, Casper and Catherine Slusher, March 24, 1788. J. Mont.
Smith, Charles and Winney Feathergill, Feb. 8, 1792. E. P.
Smith, Charles Jr. and Maria Berry, June 3, 1813. W. Hill.
Smith, Christian and Elizabeth Young, Feb. 15, 1799. C. S.
Smith, David and Susan Delong, April 13, 1815. J.B.T.
Smith, Daniel and Mary Booth, Sept. 27, 1789. C. S.
Smith, David and Elizabeth Camp, June 19, 1799. A. B.
Smith, Edward and Jane Shawer, Nov. 26, 1801. W. W.
Smith, Edward Jacqueline and Elizabeth Macky, Jan. 9, 1812. A. B.
Smith, Eli and Jenny McDonald, Aug. 21, 1800. A. B.
Smith, Fleet and Jane Holliday, April 27, 1809. A. B.
Smith, George and Frances Curlet, January 13, 1795. A. B.
Smith, George and Margaret Jarrett, January 2, 1797. W. Hill.
Smith, George and Elizabeth Ball, April 1, 1790. A. B.
Smith, George and Ann Albin, Nov. 26, 1819. J. D.
Smith, George and Mary Crum, May 13, 1822. Jas. W.
Smith, Henry and Mary Honecker, Feb. 20, 1787. S. H.
Smith, Isaac and Martha Ross, Oct. 16, 1819.
Smith, James and Catherine Taylor, April 16, 1801. A. B.
Smith, James and Mary Thompson, Jan. 2, 1817. J.B.T.

Smith, Job and Fanny Rogers, Sept. 22, 1803. L. C.
Smith, John and Kerchy Vanort, Jan. 25, 1787. J. Mont.
Smith, John and Sarah Peck, July 20, 1790. C. S.
Smith, John and Sarah Mustard, April 7, 1796. A. B.
Smith, John and Rebecka Jones, August 26, 1803. Jas. W.
Smith, John and Edy Wood, Jan. 11, 1807. B. D.
Smith, John and Hannah Hoge, September 10, 1812. A. B.
Smith, John and Eliza Pickerell, Nov. 2, 1821. Jas. W.
Smith, John L. and Mary Ash, February 12, 1817. J.B.T.
Smith, Jonathan and Lydia Kercheval, May 13, 1793. N. L.
Smith, Jonathan and Sarah Harshey, October 3, 1796. A. B.
Smith, Jonathan and Jane Hollingsworth, November 8, 1813. W. H
Smith, Joseph and Jane Davis, Jan. 18, 1807. Jas. W.
Smith, Joseph D. and Betsy Headly, Sept. 25, 1807. B. D.
Smith, Joseph and Eliza Bell, Aug. 8, 1821. W. Hill.
Smith, Kidd and Cressa Smith, Jan. 29, 1795. C. S.
Smith, Lewi and Mary Hackney, September 21, 1826.
Smith, Martin and Lydia Shaver, September 27, 1791. S. H.
Smith, Michael and Nancy McLeod, March 26, 1805. J.B.T.
Smith, Robert and Mary Freaker, July 27, 1790. C. S.
Smith, Robert and Mary Davidson, June 8, 1807. G. R.
Smith, Samuel and Julia Maria Tidings, Nov. 6, 1825. C. Sine.
Smith, Thomas and Hannah Babb, Oct. 20, 1796. A. B.
Smith, Timothy and Hannah Green, Nov. 4, 1813. G.M.F.
Smith, William and Nancy Kendrick, Jan. 24, 1792. S. H.
Smith, William and Barbara Brown, July 1, 1797. A. B.
Smithers, James and Catherine Kiger, Oct. 19, 1794. C. S.
Smoke, Henry and Hannah Williams, March 30, 1820. T. L.
Smoke, John and Lucy Crebbs, July 10, 1825. W, Hill.
Smoot, George and Nancy Gilpin, January 6, 1798. J. P.
Smoot, James and Mary Cohoon, June 4, 1793. A. B.
Snapp, George and Anna Myers, Dec. 7, 1804. C. S.
Snapp, Henry and Elizabeth Pifer, March 21, 1811. C. S.
Snapp, Joseph and Mary Rogers, October 25 1813. A. S.
Snapp, Joseph and Harriet Wilson, February 11, 1820. J.B.T.
Snapp, Lawrence and Mary Blakmore, November 1, 1804. C. S.
Snickers, William and Francis Washington, May 30, 1793. A. B.
Snider, Jacob and Margaret Hughs, Feb. 10, 1822. J.B.T.
Snyder, Daniel and Catherine Bowman, Dec. 13, 1787. C. S.
Snyder, Eli A. and Elizabeth McFarlane, Sept, 22, 1822. J.B.T.
Snyder, Jacob and Catherine Clabough, Feb. 22, 1788. J. M.
Snyder, Jacob and Eve Klyne, June 10, 1806. C. S.
Snyder, John D. and Carolyne Kline, Dec. 30, 1824. J.B.T.
Solomon, Thomas and Catherine Good, Dec. 21, 1803. A. B.
Somerset, Thomas and Mary Sholeberger, Nov. 29, 1787. C. S.
Sommers, Michael and Barbara Myers, July 22, 1788. C. S.
Sommers, William and Rebecca Glasscock, Dec. 12, 1815. A. B.
Sommerville, William and Mary Hickman, March 7, 1796. A. B.
Somer?, Henry and Eleanor Romine, Dec. 25, 1795. W. W.
Southard, William and Ann Darr, Sept. 1, 1802. L. C.
Sowers, Daniel and Martha Elizabeth Rust, Jan. 16, 1823. G.H.R
Sowers, Fielding and Sally Brownley, Dec. 20, 1810. S. O. H.
Sowers, George K. and Frances E. Mitchell, March 14, 1826. W. I
Sowers, James and Elizabeth Kerfoot, Dec. 31, 1798. J. I.
Sowers, James and Sarah Shearard, Sept. 6, 1810. A. S.
Spangler, Joseph and Margaret Kremble, April 2, 1816. C. Fry.
Spangler, Samuel and Fanny Way, Nov. 16, 1824. T. B. Jr.

Sparkes, Elijah and Elizabeth Weaver, Aug. 8, 1793. E. P.
Sparks, William and Mary Robertson, Aug. 15, 1795. W. W.
Spears, Moses and Mary Hall, April 8, 1794. A. B.
Spears, Solomon and Margaret Kerfoot, Dec. 17, 1811. W. N.
Speers, Peter and Ann Sandsbury, Jan. 22, 1797. A. B.
Spencer, Miller and Sidney Rogers, Oct. 25, 1801. J.B.
Spencer, Nicholas and Betsy Taylor, Nov. 21, 1811. G.M.F.
Sperry, Jacob and Rebecca Smith, Feb. 16, 1814. W. N.
Sperry, Nicholas and Elizabeth Brice, Feb. 22, 1810. C. S.
Sperry, Peter and Barbara Humerickhouser, Jan. 6, 1795. S. H.
Sperry, Peter E. and Rejina Austin, April 27, 1822. W. Hill.
Sperry, Peter and Mary E. Kremer, March 31, 1825. J.B.T.
Spickell, Leonard and Elizabeth Rowland, Dec. 20, 1815. G.M.F.
Spillman, Jacob and Catherine Snapp, Sept. 1, 1782. J. M.
Spoon, Peter and Peggy Hickman, June 12, 1805. C. S.
Spots, Jacob and Margaret Scott, June 8, 1820. G.M.F.
Sprag, William and Priscilla Fleming, Oct. 9, 1792. W. H.
Sprayth, Henry G. and Mary Nisewander, May 18, 1815. J.B.T.
Spring, Nicholas and Ruckey Willcox, June 26, 1787. A. B.
Sprint, Patrick and Susannah Stone, Feb. 25, 1796. A. B.
Sprout, Thomas and Jane Melor, May 24, 1798. C. S.
Sprout, William and Nelly Watson, Sept. 18, 1792. A. B.
Spur, William and Patience Withers, March 2, 1790. C. S.
Spurt, Richard and Nancy Scarff, Sept. 14, 1822. G.M.F.
Stallings, Abraham and Sarah Carr, Feb. 3, 1801. C. S.
Stallings, Hezekiah and Lethe Woodward, Jan. 26, 1802. W. W.
Stallings, Samuel and Elizabeth Pool, Nov. 5, 1801. C. S.
Stanbury, Ezekiel and Esther Kremer, Aug. 19, 1788. C. S.
Stanford, John and Susan Graves, June 29, 1820. T. L.
Stanforth, Richard and Uriah Marks, Nov. 30, 1786. A. B.
Starke, George and Barbara Bowers, Aug. 4, 1797. A. B.
Starr, Henry and Catherine Taylor, June 9, 1813. G. M. F.
Staton, Daniel and Shady Ridgeway, April 10, 1792. E. P.
Stateman, John Anthony and Catherine Polander, March 30, 1784.
                                                           J. M.
Stax, Reuben and Margaret Ann Pickerell, July 28, 1819. J.B.T.
Stedman, John and Rachel Ewing, July 28, 1796. A. B.
Steel, Adam and Elizabeth Nicholls, Oct. 28, 1813. J.B.T.
Steel, John and Ann Eaton, March 13, 1797. A. B.
Steel, Richard and Mary Nicklyn, Jan. 1, 1795. A. B.
Steel, Thomas and Jane Curry, Oct. 29, 1812. J. C.
Steele, Thomas and Sarah Carter, Feb. 24, 1816. G.M.F.
Steere, William and Hannah Clarke, March 16, 1794. A. B.
Steer, William and Louisa Brown, March 20, 1822.
Stephens, David and Susannah McGraw, April 22, 1790. C. S.
Stephens, George and Mary Ann Clark, June 12, 1822. J.B.T.
Stephens, Henry and Catherine Cooper, May 6, 1813. A. S.
Stephens, Henry and Susan Murphy, April 26, 1825 J. D.
Stephens, John and Martha Brown, Dec. 20, 1804. Jas. W.
Stephens, John and Sarah Ramey, Nov. 22, 1818. J. B. T.
Stephens, John and Nancy White, Jan. 23, 1816. J.B.T.
Stephens, Joseph and Eliza Clopton, March 7, 1822. J.B.T.
Stephens, Lewis and Catherine Brinker, Feb. 20, 1788. A. B.
Stephens, Peter Jr. and Sarah Parlett, Dec. 29, 1808. Jas. W.
Stephenson, John and Catherine Kindrick, April 4, 1822. J.B.T.
Stephenson, John and Eleanor Maclin, March 3, 1799. A. B.
Stephenson, Michael and Betsy Lett, Nov. 14, 1805. Jas. W.

Stewart, Alexander and Sarah Hill, Dec. 21, 1790. S. H.
Stewart, Archibald and Eleanor Briscoe, May, 4, 1791. A. B.
Stewart, Alexander and Polly Gassaway, June 26, 1800. A. B.
Stewart, John and Susannah Hughes, Feb. 8, 1794. B. S
Stewart, William and Hannah Wiser, Dec. 10, 1795. E. P.
Stickle, Henry and Phebe Swick, July 26, 1821. T. L.
Stickley, Joseph and Peggy Harman, April 15, 1798. J.C.H.
Stiff, John and Elizabeth Thomson, Aug. 20, 1791. C. S.
Stigley, James and Sarah Howell, June 15, 1790. A. B.
Stinson, John and Eliza Ellis, March 2, 1791. W. H.
Stip, John and Mariah Mauk, December 15, 1816. J.B.T.
Stipe, Christian and Catherine Goodykunst, Sept. 22, 1803. C.S
Stipe, George and Caty Palsor, April 23, 1789. C. S.
Stipe, George and Elizabeth Ryan, Oct. 6, 1801. A. B.
Stipe, George and Catherine Cyfret, Feb. 18, 1802. A. B.
Stipe, George and Kitty Griffin, Nov. 16, 1820. J. D.
Stipe, Henry and Margaret Lawyer, Aug. 24, 1797. A. B.
Stipp, John and Mary Ann Thompson, Aug. 22, 1805. J. W.
Stokes, John and Rachel Foley, Dec. 29, 1814. W. N.
Stone, Philip and Christianna Crum, Aug. 6, 1808. Jas. W.
Stone, Thomas and Mary Ann Hare, Dec. 29, 1825. T. W.
Stoveridge, Bethuel and Rachal Scott, Sept. 21, 1810. Jas. W.
Strahan, William and Jane Sutton, Oct. 21, 1792. A. B.
Stratton, Seth and Mary Greenway, April 10, 1787. C. S.
Streit, Charles and Catherine Freize, Aug. 16, 1804. C. S.
Streit, Christian and Susannah Barr, Oct. 15, 1789. A. B.
Streit, William and Rosana Smith, Oct. 21, 1795. C. S.
Stribling, Francis Jr. and Rebecca Littler, June 17, 1823. J.
Striblings, John and Sarah Drummond, Jan. 20, 1792. A. B.
Stribling, Sigismund and Elizabeth Sarah Taliaferro Ware,
                                November 7, 1820. A. B.
Stribling, Thomas and Elizabeth Snickers, Dec. 18, 1788. A. B
Stribling, William and Sally Humphries, April 23, 1789. A. B.
Strickell, Daniel and Mary Lanham, May 30, 1811. T. L.
Strickling, Alexander and Jane Bowman, Nov. 27, 1788. A. B.
Strickling, John and Mary Tay(l)or, Nov. 11, 1819. J. D.
Stringfellow, George and Susannah Gray, March 12, 1807. B. D.
Strohsnider, John and Elizabeth Shriver, Feb. 18, 1794. C. S.
Strosnider, Adam and Frances Savage, Sept. 13, 1787. S. H.
Strosnyder, Isaac and Loah Tewalt, Jan. 9, 1812. J.B.T.
Strong, Richard and Sarah Scarf, March 29, 1791. C. S.
Strother, John and Elizabeth W. Clopton, May 13, 1818. W. Hil.
Stroud, Thomas and Sally Kean, June 7, 1788. A. B.
Stubblefield, John and Frances Jones, June 17, 1806. W. Hill.
Stubblefield, William T. and Susan Kenon, Sept. 16, 1817. T.L.
Stump, Abraham and Margaret Shambaugh, April 24, 1812. J.B.T.
Stump, David and Mary Lowrey, Oct. 1, 1793. E. P.
Stump, David and Vina Stokes, March 16, 1813. J.B.T.
Stump, Daniel and Mary Ramy, Oct. 27, 1789. C. S.
Stump, George and Elizabeth Ewan, March 24, 1814. J.B.T.
Stump, John and Jane Lowry, Oct. 1, 1793. E. P.
Stump, Lewis and Hannah Shambaugh, June 24, 1793. S. H.
Stump, Lewis and Elizabeth Wright, Feb. 19, 1809. J.B.T.
Stutz, John and Mary Chissel, Oct. 14, 1794. A. B.
Sullivan, John and Margaret Hare, April 4, 1786. C. S.
Sullivan, James and Mary Martin, April 15, 1800. J.B.
Sullivan, Lewis and Sarah Clark, March 20, 1822. Jas. W.

Summers, Thomas L. and Sarah Glasscock, April 20, 1813. J.B.T.
Supinger, Abraham and Magdalen Nizberger, Sept. 5, 1797. W. W.
Suter, William and Peggy Pierce, Jan. 19, 1811. Jas. W.
Sutherland, Uriah and Rebecca Bently, Feb. 19, 1787. S. H.
Suttlemire, Gaspar and Mary Martin, Aug. 25, 1795. A. B.
Swan, Mr. and Mrs. Richardson, May 30, 1816. A. S.
Swann, William and Eliza Kiger, March 8, 1821. T. L.
Swangs, Samuel and Elizabeth Johnston, Dec. 24, 1789. C. S.
Swartz, Phineas and Nancy McCall, June 4, 1795. A. B.
Swarm, Joseph and Christianna Lindy, Nov. 7, 1787. C. S.
Swearingen, Eli and Ann Noble, June 21, 1798. A. B.
Swearingen, John and Elizabeth A. Bond, April 12, 1803. W. Hill.
Swartz, Henry and Elizabeth Day, May 21, 1820. J. W.
Swartz, Lewis and Elizabeth Jones, Aug. 7, 1820. Jas. W.
Swarts, Notley and Sarah Beaty, Nov. 25, 1826. Jas. Withers.
Swatz, George and Phoebe Mersser, April 30, 1818. E. G.
Swhiar, Jacob and Mary Bowman, July 25, 1797. A. B.
Swhitzich, Jacob and Sarah Cameron, Sept. 25, 1822. C.P. K.
Swieer, George and Elizabeth Friess, Aug. 30, 1791. C. S.
Swift, Leroy W. and Deliah Dent, Dec. 20, 1821. J. D.
Swift, Richard and Mary M. McGroynor, May 26, 1822. Jas. W.
Swimley, Jacob Jr. and Sarah Cochran, Dec. 4, 1823. J. W.
Switzer, John and Rebecca Fry, January 10, 1786. J. M.
Switzer, Michael and Mary Magdalene Klyne, Aug. 27, 1795. A.B.
Switzer, Peter and Mary Hoover, Oct. 21, 1794. C. S.
Swope, John and Mary Bishop, June 28, 1796. A. B.
Sworts, William and Frances Beaty, Dec. 30, 1825. Jas. Withers.
Sydor, William and Sarah Redman, December 16, 1810. A. S.
Syfert, Philip and Mima Johnson, November 30, 1808. Jas. W.
Sylvia, James and Elizabeth Rankin, May 4, 1789. A. B.
Sypher, George and Rachel Hamilton, December 16, 1816. W. Hill.

Tait, James and Jane Sutherland, April 10, 1821. W. Hill.
Talbott, Daniel and Mary Blakemore, Jan. 23, 1798. A. B.
Talbott, Presly and Mary Brent, March 16, 1800. W. H.
Tally, Anson and Elizabeth Lidia White, Oct. 25, 1811. A.B.
Tanquary, James and Anna McClure, Jan. 24, 1820. W. Hill.
Tanquary, James and Rachel Royer, June 10, 1803. Jas. W.
Tap, Isaac and Elizabeth Pritchett, June 7, 1798. W. W.
Tap, Samuel and Rebecca Shipley, March 31, 1799. J. I.
Tapp, John and Margaret Smith, Feb. 14, 1810. J.B.T.
Tapscott, William and Frances Washington, Feb. 1, 1789. A. B.
Tarflinger, Jacob and Barbara Kline, April 16, 1798. J. H.
Tate, William and Priscilla Fenton, Oct. 15, 1823.
Taylor, Amos and Mildred Fenton, Jan. 21, 1796. A. B.
Taylor, Benjamin and Ann Horner, May 18, 1790. C. S.
Taylor, Benjamin and Sarah Hastings, June 1, 1797. A. B.
Taylor, Benjamin and Rebecca Sidwell, April 11, 1822.
Taylor, Bushrod and Elizabeth Stribling Milton, Nov. 13, 1817.
                                                        A. B.
Taylor, Bushrod and Patsey Stubblefield, Jan. 29, 1801. A. B.
Taylor, David and Martha Hott, March 12, 1801. C. S.
Taylor, Edmund H. and Eloisa Thruston, Feb. 23, 1797. A. B.
Taylor, George and Margaret Wolverton, April 21, 1791. W. H.
Taylor, Griffin and Molly Cannon, Sept. 10, 1789. A. B.

Taylor, Griffin and Rhoda Kingore, Jan. 1, 1824.   T. K.
Taylor, Henry and Elizabeth Carr, Aug. 24, 1801.   C. S.
Taylor, Hiram and Phoebe Lee, Oct. 31, 1822.   G. R.
Taylor, Jacob and Polly Lemons, Feb. 25, 1789.   C. S.
Taylor, James and Willy Ann Gray, April 4, 1805.   J.B.T.
Taylor, Jesse and Mary Jacquelin Smith, Jan. 31, 1793.   A. B.
Taylor, John and Elizabeth Davis, Oct. 3, 1796.   A. B.
Taylor, John and Mary Snyder, Feb. 3, 1825.   J.B.T.
Taylor, John and Mary C. Kercheval, Jan. 15, 1822.   J.B.T.
Taylor, Mandly and Catherine Williams, Oct. 21, 1801.   A. B.
Taylor, Richard and Dorcus Thomas, March 1, 1796.   A. B.
Taylor, Samuel and Mary Macky, May 21, 1801.   A. B.
Taylor, Samuel and Elizabeth White, June 21, 1826.   W. Hill.
Taylor, Septimus and Mary McMahon, Aug. 10, 1797.   A. B.
Taylor, Walter Jr. and Polly Jones, Oct. 10, 1799.   C. S.
Taylor, William and Ann Miller, Dec. 30, 1791.   R. S.
Taylor, William and Jane Chitter, Dec. 18, 1792.   C. S.
Taylor, William and Elizabeth Dunlap, Oct. 19, 1797.   A. B.
Taylor, William Jr. and Harriet McIlhenny, Nov. 8, 1812.   W. Hill.
Taylor, William and Hannah McCormick, Jan. 26, 1826.   J. L.
Tedford, John and Susanna Brown, June 5, 1804.   W. Hill.
Tenchell, Ninion and Martha Leith, Feb. 23, 1788.   A. B.
Tewalt, Abraham and Rebecca Bly, March 5, 1812.   J.B.T.
Tewald, George and Elizabeth Henry, Feb. 28, 1791.   C. S.
Tewalt, Peter and Margaret Brill, Jan. 20, 1795.   C. S.
Thacker, Isaac and Elizabeth Locke, July 10, 1807.   W. H.
Thatcher, Mark and Hannah Thomas, April 16, 1823.
Thibault, Conrad and Rebecca Dunlap, Jan. 5, 1797.   A. B.
Thomas, George and Mary Marr, Nov. 17, 1796.   A. B.
Thomas, George and Elizabeth Freeman, Nov. 11, 1798.   A. B.
Thomas, Grandison and Sarah Frost, June 26, 1819.   W. Hill.
Thomas, Jacob and Sarah Kercheval, Oct. 3, 1793.   N. L.
Thomas, John and Jean Madden, Nov. 25, 1795.   W. Hill.
Thomas, John Hanson and Mary Isham Colston, Oct. 5, 1809.   A. B.
Thomas, Joshua H. and Lucy L. C. Colston, April 12, 1826.   T. W.
Thomas, Levi and Mary Moore, October 24, 1796.   A. B.
Thomas, Philip and Mary Swope, June 30, 1804.   Jas. W.
Thomas, Townsend W. and Evelina O'Shackleford, Oct. 28, 1822.J.W.
Thompson, Greenberry and Elizabeth Bostyon, May 12, 1825.   T.K.
Thompson, Jacob and Mary Grady, Dec. 8, 1795.   A. B.
Thompson, James and Lettice Beattey, Sept. 25, 1800.   J. B.
Thompson, James and Susannah Scott, Nov. 14, 1807.   G. R.
Thompson, Samuel and Hannah Noland, January 5, 1823.   J. S.
Thompson, William and Mary David, Nov. 3, 1788.   A. B.
Thomson, Abel and Elizabeth Scarf, October 16, 1804.   J. W.
Thomson, John and Sarah Campbell, October 19, 1792.   C. S.
Thornburg, John and Lydia Carter, January 25, 1817.   G.M.F.
Thornburg, William and Hannah Lloyd, September 14, 1812.   Jas. W
Thornton, Francis Jr. and Susan B. Wormeley, Sept. 10, 1820.   W H
Thorp, Charles M. and Maria L. Darlington, April 3, 1823.   G.M.F
Throckmorton, Albion and Mildred Washington, Dec. 13, 1785.   A.B
Throckmorton; John and Maria Lauck, November 27, 1820.   G.M.F.
Throckmorten, Mordecai and Mildred Throckmorten, February 15,
                                                    1799.   W. H.
Throckmorton, Robert and Elizabeth Abrill, Dec. 26, 1791.   W. H.
Throckmorton, William and Magdeline Burn, July 27, 1791.   W. H.
Tidball, James and Eleanor McDonald, Feb. 7; 1799.   A. B.
Tignor, Edward and Elizabeth Swartz, May 31, 1817.   G.M.F.

Tilman, George and Mary Denny, Oct. 22, 1801. C. S.
Timberlake, William and Esther Sherman, April 25, 1792. E.P.
Timmons, Peter and Elizabeth Dyer, July 5; 1806. W. D.
Tine? Robert and Anna Payne Jones, Nov. 8; 1787. C. S.
Tipple, Henry and Elizabeth Stump, May 22, 1806. C. S.
Todd, James and Lane? Lowry, June 17, 1794. C. S.
Touchstone, Sampson and Peggy Boles, March 27, 1820. G.R.
Townsend, George T. A. and Sarah Graves, Jan. 9, 1816. J.T.
Townsend, John and Elizabeth Davis, Dec. 20, 1795. E. P.
Trenary, Samuel and Sarah Grimes, Sept. 5, 1786; C. S.
Trenary, Hezekiah and Elizabeth Handle, July 14, 1823. T.K.
Trigger, James and Jane Chandler, Sept. 5, 1815. W. Hill.
Trimble, James W. and Mary Ann Hackney, Dec. 14, 1826.
Trimmer, Richard and Elizabeth White, July 22, 1794. A..B.
Triplett, Arthur and Nancy Oliver, Jan. 1, 1795. C. S.
Triplett, Nathaniel B. and Mary Henry, Jan. 16, 1816. J. W.
Trisler, George and Ann Bulger, Dec. 25, 1792. A. B.
Trisler, George and Rosannah Wetzel, Jan. 2, 1800. C. S.
Trowbridge, David and Mary Grady, Sept. 28, 1797. A. B.
Tucker, Joseph and Margaret Barry, July 21, 1791. C. S.
Tuley, Joseph and Nancy Brownley, Dec. 25, 1787. J. M.
Tullis, David and Hannah Longacre, Jan. 22, 1788. J. Mont.
Turk, Samuel and Nancy Ong, May 25, 1786. A. B.
Turner, Edward and Tabitha McPherson, Jan. 10, 1797. J. I.
Turner, Jacob and Airy Young, Nov. 5, 1810. C. S.
Turner, Samuel and Matilda Beckley, Oct. 6, 1816. J.B.T.
Turner, Thomas and Hannah Anderson, April 6, 1823. G.H.R.
Turner, William and Charlotte Ashby, July 25, 1822. T. L.
Tuttle, John and Catherine Farrell, Jan. 31, 1801. J. B.
Tyler, Edward and Charity Welsh, Dec. 25, 1788. A. B.

Ulery, Henry and Barbara Polen, Dec. 9, 1794. C. S.
Upp, John and Sarah Chin, Nov. 19, 1792. E. P.
Utterback, Nimrod and Gereney Perry, Oct. 6, 1796. W. W.

Vanacka, William H. and and Sarah Sullivan, Feb. 12, 1823. J.
Vance, Andrew and Margaret Batchelor, Aug. -- 1805. J.B.T.
Vance, James and Nancy Hiett, January 6, 1791. W. Harvey.
Vance, Robert and Catherine Frye, Aug. 21, 1789. C. S.
Vance, William and Rebecca Hinton, Feb. 6, 1787. C. S.
Vance, William and Ann Glass, Aug. 18, 1791. C. S.
Vance, William and Margaret Moiers, Dec. 7, 1809. A. S.
Vanhorn, John and Elizabeth Rutter, January 27, 1802. Jas. W.
Vanhorn, William and Eleanor Hiett, May 6, 1790. W. Harvey.
Vanhorn, William H. and Nancy Carter,Nov.24, 1826. T. K.
Vanlandingham, William and Elizabeth Fetheringale, May 5, 1800.
                                                            J. I.
Vanort, William and Betsy Maltimore, Dec. 24, 1800. W. W.
Vanourt, John and Lydia Ramey, Feb. 21, 1800. J. I.
Vanskivers, David and Catherine Bealis, Sept. 2, 1823. T. L.
Vaughan, Vincent and Mary Shipe, Dec. 14, 1797. W. W.
Vaugharn, Thomas and Rebecca Cain, Dec. 12, 1796. A. B.
Vaughin, George and Mary Seaborn, July 16, 1789. C. S.
Venable, John and Nancy Day, May 18, 1819. T.B.Jr.
Vice?, William and Tabitha McCann, Oct. 16, 1786. A. B.

Vickers, Charles and Parthenia Riley, December 16, 1824. T. I
Vincent, Cornelius and Mary Winser, March 30, 1792. A. B.
Vincent, William and Mary Smith, November 6, 1822. G. R.

Wade, John and Martha Brabham, April 24, 1821. T. L.
Wade, Thomas and Mary Souvain, June 9, 1787. A. B.
Waite, Obed and Mary Ann Harrison, Feb. 27, 1794. C. S.
Walder, Thomas and Ruth Henning, Sept. 16, 1794. A. B.
Walker, Jeremiah G. and Evelina Bedinger, Aug. 31, 1824. J.A.
Wall, George and Abagail Northern, Jan. 24, 1788. S. H.
Wall, Richard and Doshe Grigsby, July 29, 1798. W. W.
Waller, Elijah and Elizabeth Bowers, June 8, 1806. A. B.
Waln, Jesse and Nancy Hubbard, Jan. 23, 1816. G. M. F.
Waln, Obed and Mary Parlett, Aug. 28, 1811. Jas. W.
Walter, William L. and Henrietta Shull, Dec. 30, 1825. J. W.
Walters, John and Dorothy Ashby, Aug. -- 1806. J. B. T.
Walters, Tobias and Sally Walker, Aug. 27, 1803. J. I.
Walton?, Vanus and Sarah Brewer, Dec. 25, 1783. J. M.
Ward, Henry Pendleton and Elizabeth Ann Riely, Nov. 26, 1826.
Ward, Joel Jr. and Rachel Donaldson, April 27, 1821. Jas. W.
Ware, Charles and Frances Whiting, Nov. 29, 1803. A. B.
Ware, James and Elizabeth Alexander, Nov. 10, 1796. A. B.
Ware, James and Harriet Taylor, March 16, 1808. W. Hill.
Warmer?, Godfrey and Nancy Clevenger, Oct. 1, 1814. G.M.F.
Warren, William and Ann Nichols, Jan. 5, 1804. A. B.
Warrener, Robert and Susannah Williams, July 27, 1791. W. H.
Washington, Fairfax and Sarah Armstead, Oct. 18, 1798. A. B.
Washington, John and Frances Baylor, Jan. 16, 1799. A. B.
Washington, Lawrence Augustine and Mary Dorcas Wood, Nov. 6
1797. A. B.
Washington, Whiting and Rebecca Smith, Feb. 23, 1804. A. B.
Waters, John and Winney Poston, Jan. 28, 1806. Wm. D.
Watkins, Nicholas and Mary Freeman, Nov. 27, 1797. A. B.
Watson, Abraham and Ruth Cloud, Jan. 1, 1813. G.M.F.
Watson, James and Lettice Burnett, Oct. 17, 1797. A. B.
Watson, James and Rebecca Kendrick, Oct. 10, 1810. Jas. W.
Watson, Joshua and Lucy Dowdon, Sept. 15, 1816. G.M.F.
Watson, Moses and Polly Kello, Dec. 29, 1808. J.B.T.
Watson, Walter and Cassandra Gill, Sept. 12, 1822. Jas. W.
Wax, Peter and Margaret Allis, Aug. 7, 1790. A. B.
Way, Stephen and Mary Richardson, April 25, 1793. C. S.
Weathers, Thomas and Elizabeth Bonham, Jan. 20, 1791. W. H.
Weathers, William and Nancy Trote, Jan. 28, 1794. E. P.
Weaver, David and Ann Beall, March 7, 1826. T. W.
Weaver, George and Polly Wilson, June 29, 1790. S. H.
Weaver, Jacob and Elizabeth Boydeman, Sept. 7, 1794. C. S.
Weaver, Jacob and Olivia McCooe, Jan. 17, 1811. C. S.
Weaver, Jacob and Eleanor Beall, Nov. 6, 1823. J. F.
Weaver, John and Rebecca Cartmell, Aug. 8, 1790. S. H.
Weaver, John and Elizabeth Stump, Sept. 27, 1791. S. H.
Weaver, Leonard and Ingle Slusher, Aug. 13, 1793. C. S.
Weaver, Thomas and Eleanor Hughs, April 13, 1809. C. S.
Weaver, William and Peggy Carson, March 9, 1802. A. B.
Webb, Charles and Polly T. Ware, Feb. 24, 1791. A. B.
Webb, Eli and Christianna App, May 2, 1787. C. S.
Webb, Isaac and Lucy Ware, Dec. 23, 1790. A. B.

74.

Webb, William and Catherine Evans, Aug. 8, 1799. J.W.
Webber, Robert and Eleanor Holland, March 21, 1797. A. B.
Webster, Thomas T. and Elizabeth Pulse, March 26, 1816. G.M.F.
Weedon, John and Eleanor Vincent, Jan. 23, 1791. A. B.
Weeks, Samuel and Elizabeth Ireson, April 5, 1784. J. M.
Weiner, John and Ann Warf, Oct. 9, 1792. C. S.
Weiser, George and Mary Luckleiter, March 28, 1786. C. S.
Wells, Edward and Rebecca Powell, Dec. 3, 1785. C. S.
Wells, Richard and Jane Reddice Carson, Aug. 28, 1823. T.B.Jr.
Welpon, John B. and Sarah Flore, Feb. 28, 1822. T. L.
Welsh, Edward and Fanny Turner, Oct. 4, 1789. A. B.
Welsh, William and Mary Bishop, Oct. 21, 1820. G. R.
Wendle, Peter and Rebecca Lang, June 26, 1787. S. H.
Wammer, Isaac and Catherine Bastion, April 8, 1786. C. S.
West, Thomas and Sarah Wright, Jan. 28, 1790. C. S.
Westbrook, William and Dorcas Morfett, Jan. 1, 1811. W. H.
Wetzell, Christopher and Sally Gaunt, Dec. 29, 1802. C. S.
Wetzell, John and Barbara Shaver, Sept. 24, 1786. C. S.
Weylie, John Vance and Martha Maria Jacqueline Robinson, Oct.
                                        26, 1812. A. B.
Whetzell, Charles and Cinty Gregory, March 8, 1816. J. W.
Whilley, John and Ann Hart, April 10, 1812. Jas. W.
Whilson, Charles and Rebecca Cole, May 28, 1791. C. S.
Whissent, Joseph and Elizabeth Carr, Feb. 12; 1812. Jas. W.
Whitacre, George and Elizabeth McKee, May 13, 1818. J.D.
Whitacre, Wilson and Rachel Kerns, Dec. 27, 1821. J. D.
White, Alexander 3rd. and Sarah Cotter Gassaway, Dec. 1, 1796. A
White, Augustus and Abigail Hicks, Aug. 25, 1791. C. S.
White, Clemon and Ann Rayon, Sept. -- 1806. J.B.T.
White, David and Sarah Newbrough, Feb. 28, 1793. A. B.
White, Edward and Mary Alloway, Jan. 16, 1811. Jas. W.
White, Francis and Margaret White, Dec. 5, 1787. J. M.
White, Garrison and Elizabeth Reiser, March 9, 1786. C. S.
White, James and Polly Spotts, Nov. 20, 1822. G. M. F.
White, John and Peggy Frye?, Oct, 29, 1788. A. B.
White, John and Elizabeth Carver, June 16, 1810. Jas. W.
White, John and Hannah Redd, Mar. 31, 1824. J.B.T.
White, Joseph and Elizabeth Brill, Aug. 26, 1806. C. S.
White, Michael and Elizabeth Frye, Sept. 9, 1783. J. Mont.
White, Michael and Malinda Crupper, Oct. 17, 1816. J.B.T.
White, Thomas and Sarah McKonkey, Feb. 26, 1784. J. M.
White, Warner and Mary Taylor, April 29, 1783. J. Mont.
White, William and Polly White, Jan. 1, 1790. C. S.
Whiteman, Henry and Elizabeth Clark, Oct. 16, 1804. Jas. W.
Whitemore, William and Elizabeth Conner, Jan. 18, 1810. W. N.
Whiting, Peter and Hannah Washington, June 10, 1788. A. B.
Whitlock, William and Nancy Montgomery, Jan. 23, 1814. Jas. W.
Whitlow, William G. and Elizabeth Simpson, Nov. 14, 1816. W.H.
Whittington James and Orrata Mitchell, Dec. 18, 1823. J. W.
Whittington, Joseph and Susannah Gibbons, Sept. 25, 1815. G. M.
Whittington, William and Rebecca Mullinicks, Oct. 31, 1802. C.S.
Wickersham, Enoch and Elizabeth Williams, Aug. 26, 1806. Jas. W
Wickersham, Enoch and Catherine Connelly, Aug. 27, 1810. Jas. W
Wickersham, Isaac and Jane Gorley, Oct. 3, 1811. J.B.T.
Wickersham, Jonathan and Mary Scarf, March 1, 1816. G.M.F.
Wickersham, Josiah and Susannah Owgen, Aug. 7, 1792. A. B.
Wiley, Cornelius and Catherine Anderson, Feb. 17, 1820. T. L.

Wiley, Frederick·and Glinda Poole, Oct, 14, 1806. Jas. W.
Wiley, John and Ann Phillips, June 2; 1811. T. L.
Wiley, William and Priscilla Marquis, May 4, 1789. A. B.
Wilkins, Daniel and Sarah Ellis, March 29, 1804. C. S.
Wilkins, James and Betsy Hastings, Jan. 24, 1811. A. S.
Wilkins, John and Polly Breedlove, March 3, 1811. J. B. T.
Wilkins; Thomas and Mary Clark, Nov. 6, 1787. A: B.
Wilkins, William and Isabella I. Steele, Jan. 20, 1812. W. Hi.
Wilkinson, Abel and Mary Dowell, Dec. 3, 1813. Jas. W.
Wilkinson, Abel and Sarah Scarf, March 1, 1816. G.M.F.
Wille, John and Rosanna Teboe, Jan. 31, 1790. C. S.
Willey, Moses and Rachel Lehue, April 17, 1788. S. H.
Williams, Allen and Helen M. Helm, Jan. 9, 1823. J.J.R.
Williams, Benjamin and Elizabeth Wolfe, March 10, 1792. C. S.
Williams, Charles and Elizabeth Redd, Dec. 28, 1786. A. B.
Williams, Daniel and Milly Ann Nolen, Dec. 3, 1820. J.B.T.
Williams, Daniel Webb and Jemima Lewis, March 16, 1809. Jas.
Williams, Ebenezer and Rachel Smith, Sept. 6, 1792. C. S.
Williams, Edward and Mary Green, Aug. 9, 1788. C. S.
Williams, Edward and Rebecca Rees, Nov. 27, 1823. J. W.
Williams, Elias and Honer Trenary, March --, 1807. J.B.T.
Williams, Elijah and Elizabeth Hayse, June 26, 1791. W. H.
Williams, Elisha and Selina Helm, Dec. 14, 1809. A. B.
Williams, Enoch and Lydia Felton, Sept. 14, 1797. A. B.
Williams, Jacob and Elizabeth Greenlee, Nov. 16, 1801. Jas. W.
Williams, Jacob and Ruth Wilson, Dec. 19; 1811. C. S.
Williams, James and Sarah Grubbs, June 9, 1805. J.B.T.
Williams, James and Catherine Myers, Sept. 23, 1822. J. S.
Williams, John and Mary Ashby, Feb. 22, 1786. C. S.
Williams, John and Mary Thompson, Feb. 4, 1808. W. Hill.
Williams, John and Martha Chrisman, Sept. 18. ----. J. D.
Williams, John S. and Maria Littler, June 1, 1809. C. S.
Williams, Limas and Nancy Cunningham, Jan. 14, 1806. Jas. W.
Williams, Robert and Sarah Ellis, Feb. 7, 1805. G. R.
Williamson, Ralph and Catherine McConnell, July 27, 1807. G.R.
Williamson, Thomas S. and Margaret Spurr, March 4, 1797. A. B.
Williamson, Thomas and Elizabeth Fisher, April 19, 1822. J.D.
Williamson, William and Elizabeth Brannon, Nov. 7, 1797. A. B.
Willis, Nathaniel and Mary Cartmell, Jan. 15, 1789. A. B.
Wilson, David and Mary Henning, March 11, 1783. J. Mont.
Wilson, James and Sarah Brown, Dec. 25, 1783. John Mont.
Wilson, James and Hannah Jamison, Jan. 27, 1789. S. H.
Wilson, James and Mary Thomas, May 6, 1804. Wm. Hill.
Wilson, John and Sarah Wilson, Dec. 2, 1790. C. S.
Wilson, John and Rachel Bryan, June 27, 1791. A. B.
Wilson, John and Mary Ann Wilkey, May 19, 1819. G.M.F.
Wilson, Joseph and Lydia Supinger, June 1, 1815. J.B.T.
Wilson, Russell and Alice Timberlake, Nov. 7, 1820. J.B.T.
Wilson, Stacy M. and Frances Glenn, Oct. 25, 1810. A. B.
Wilson, Thomas and Elizabeth Stephenson, March 6, 1800. A. B.
Wilson, Thomas M. and Mary Ann Wilson, Dec. 13, 1815. G.M.F.
Wilson, Thomas and Catherine Smith, April 12, 1825. T. B. Jr.
Windle, John and Eve Anderson, Jan. 21, 1794. C. S.
Windle, Samuel and Catherine Coyle, Jan. 20, 1804. W. Hill.
Wingfield, John and Elizabeth Good, Jan. 3, 1805. J.B.T.
Wingfield, William and Sarah Myers, Aug. 22, 1803. J. I.
Winpiglar, George and Elizabeth Watson, March 5, 1813. G.M.F.

Winsburg, George and Ann McDonald, Oct. 24, 1793. C. S.
Wire?, John and Eve Levergood, Dec. 2, 1782. J. Mont.
Wisecarver, Henry and Leah Snapp, April 19, 1807. C. S.
Withers, James and Margaret Critsinger, Jan. 7, 1786. J. Mont.
Withers, James and Frances Funston, Dec. 12, 1822. J. L. D.
Withrow, John and Sarah Rowland, April 9, 1801. A. B.
Witherow, John and Minty Johnston, June 5, 1818. T. L.
Witmon, Andrew and Elizabeth Stephens, Nov. 26, 1782. J. M.
Wizer, John and Priscilla Hall, May 6, 1813. W. H.
Wolfe, Isaac and Susannah Dehaven, March 25, 1819. J. D.
Wolfe, Jacob and Hannah Vance, Dec. 17, 1793. S. H.
Wolfe, Jonathan and Ann Smith, Oct. 7, 1789. C. S.
Wolfe, John and Hester Triplett, May 18, 1796. A. B.
Wolf, John and Mary Holliday, Dec. 15, 1793. C. S.
Wolf, Peter and Clary Ridgeway, Nov. 19, 1799. Jas. W.
Wood, David and Louisa Smith, Feb. 15, 1793. C. S.
Wood, John and Barbara Myer, Jan. 22, 1787. S. H.
Wood, William K. and Mary Campbell, March 21, 1820. W. H.
Woody, Tarlton and Molita Folger, Oct. 1, 1812. A. B.
Woodford, John and Sarah Mann, May 11, 1809. Jas. W.
Woodward, Stephen and Mary Allensworth, Dec. 24, 1812. W. N,
Woolery, Henry and Elizabeth Rogers, Oct. 17, 1811. E. H.
Wrenn, John and Sarah Hite, Jan. 14, 1790. E. P.
Wright, David and Mary Griffith, Dec. 12, 1822.
Wright, George and Mary Carpenter, Jan. 22, 1789. C. S.
Wright, George and Susannah Hott, Oct. 12, 1809. C. S.
Wright, James and Mary Druggett, Sept. 1, 1791. C. S.
Wright, James and Charlotte Madden, Nov. 10, 1812. W. Hill.
Wright, Jesse and Sarah Crummley, Feb. 13, 1800. C. S.
Wright, John Jr. and Elizabeth Stephens, Jan. 14, 1807. W. Hil
Wright, John and Rebecca Lockheart, June 14, 1810. C. S.
Wright, Reid and Sarah T. Mastin, July 25, 1805. L. C.
Wright, William and Mary Carns, Oct. 4, 1784. J. M.
Wright, William and Maria Churchill, Jan. 3, 1826. J. K.
Wyatt, Edward and Deliverance Bryarly, Jan. 16, 1817. A. B.
Wyatt, John and Ann Turner, April 15, 1795. W. W.
Wyndham, Thomas C. and Elizabeth Everheart, Aug. 25, 1816. T.

Yates, Joseph and Polly McBride, July 28, 1797. A. B.
Yately, John and Mary Freese, Dec. 9, 1794. C. S.
Yenders, Nicholas and Catherine Foglesong, Jan. 5, 1789. C. S.
Yeo, John and Catherine Shambaugh, Aug. 4, 1814. J.B.T.
Yoe, Michael and Rachel Keckley, May 5, 1793. C. S.
Yoe, Peter and Mary Seacrist, June 18, 1807. C. S.
Young, Archibald and Lettice Morgan, Sept. 3, 1801. A. B.
Young, Henry and Peggy Noal, June 5, 1812. Jas. W.
Young, John and Hester Hollingsworth, Nov. 15, 1803. C. S.
Young, Latham and Rebecca Eckles, July 1, 1788. A. B.
Young, Nathan and Amelia Noland, Dec. 16, 1806. T. A.
Young, Samuel and Mary Britton, Dec. 30, 1806. Jas. W.
Young, Thomas and Susannah Barnet, June 8, 1786. A. B.
Young, Thomas and Ann Carroll, Oct. 16, 1800. A. B.

Zaach, John and Catherine McDonald, July 16, 1791. W. H.
Zigler, Andrew and Miss Holloway, July 23, 1815. A. S.

INDEX
Of
Names of Women in Marriage Bonds.

Abrill, ----------
    Elizabeth (widow)-- 4.
    Liddy------------- 11.
Adamson,
    Sarah ------------ 3.
Alexander,
    Eleanor ---------- 7.
    Elizabeth --- 7, 10.
Aires,
    Ann -------------- 15.
Allenworth,
    Ann -------------- 5.
Anderson,
    Betsy ------------ 5.
    Nancy ------------ 11.
Archy,
    Elizabeth -------- 13.
Armistead,
    Sarah ------------ 14.
Arnold,
    Nancy ------------ 13.

Babb,
    Charlotte -------- 5.
Bailey,
    Elizabeth -------- 8.
    Polly ------------ 6.
    Priscilla -------- 11.
Barger,
    Mary ------------- 5.
Barnett,
    Rachel ----------- 7.
Barrett,
    Sidney ----------- 3.
Bealer,
    Mary ------------- 12.
Beall,
    Mazy ------------- 14.
Bean,
    Mary ------------- 12.
Beaty,
    Esther ----------- 10.
Bell,
    Jane ------------- 1.
    Mary ------------- 2.
    Sarah ------------ 1.
Berry,
    Sally ------------ 6.

Black,
    Kitty -------- 1.
Blakemore,
    Ann ------- 7.
Boman,
    Dolly ----- 7.
Bonard,
    Jane ------ 12.
Bonham,
    Catherine - 9.
Booker,
    Elizabeth - 5.
Bowen,
    Elizabeth - 11.
Brecount,
    Sarah ----- 2.
Brenan,
    Elizabeth - 15.
Brinker,
    Rebecca --- 8.
Britain,
    Jemima ---- 4.
Brown,
    Martha ---- 9.
    Sarah ------ 12.
Bruin,
    Susannah --- 9.
Burnett,
    Lettice --- 14.
Bush,
    Elizabeth - 13.

Cackley,
    Elizabeth - 10.
Cahoon,
    Mary ------ 13.
Campbell,
    Elizabeth - 11.
Callen,
    Elizabeth - 10.
Carter,
    Jemima ---- 8.
Cartmell,
    Regina ---- 3.
Cather,
    Jane ------ 9.
Catlett,
    Elizabeth - 1.

Chinn,
    Agatha -------------- 7.
Clark,
    Mary ---------------- 13.
Clevenger,
    Lydia --------------- 7.
Cockran,
    Elizabeth ----------- 8.
Cooley,
    Elizabeth ----------- 10.
Cooper,
    Hannah -------------- 10.
    Rachel -------------- 3.
Cornwell,
    Anne ---------------- 15.
Craig,
    Mary ---------------- 5.
Crawford,
    Ediah --------------- 4.
Crider,
    Catherine ----------- 8.
Curlett,
    Elizabeth 2---------- 2.
Cochran,
    Jane ---------------- 1.
Cohagan,
    Catherine ----------- 6.
Cusych,
    Mrs. Elizabeth ------ 13.
Cyphert,
    Sarah --------------- 13.

Dailey,
    Elizabeth ----------- 15.
Daugherty,
    Susannah ------------ 10.
Davis,
    Elizabeth ----------- 1.
    Mary ---------------- 6.
Dean,
    Peggy --------------- 6.
Dearmont,
    Margaret ------------ 12.
Decker,
    Lydia --------------- 4.
Denes,
    Mary ---------------- 10.
Dixon,
    Mildred ------------- 3.
Doby,
    Milisent ------------ 9.
Donaldson,
    Sally --------------- 14.

Dragoe,
    Mary -------- 7.
Drake,
    Elizabeth --- 11.
Duffield,
    Jane -------- 6.
Dunlop,
    Elizabeth --- 14.
Dunn,
    Abigail ----- 10.

Earle,
    Mary Ann ---- 2.
Ellis,
    Eleanor ----- 8.
Everns,
    Mary -------- 8.

Farmer,
    Daisey ------ 3.
    Jane -------- 4.
Fisher,
    Eleanor ----- 12.
    Elizabeth --- 2.
    Rebecca ----- 12.
Freeman,
    Elizabeth --- 14.
    Mary -------- 14.
Frisbee,
    Catherine --- 8.
Frost,
    Hannah ------- 9.
Fry,
    Ann --------- 13.
    Mary -------- 9.
Fulton,
    Lydia ------- 15.

Garrett,
    Leah -------- 3.
Gay,
    Sarah ------- 4.
Gilkerson,
    Peggy ------- 12.
Gillbreath,
    Eleanor Talbott 1.
Glass,
    Ruth -------- 14.
    Sarah ------- 8.

Good,
　　Judith ------------ 2.
Goodekuntz,
　　Margaret -----------12.
Gorley,
　　Mary -------------- 4,
Grady,
　　Mary ---------------14.
Graham,
　　Ginnie ------------ 4.
Gray,
　　Susannah -----------10.
Griffiths,
　　Ann Maria ----------- 2.
　　Priscilla ---------- 5.
Griggsby,
　　Dosie --------------14.
Groves,
　　Anna ---------------13.
　　Sarah --------------10.

Harman,
　　Peggy --------------13.
Harper,
　　Mary --------------- 1.
Harny,
　　Rachel ------------- 9.
Helphenstine,
　　Nancy ------------- 6.
Heth,
　　Susanna ------------ 5.
Hicks,
　　Lucy ---------------10.
Hickman,
　　Margaret ----------- 3.
Hoff, (spinster) -------12.
Hog,
　　Ann ---------------- 7.
Hoier,
　　Barbara ------------ 2.
Horn,
　　Mary ---------------12.
Horton,
　　Chloe -------------- 2.
Hotsinfiller,
　　Christianna --------13.
How,
　　Margaret ----------- 8.
Huffman,
　　Catherine ---------- 1.

Jackson,
　　Hanner ------------- 8.

Jennings,
　　Mary ------------ 7.
Jewell,
　　Margaret -------- 4.
Johnston,
　　Mary ----------- 3.
Joliffe,
　　Elizabeth ------- 8.

Kean,
　　Alsey -----------14.
Keller,
　　Mary ----------- 3.
Kendall,
　　Elizabeth -------11.
Kercheval,
　　Lydia -----------13.
Keys,
　　Elizabeth ------- 9.
Kline,
　　Barbara --------- 4.

Latty,
　　Agnes ----------- 6.
Lemley,
　　Elizabeth ------- 3.
Lewis,
　　Dilly ----------- 5.
Lindsay,
　　Sarah -----------12.
Littler,
　　Lydia ----------- 7.
Loftin,
　　Sarah ----------- 4.
Lupton,
　　Phebe ----------- 4.

McAnnully,
　　Elizabeth ------- 6.
McDonald,
　　Rebecca ---------10.
McFessor,
　　Milly -----------10.
McKay,
　　Hannah ----------11.
Malin,
　　Mary ------------13.
March,
　　Ann ------------- 9.

Smith,
    Beady --------------- 11.
    Elizabeth ----------- 8.
    Mary --------------- 2.²
Snickers,
    Sarah -------------- 1.
Spoar
    Christiana ---------- 10.
Spurrier,
    Arianna ------------- 2.
Stanford,
    Margaret ------------ 3.
Staze,
    Ann ---------------- 12.
Steer,
    Mary Dinah ---------- 9.
Stephens,
    Tabitha ------------- 9.
Sterlings,
    Jane ---------------- 6.
Stewart,
    Sally -------------- 15.
Stone,
    Katey --------------- 9.
    Mary ---------------- 2.
Stuart,
    Grace --------------- 3.
Stump,
    Mary ---------------- 4.
Sumrall,
    Frances ------------- 9.
Sugars,
    Elizabeth ----------- 9.

Taylor,
    Elizabeth ----------- 1.
Thomas,
    Elizabeth ----------- 6.
Thompson,
    Elizabeth ----------- 3.
Thruston,
    Elizabeth Mynn ------- 4.
    Frances ------------- 3.

Undrell,
    Deborah ------------- 13.

Washington,
    Catherine ----------- 10.
    Frances ------------- 13.
Weaver,
    Eliza --------------- 13.
    Elizabeth ----------- 1.
Welsh,
    Comfort ------------- 15.

Wenkland,
    Elizabeth ----- 11.
Wharf,
    Ann ----------- 15.
Whetsel,
    Mary ---------- 2.
Wickersham,
    Rebecca ------- 4.
Wilcooke,
    Elizabeth ----- 3.
Williams,
    Eleanor E. ---- 8.
    Margaret ------ 8.
Wilson,
    Hannah -------- 4.
    Mary ---------- 15.

OMITTED NAMES

Cullen, Elizabeth -- 10.
Littler, Anna ------ 8.
Spoar, Christiana --- 10.

INDEX
of
Women in Ministers' Returns.

Archey,
    Elizabeth ---------- 64.
Armstead,
    Sarah --------------- 73.
Arnold,
    Jane ---------------- 23.
    Pheby --------------- 37.
    Sarah --------------- 39.
Asbill,
    Sarah --------------- 33.
Ash,
    Ann ----------------- 51.
    Elizabeth ----------- 17.
    Ellen --------------- 56.
    Mary ---------------- 67.
Ashahurst,
    Margaret ------------ 44.
Ashby,
    Dorothy ------------- 73.
    Charlotte ----------- 72.
    Kitty --------------- 54.
    Lucy ---------------- 24.
    Mary ------------61, 75.
    Milly --------------- 27.
    Philadelphia -------- 24.
    Rachel -------------- 27.
    Sidney -------------- 52.
Atchison,
    Elizabeth ----------- 47.
Atherton,
    Jane ---------------- 28.
Atwood,
    Jane ---------------- 21.
Audedell,
    Hannah -------------- 45.
Andle,
    Nancy --------------- 41.
Aulick,
    Mary E. ------------- 35.
Austin,
    Alice --------------- 16.
    Regina -------------- 68.
Awbry,
    Nelly --------------- 20.

Babb,
    Ann ----------------- 53.
    Charlotte ----------- 36.
    Eliza Ann ----------- 60.
    Elizabeth ----------- 17.
    Hannah -------------- 67.
    Harriet ------------- 56.
    Mary ---------------- 32.
    Sampson ------------- 53.
    Susannah ------------ 16.

Bachelor,
    Elizabeth ---------- 21.
Bailes,
    Nancy -------------- 60.
Bailey,
    Ann ---------------- 27.
    Elizabeth ---------- 49.
    Eve Maria ---------- 22.
    Martha ------------- 33.
    Polly -------------- 42.
    Porsinna ----------- 24.
    Priscilla ---------- 56.
    Rachel ------------- 17.
    Sarah -------------- 48.
Baker,
    Abigail ------------ 46.
    Christiana --------- 31,
    Elizabeth --------27, 55.
    Louisa ------------- 23.
    Mary --------------- 59.
    Susannah ----------- 23.
Balding,
    Mary --------------- 27.
Baldwin,
    Eliza ------------18, 61.
    Margaret ----------- 40.
    Mary --------------- 26.
    Rebecca ------------ 52.
Balees,
    Susan -------------- 41.
Balentine,
    Mary --------------- 20.
Ball,
    Ann ---------------- 24.
    Catherine ---------- 33.
    Elizabeth --------66, 67.
    Frances W. --------- 32.
    Judith ------------- 66.
    Mildred ------------ 32.
    Phebe -------------- 54.
    Sallie ------------- 27.
Bandil,
    Mary --------------- 33.
Barger,
    Mary --------------- 36.
Barley,
    Charlotte ---------- 66.
Barner, (Banner)
    Eve ---------------- 55.
Barnes,
    Elizabeth ---------- 27.
Barnett,
    Jane Helm ---------- 33.
    Rachel ------------- 45.
    Susannah ----------- 76.
Barney,
    Elizabeth ---------- 36.

Barns,
Elizabeth ------------ 24.
Fanny ---------------- 27.
Mary ----------------- 58.
Rachel --------------- 46.
Sarah ---------------- 26.
Barr,
Catherine ------------ 53.
Elizabeth ------------ 59.
Hannah --------------- 28.
Mary ----------------- 65.
Miss Barr ------------ 57.
Sarah ------------- 38, 59.
Susannah ------------- 69.
Barrett,
Lysia ---------------- 53.
Mary ----------------- 35.
Rebecca -------------- 35.
Barrow,
Nancy ---------------- 64.
Rebecca -------------- 54.
Barry,
Margaret ------------- 72.
Barton,
Catherine ------------ 50.²
Eliza ---------------- 28.
Elizabeth ---------40, 53.
Juliana S. P. ------- 36.
Bastion,
Catherine ------------ 74.
Batchelor,
Margaret ------------- 72.
Batton,
Martha --------------- 48.
Baughman,
Barbara -------------- 37.
Baylis,
Henrietta ------------ 39.
Baylor,
Frances -------------- 73.
Bazzle,
Catherine ------------ 21.
Bazzell,
Elizabeth ------------ 19.
Badles,
Sally ---------------- 25.
Bealis,
Catherine ------------ 72.
Beall,
Ann ------------------ 73.
Eleanor -------------- 73.
Marcey --------------- 62.
Bealle,
Mary ----------------- 46.
Bean,
Betsy ---------------- 34.
Harriet -------------- 31.
Mary ----------------- 61.

Bean,
Sarah ------- 17, 24.
Beasley,
Nelly ------- 35, 36.
Beatty,
Lettice --------- 71.
Beaty,
Elizabeth ------ 45.
Frances -------- 70.
Sarah ---------- 70.
Beatty,
Mary --------37, 63.
Sarah Irvin ----- 40.
Beavers,
Elizabeth ------ 52.
Beckham,
Nancy ---------- 66.
Beckley,
Elizabeth ------ 28.
Matilda -------- 72.
Beddinger,
Sarah ---------- 60.
Bedenger,
Maria ---------- 54.
Bedinger,
Elizabeth ------ 36.
Evelina -------- 73.
Mary ----------- 58.
Beese,
Mary ----------- 65.
Beevers,
Mary ----------- 38.
Beiry,
Sarah ---------- 48.
Bell,
Ann ------------ 60.
Elizabeth ------ 53.
Hannah --------- 54.
Jane --------17, 26.
Rachel --------- 48.
Sally D. ------- 35.
Bellert,
Margaret -------- 49.
Benegar,
Jane ----------- 29.
Benham,
Alice ---------- 36.
Benn,
Maria ---------- 60.
Tereza --------- 61.
Bennett,
Ann ------------ 41.
Cecelia -------- 46.
Elizabeth ------ 46.
Mary --------19, 20.
Rachel --------- 54.
Rebecca -------- 33.

Bowman,		
	Catherine	67.
	Jane	69.
	Mary	70.
Boxwell,		
	Winnifred	45.
Boyce,		
	Nancy	48.
Boyd,		
	Charity	55.
	Jane	38.
Boydeman,		
	Elizabeth	73.
Brabham,		
	Martha	73.
Brady,		
	Rachel	37.
Braham,		
	Patty	18.
Braithwaite,		
	Helen	52.
	Susannah	28.
Brannon,		
	Elizabeth	75.
Branson,		
	Hannah	47.
	Sarah	57.
Brecount,		
	Sarah	24.
Breech,		
	Hannah	23.
Breedlove,		
	Judith	41.
	Polly	75.
Brent,		
	Eliza	22.
	Elizabeth	22. 36.
	Mary	70.
Brewer,		
	Sarah	16, 73.
Briant,		
	Elizabeth	38.
Brice,		
	Elizabeth	68.
Brill,		
	Catherine	40.
	Elizabeth	65, 74.
	Margaret	71.
Brim,		
	Molly	45.
Brinker,		
	Catherine	68.
	Mary	63.
Briscoe,		
	Eleanor	69.
	Elizabeth	42.

Briscoe,		
	Mary	18.
Brison,		
	Margaret	18.
Britain,		
	Elizabeth	17.
Britton,		
	Abigail	42.
	Catherine	31.
	Mary	59, 76.
	Rachel	35.
Brook,		
	Mary Page	40.
Brooks,		
	Elizabeth'W.	20.
	Hannah	45.
	Mary	20.
	Sarah	58.
Brookover,		
	Ann	24.
Brown,		
	Airy	52.
	Barbara	67.
	Elizabeth 40,60,	64.
	Jane	53.
	Louisa	68.
	Lydia	39.
	Maria R.	32.
	Martha	68.
	Mary	54, 60.
	Polly	39.
	Sarah 42,61,63,	75.
	Sary	51.
	Susannah	71.
Brownfield,		
	Martha	61.
Brownly,		
	Emily	44.
Brownley,		
	Nancy	72.
	Sally	67.
	Sarah	31.
Bruce,		
	Eliza	39.
	Elizabeth	58.
	Rachel	50.
	Rebecca	25.
Bruin,		
	Susannah	51.
Brumback,		
	Helen	56.
	Polly	56.
Bruner,		
	Barbara	64.
	Catherine	44.
	Mary Ann	30.

Chisel,
Susannah ------------ 53.
Chissel,
Mary ---------------- 69.
Chitter,
Jane ---------------- 71.
Chrisman,
Henrietta ----------- 48.
Jane ---------------- 25.
Martha -------------- 75.
Christey,
Ann ----------------- 61.
Christian,
Ann ----------------- 20.
Mary ---------------- 55.
Churchill,
Maria --------------- 76.
Ciner,
Polly --------------- 39.
Clabough,
Catherine ----------- 67.
Clark,
Betsy --------------- 26.
Elizabeth ----------- 74.
Hannah -------------- 68.
Henrietta M. -------- 63.
Louisa -------------- 61.
Mary ---- 25, 29,   75.
Mary Ann ------------ 68.
Nancy --------------- 47.
Olivia -------------- 29.
Rachel -------------- 53.
Sarah ------- 30, 64, 69.
C(G)laspill,
Elizabeth ----------- 36.
Clayton,
Phoebe -------------- 41.
Cleavenger,
Ann ----------------- 20.
Clemin,
Catherine ----------- 45.
Cleveland,
Nancy --------------- 43.
Clevenger,
Achsah -------------- 17.
Delia --------------- 24.
Edith ----------- 19, 25.
Joanna -------------- 33.
Mary ---------18, 61, 62.
Nancy --------------- 73.
Ruth ---------------- 46.
Theodosia ----------- 21.
Clinch,
Mary ---------------- 45.
Cline,
Catherine -------- 29, 38.
Mary ------------- 21, 29.

Clopton,
Eliza ------------ 68.
Elizabeth W. ----- 69.
Cloud,
Edith ------------ 23.
Ruth ------------- 73.
Susan ------------ 43.
Clowser,
Catherine -------- 64.
Sarah ------------ 38.
Clyne,
Barbara ---------- 36.
Elizabeth -------- 61.
Coale,
Betsy ------------ 52.
Coates,
Clara ------------ 54.
Cobens,
Margaret --------- 47.
Cochran,
Agnes ------------ 46.
Ann -------------- 47.
Jane ------------- 17.
Martha ----------- 46.
Mary ------------- 59.
Polly ---------56, 64.
Sarah ---------60, 70.
Susannah --------- 28.
Cockrell,
Edy -------------- 21.
Coe,
Elizabeth -------- 64.
Mary ------------- 22.
Cogill,
Hannah ----------- 52.
Cohagan,
Catherine -------- 41.
Cohoon,
Mary ------------- 67.
Cole,
Charity ---------- 63.
Eleanor ---------- 63.
Mary Ann --------- 25.
Rebecca ---------- 74.
Coleman,
Phebe ------------ 30.
Collings,
Ann -------------- 63.
Collins,
Ann -------------- 17.
Jenny ------------ 31.
Linney ----------- 43.
Nancy ------------ 31.
Colston,
Lucy L. C. ------- 71.
Mary Isham ------- 71.

Delong,
Catherine ----------- 38.
Margaret ----------- 63.
Mary --------------- 55.
Susan -------------- 66.
Demoss,
Nancy -------------- 38.
Denny,
Mary --------------- 72.
Dent,
Cassandra ----------- 49.
Delia -------------- 70.
Derflinger,
Elizabeth ----------- 65.
Derrough,
Mary --------------- 43.
Devoe,
Sarah -------------- 57.
Devore,
Sarah -------------- 44.
Dewell,
Hester ------------- 41.
Dick,
Nancy -------------- 40.
Sarah -------------- 22.
Dicks,
Mary D. ------------ 31.
Dillon,
Liddia ------------- 17.
Mary --------------- 31.
Dinges,
Mary --------------- 62.
Sarah -------------- 75.
Disk, (Dick)
Catherine ----------- 16.
Disponet,
Elizabeth ----------- 59.
Dixon,
Martha ------------- 29.
Dodson,
Margaret ----------- 64.
Donaldson,
Rachel ------------- 73.
Sally -------------- 66.
Dooley,
Cordelia ----------- 39.
Dore,
Mary --------------- 46.
Doster,
Mary --------------- 29.
Sarah -------------- 29.
Doughty,
Ann ---------------- 49.
Elizabeth ----------- 27.
Douglass,
Ann ---------------- 34.

Douglass,
Mary ---------- 57.
Sally --------- 51.
Dowdon,
Lucy ---------- 73.
Dowell,
Elizabeth ----- 54.
Jane ---------- 60.
Mary ---------- 75.
Nancy --------- 17.
Dowling,
Eleanor ------- 50.
Isabella ------ 59.
Drake,
Lucy ------- 20, 47.
Mary ---------- 34.
Rachel -------- 24.
Sarah -------42, 46.
Drisk,
Catherine ----- 44.
Druggett,
Mary ---------- 76.
Drummond,
Sarah --------- 69.
Ducker,
Mary ---------- 53.
Sarah --------- 23.
Duff,
Alice --------- 46.
Mary ---------- 59.
Duffey,
Ann ----------- 64.
Dun,
Elizabeth ----- 63.
Dunbar,
Grace --------- 33.
Dunlap,
Elizabeth ----- 71.
Rebecca ------- 71.
Dunn,
Isabel -------- 29.
Dutton,
Mary ---------- 48.
Dyer,
Elizabeth ----- 72.
Julliet ------- 33.
Sarah --------- 34.
Susannah ------ 36.
Dyson,
Jane B. ------- 45.

Earhart,
Lydia --------- 34.
Susannah ------ 35.

Earheart,
    Catherine ---------- 65.
    Nancy ------------- 31.
Earle,
    Betsy ------------- 38.
    Matilda B. -------- 30.
Eastin,
    Mary -------------- 49.
Eaton,
    Ann --------------- 68.
Eckles,
    Rebecca ----------- 76.
Eckstine,
    Elizabeth --------- 16.
    Mary -------------- 48.
Eddy,
    Elizabeth --------- 22.
Edmonds,
    Sarah ------------- 65.
Edmondson,
    Ann --------------- 56.
    Eleanor ----------- 58.
    Mary -------------- 30.
Edwards,
    Margaret ---------- 29.
    Nancy ------------- 33.
    Polly ------------- 29.
    Sarah ------------- 18.
Egar,
    Elizabeth --------- 59.
Ehrheart,
    Mary -------------- 23.
Elkins,
    Lucy -------------- 57.
    Mary -------------- 65.
    Sarah ------------- 31.
    Thurza ------------ 24.
Elliott,
    Elizabeth --------- 48.
Ellis,
    Eleanor ----------- 53.
    Eliza ------------- 69.
    Elizabeth --------- 20.
    Mary ----- 29, 32, 53.
    Rachel ------------ 52.
    Sarah ------------- 75.
Ellsey,
    Lyna -------------- 62.
Eltin,
    Elizabeth --------- 47.
Elzey,
    Dorcas ------------ 60.
    Rebecca ----------- 52.
Emett,
    Elizabeth --------- 23.
Emmons,
    Hannah ------------ 66.

Emmons,
    Marian ----------- 31.
Emmonds,
    Susannah -------- 57.
Enghan,
    Sebely ---------- 53.
England,
    Sarah ----------- 22.
Ensley,
    Elizabeth ------- 52.
Eo, (Yeo)
    Catherine ------- 57.
Eskridge,
    Rebecca --------- 19.
Estes,
    Elizabeth ------- 65.
Evans,
    Catherine ------- 74.
    Elizabeth ------- 32.
    Peggy ----------- 50.
Everett,
    Mary ------------ 52.
Everheart,
    Elizabeth ------- 76.
    Minia ----------- 28.
Ewan,
    Elizabeth ------- 69.
Ewe,
    Catherine ------- 53.
    Margaret -------- 33.
Ewens,
    Elizabeth ------- 38.
Ewin,
    Mary ------------ 48.
Ewing,
    Catherine ------- 25.
    Elizabeth ------- 20.
    Rachel ---------- 68.
Ewings,
    Jenny ----------- 26.
    Sarah ----------- 44.
Eyre,
    Hannah ---------- 63.

Fair,
    Dinah ----------- 47.
Farmer,
    Daisey ---------- 25.
    Jane ------------ 33.
    Mary -------- 36, 39.
    Peggy ----------- 44.
    Phebe ----------- 51.
    Sarah ------- 29, 40.
Farrell,
    Catherine ------- 72.

Farrell,
Rebecca ------------ 45.
Fauntleroy,
Emily -------------- 32.
Fawcett,
Elizabeth ---------- 48.
Polly -------------- 25.
Featheringale,
Nancy -------------- 35.
Feathergill,
Winny -------------- 66.
Featherling,
Polly -------------- 46.
Fegans,
Elizabeth ---------- 33.
Felton,
Lydia -------------- 75.
Fenton,
Mary --------------- 33.
Mildred ------------ 70.
Priscilla ---------- 70.
Ruth --------------- 58.
Sarah ---------- 29, 58.
Sydney ------------- 29.
Ferguson,
Lucinda --------- 29, 50.
Mary ------------ 19, 50.
Nancy -------------- 17.
Ferrell,
Sarah -------------- 40.
Fetheringale,
Elizabeth ---------- 72.
Hannah ------------- 60.
Fetherling,
Catherine ---------- 16.
Figgins,
Sarah -------------- 30.
Finchman,
Elizabeth ---------- 57.
Finley,
Elizabeth ---------- 56.
Fish,
Matilda ------------ 47.
Fisher,
Catherine --------41, 59.
Eleanor ------------ 60.
Ellen -------------- 48.
Eliza -------------- 16.
Elizabeth ---- 22,40, 75.
Esther ------------- 23.
Hannah ------------- 32.
Mary --------------- 24.
Rebecca ------------ 59.
Susannah ----------- 31.
Fleet,
Margaret ----------- 47.

Fleming,
Elizabeth ---------- 34.
Priscilla ---------- 68.
Sarah -------------- 27.
Flint,
Margaret ----------- 35.
Flore,
Sarah -------------- 74.
Foglesay,
Catherine ---------- 76.
Foley,
Mary --------------- 42.
Polly -------------- 63.
Rachel ------------- 69.
Folger,
Molita ------------- 76.
Follis,
Rachel ------------- 36.
Foss,
Eve ---------------- 21.
Fossett, _____ ---- 51.
Foster,
Elizabeth ---------- 18.
Francis,
Jane --------------- 32.
Margaret ----------- 17.
Franks,
Nancy -------------- 33.
Frazier,
Mary --------------- 21.
Freaker,
Mary --------------- 67.
Fred,
Rebecca ------------ 20.
Freefar,
Sarah -------------- 46.
Freeman,
Elizabeth ---------- 71.
Mary --------------- 73.
Frees,
Margaret ----------- 42.
Freese,
Mary --------------- 76.
Freestone,
Deborah ------------ 64.
Freeze,
Anna --------------- 42.
Freidley,
Sarah -------------- 32.
Freize,
Catherine ---------- 69.
French,
Ann ---------------- 55.
Polly -------------- 37.
Fridley,
Elizabeth --------36, 39.

Fridley,
  Mary --------------- 17.
Freidley,
  Susannah ----------- 57.
Friess,
  Elizabeth ---------- 70.
Frister,
  Catherine ---------- 49.
Frost,
  Bushrod ------------- 24.
  Elizabeth ---------- 44.
  Sarah -------------- 71.
Frum,
  Catherine ---------- 34.
Fulk,
  Barbara ------------ 24.
  Mary --------------- 22.
Fuller,
  Ann ---------------- 52.
  Elizabeth ---------- 30.
Funk,
  Ann ---------------- 45.
  Rosannah ----------- 26.
Funston,
  Frances ------------ 76.
Furr,
  Hannah ------------- 47.
Fustnerin,
  Elizabeth ---------- 21.
Fry,
  Ann ---------------- 64.
  Catherine ------ 34, 65.
  Rachel ---------- 59, 70.
  Rebecca ------------ 55.
Frye,
  Catherine --------34, 72.
  Christiana ---------- 24.
  Elizabeth ---------- 74.
  Mary --------------- 52.
  Peggy -------------- 74.
  Rebecca ------------ 56.
  Sarah ---- 26, 34, 65.

Gall,
  Judith ------------- 56.
Gantt,
  Fanny -------------- 22.
Garber,
  Nancy -------------- 64.
Gardiner,
  Mary --------------- 42.
Gardner,
  Christianna -------- 66.
  Elizabeth ---------- 28.

Garman,
  Sophia ------------- 23.
Garmong,
  Nancy -------------- 55.
Garner,
  Ann ---------------- 38.
  Jane --------------- 35.
  Nancy ----------- 30, 36.
  Peggy -------------- 25.
  Rhoda -------------- 27.
Garnet,
  Ann ---------------- 31.
Garnett,
  Elizabeth ---------- 35.
Garrett,
  Ann ---------------- 58.
  Elizabeth ---------- 61.
  Judith ------------- 36.
  Margaret ----------- 39.
  Nancy -------------- 31.
Garrison,
  Mildred ------------ 33.
  Sally E. ----------- 50.
Gassaway,
  Polly -------------- 69.
Gaunt,
  Ann ---------------- 65.
  Elizabeth -------- 54, 55.
  Fanny ----------- 22, 33.
  Sally -------------- 74.
Gawthrop,
  Rachel ------------- 29.
Gebheart,
  Elizabeth ---------- 46.
Gemmell,
  Catherine A. ------- 43.
George,
  Elizabeth B. ------- 18.
  Rachel ------------- 18.
Gibbons,
  Eleanor ------------ 25.
  Phebe -------------- 41.
  Susannah ----------- 74.
Gibbs,
  Eliza -------------- 25.
  Mary --------------- 39.
Gibons,
  Sarah -------------- 25.
Gibson,
  Martha ----------- 33, 56.
Gier,
  Sophia ------------- 55.
Gilbert,
  Eve ---------------- 53.
  Rachel ------------- 65.
Gilham,
  Hannah ------------- 39.

Gilham,
Martha ------------ 26.
Mary -----------41, 61.
Gilhan,
Sarah ------------- 57.
Gilkeson,
Gennett ----------- 52.
Gilkerson,
Sally ------------- 35.
Gill,
Cassandra --------- 73.
Sarah ------------- 38.
Gilpen,
Nancy ------------- 67.
Glass,
Ann --------------- 72.
Catherine --------- 36.
Martha ------------ 65.
Mary -------------- 41.
Glasscock,
Fannie ------------ 53.
Rebecca ----------- 67.
Sarah ------------- 70.
Stacy ------------- 25.
Glasgow,
Jane -------------- 56.
Glen,
Eleanor ----------- 53.
Glenn,
Frances ----------- 75.
Goar,
Tasia ------------- 26.
Goff,
Elizabeth --------- 24.
Hannah ------------ 33.
Gold,
Mary -------------- 51.
Good,
Catherine --------- 67.
Elizabeth --------- 75.
Judith ------------ 20.
Judy -------------- 33.
Goodekunts,
Margaret --------33, 58.
Gooden,
Margaret ---------- 36.
Goody,
Eliza ------------- 33.
Goodykunst,
Catherine --------- 69.
Gordon,
Elizabeth ------ 33, 49.
Matilda Ann ------- 22.
Gorley,
Ann --------------- 28.
Jane -------------- 74.

Grace,
Sarah ------------- 37.
Grady,
Mary ------------ 71, 72.
Graham,
Pattey ------------ 66.
Rebecca ----------- 66.
Grapes,
Hannah ------------ 64.
Grasman,
Dorcas ------------ 47.
Grantham,
Phebe ------------- 59.
Graves,
Ann --------------- 58.
Elizabeth --------- 50.
Sarah ------------- 72.
Susan ------------- 68.
Gray,
Elizabeth --------- 60.
Isabella ---------- 45.
Nancy ------------- 66.
Rachel ------------ 61.
Ruth -------------- 37.
Susannah --------46, 69.
Willie Ann -------- 71.
Green,
Ann --------------- 47.
Elizabeth --------- 26.
Hannah ------------ 67.
Mary -------------16, 75.
Greenlee,
Elizabeth -------20, 75.
Greenway,
Hannah ------------ 62.
Mary -------------- 69.
Greggory,
Susan ------------- 18.
Gregory,
Cinty ------------- 74.
Grice,
Susannah ---------- 23.
Griffin,
Elizabeth --------- 45.
Jane -------------- 35.
Kitty ------------- 69.
Margaret ---------- 21.
Nancy ------------- 46.
Priscilla --------- 37.
Rachel ------------ 55.
Rebecca ----------- 63.
Griffith,
Ann --------------- 39.
Anna Maria -------- 25.
Mary -------------- 76.
Mary (widow) ------ 23.

Griffy,
     Sarah -------------- 43.
Griggs,
     Ann -------------- 39.
Greeding,
     Elizabeth ---------- 37.
Grigsby,
     Doshe -------------- 73.
     Elizabeth ---------- 35.
     Rebecca ------------ 47.
Grim,
     Catherine ---------- 37.
     Maria Chloe -------- 54.
     Mary --------------- 27.
     Mary Ann ----------- 21.
     Sally -------------- 40.
Grimes,
     Sarah -------------- 72.
Groober,
     Catherine ---------- 64.
Grosman,
     Mary --------------- 44.
Grove,
     Catherine ---------- 41.
     Elizabeth ---------- 52.
     Fanny -------------- 49.
     Mary --------------- 47.
Groves,
     Ann ------------- 45,63.
     Catherine ---------- 60.
     Elizabeth --------56,59.
     Mary --------------- 35.
     Susannah ----------- 57.
Grubbs,
     Edy ---------------- 43.
     Eleanor ------------ 18.
     Eliza -------------- 64.
     Joely -------------- 25.
     Rachel ------------- 41.
     Sarah ----- 32, 38, 75.
     Sally -------------- 37.
     Sidney ------------- 54.
Grum,
     Rebecca ------------ 49.
Gustine,
     Mary --------------- 61.
Guthridge,
     Eleanor ------------ 29.
Gwynn,
     Mary B. ------------ 63.

Haburn,
     Mary Ann ----------- 32.
Hackley,
     Fanny -------------- 26.

Hackney,
     Mary --------------- 67.
     Mary Ann ---------- 72.
Haddox,
     Betsy ------------- 46.
     Dorcas ----------- 56.
Hagerty,
     Sarah ------------- 63.
Haines,
     Lydia N. --------- 43.
Hainey,
     Jenny ------------ 51.
Halbert,
     Hannah ------------ 19.
     Sarah ------------ 56.
Halfpenny,
     Ann --------------- 41.
Hale,
     Elizabeth Frances -- 21.
Hall,
     Ann --------------- 23.
     Eleanor ----------- 59.
     Elizabeth ------ 50, 54.
     Hannah ------------ 27.
     Martha ------------ 30.
     Mary -------------- 68.
     Priscilla --------- 76.
     Ruth -------------- 42.
     Sarah ------------- 19.
     Susannah ---------- 61.
Hamilton,
     Elizabeth --------- 63.
     Mary ---------- 49, 59.
     Rachel ------------ 70.
     Sarah ------------ 49.
Hammock,
     Elizabeth --------- 62.
Hammond,
     Jane -------------- 47.
     Martha ------------ 50.
Hampton,
     Elizabeth -------26, 27.
     Frances ----------- 59.
     Mary -------------- 25.
Hamson,(Harrison)
     Mary -------------- 59.
Hancher,
     Elizabeth --------- 28.
     Janey ------------- 21.
     Rebecca ----------- 54.
Hancock,
     Nancy D. ---------- 19.
Hand,
     Betsy ------------- 17.
     Nancy ------------- 65.
     Sarah ------------- 40.
Handle,
     Elizabeth --------- 72.

Handle,
Sarah --------------- 19.
Haney,
Elizabeth ----------- 21.
Hankins,
Elizabeth ----------- 60.
Rebecca ------------- 64.
Winney -------------- 20.
Hanley,
Hannah -------------- 47.
Hannans,
Nancy --------------- 65.
Hannon,
Catherine ----------- 49.
Hanshaw,
Lydia --------------- 25.
Harbert,
Margaret ------------ 62.
Harden,
Mary ---------------- 63.
Susannah ------------ 58.
Hardin,
Ann ----------------- 47.
Hardy,
Eleanor ------------- 53.
Hare,
Mary Ann ------------ 69.
Margaret ------------ 69.
Harkins,
Dianna -------------- 46.
Hargrave,
Elizabeth ----------- 66.
Harman,
Margaret ------------ 48.
Peggy --------------- 69.
Harper,
Elizabeth ----------- 60.
Hannah -------------- 42.
Mary ---------------- 18.
Harr,
Catherine ----------- 64.
Harrell,
Hannah -------------- 45.
Harris,
Rebecca ------------- 61.
Harrison,
Betsy --------------- 25.
Jane ---------------- 18.
Mary Ann ------------ 73.
Patsy --------------- 25.
Harry,
Rachel -------------- 51.
Harshey,
Sarah --------------- 67.
Hart,
Ann ----------------- 74.
Anne ---------------- 21.

Harry,
Nancy --------------- 34.
Hass,
Ann ----------------- 43.
Eve Ann ------------- 43.
Peggy --------------- 55.
Hastings,
Betsy --------------- 75.
Mary ---------------- 43.
Sarah --------------- 70.
Hatgen, _____ ----- 47.
Hatt,(Hott)
Catherine ------ 29, 39.
Haymaker,
Elizabeth ----------- 25.
Magdalene ----------- 47.
Margaret ------------ 66.
Mary ---------------- 41.
Haynie,
Margaret ------------ 27.
Sallie -------------- 60.
Hays,
Elizabeth ----------- 55.
Ruth ---------------- 48.
Hayse,
Elizabeth ----------- 75.
Headley,
Betsy --------------- 67.
Lucinda ------------- 45.
Polly --------------- 53.
Rebecca ------------- 45.
Sarah --------------- 45.
Winifred ------------ 22.
Heard,
Ann Morgan ---------- 58.
Matilda ------------- 57.
Helm,
Dorothea ------------ 19.
Elizabeth -------30, 55.
Frances ------------- 44.
Harriett T. --------- 27.
Helen M. ------------ 75.
Lucy ---------------- 22.
Margaret ------------ 18.
Peggy --------------- 62.
Selina -------------- 75.
Helpbringer,
Dorothy ------------- 44.
Helpenstine,
Susana -------------- 64.
Elizabeth ----------- 66.
Helt,
Nancy --------------- 35.
Henderson,
Mary ---------------- 48.
Hendrick,
Elizabeth ----------- 49.

Henning,
    Ann ---------------- 17.
    Mary --------------- 75.
    Ruth --------------- 73.
Henry,
    Elizabeth --------62, 71.
    Mary --------------- 72.
    Susannah ----------- 58.
Hensell,
    Mary --------------- 17.
    Sarah -------------- 33.
Henshaw,
    Hannah ------------- 52.
    Rhuamy ------------- 31.
    Sarah -------------- 20.
Henson,
    Rachel ------------- 21.
Hersha,
    Elizabeth ---------- 29.
    Martha ------------- 16.
Hess,
    Ann ---------------- 19.
    Betsy -------------- 21.
Hesser,
    Elizabeth ---------- 57.
Hickle,
    Elizabeth ---------- 60.
Hickman,
    Caty ------------48, 52.
    Christiana --------- 45.
    Elizabeth ---------- 45.
    Fanny -------------- 61.
    Mary --------------- 67.
    Peggy -------------- 68.
    Rebecca H. --------- 26.
Hicks,
    Abigail ------------ 74.
    Lucy --------------- 53.
Hicky,
    Elizabeth ---------- 55.
Hiett,
    Eleanor ------------ 72.
    Nancy -------------- 72.
Higgins,
    Elizabeth ---------- 47.
Hill,
    Nelly -------------- 18.
    Ruth --------------- 32.
    Sarah -------------- 69.
Hinton,
    Deborah ------------ 17.
    Polly -------------- 23.
    Rebecca ------------ 72.
Hite,
    Katherine ---------- 47.
    Mary --------------- 34.
    Sarah ---------- 22, 76.

Hittle,
    Lydia ------------- 50.
Hobson,
    Jane -------------- 25.
Hodge,
    Mary -------------- 21.
Hodgson,
    Abigail ----------- 58.
    Delilah Ann ------- 60.
    Elizabeth --------- 49.
    Hannah ------------ 56.
    Ruth -------------- 23.
Hodson,
    Elizabeth --------- 49.
    Mary -----------46, 48.
Hoffman,
    Margaret ---------- 27.
    Maria ------------- 21.
Hogan,
    Mary -------------- 26.
Hoge,
    Hannah ------------ 67.
    Martha ------------ 33.
    Mary -------------- 63.
    Susannah ---------- 47.
Hoier,
    Barbara ----------- 24.
Holden,
    Margaret ---------- 43.
Holding,
    Honor ------------- 57.
Holker,
    Catherine Cooper -- 42.
Holland,
    Eleanor ----------- 74.
Holliday,
    Elizabeth --------- 35.
    Jane ----------- 23, 66.
    Mary -------------- 76.
    Sarah ------------- 23.
Hollinback,
    Elizabeth --------- 19.
Hollingshead,
    Elizabeth --------- 55.
    Polly ------------- 52.
Hollingsworth,
    Hester ------------ 76.
    Jane -------------- 67.
    Sarah ------------- 59.
Holloway,
    Miss Holloway ----- 76.
    Phoebe ------------ 32.
Holmes,
    Elizabeth --------- 27.
    Peggy ------------- 47.
Honecker,
    Mary -------------- 66.

Hons,
    Susannah ------------- 44.
Hood,
    Ann --------------- 20, 62.
Hooper,
    Elizabeth ------------ 45.
    Mary ----------------- 47.
Hoover,
    Elizabeth ------------ 38.
    Mary ----------------- 70.
    Susannah ------------- 63.
Horn,
    Eve ------------------ 48.
Horner,
    Ann ------------------ 70.
    Deliverance ---------- 17.
Horseman,
    Elizabeth ------------ 44.
    Mary ----------------- 49.
Horton,
    Chloe -------------23, 30.
Hott,
    Barbara -------------- 18.
    Kitty ---------------- 42.
    Martha --------------- 70.
    Rebecca -----------23, 47.
    Susannah ------------- 76.
Hotsbeiler,
    Elizabeth ------------ 34.
Hotsebeiler,
    Christiana ----------- 62.
Hotzenpiller,
    Amelia --------------- 66.
    Catherine ------------ 16.
    Elizabeth ------------ 47.
    Mary ----------------- 27.
House,
    Eve ------------------ 20.
Houseman,
    Elizabeth ------------ 31.
    Libby ---------------- 22.
Houston,
    Jenny ---------------- 28.
Hover,
    Kitty ---------------- 40.
Howard,
    Mary ----------------- 58.
    Nancy ---------------- 20.
Howell,
    Franky --------------- 24.
    Hannah --------------- 16.
    Sarah ---------------- 69.
    Sucresa -------------- 17.
    Winney --------------- 38.
Hoyle,
    Catherine ------------ 55.

Hubbard,
    Nancy ------------ 73.
Hueston,
    Mary ------------- 20.
Huft,
    Gertrant --------- 64.
Hughs,
    Eleanor ---------- 73.
Hughes,
    Elizabeth ------ 39,58.
    Margaret ---------- 67.
    Nancy ------------ 36.
    Susannah --------- 69.
Hulett,
    Ann -------------- 51.
Hull,
    Betsy ------------ 46.
    Margaret --------- 29.
Humerickhouser,
    Barbara ---------- 68.
Humphries,
    Nancy ------------ 32.
    Sally ------------ 69.
Hunsicker,
    Catherine -------- 55.
Huntsacre,
    Elizabeth -------- 38.
Huntsberry,
    Catherine -------- 46.
Hurford,
    Elizabeth -------- 35.
Hutchinson,
    Dorothea --------- 65.
Hyatt,
    Phebe ------------ 66.

Ireland,
    Lucinda ---------- 26.
Ireson,
    Elizabeth -------- 74.
Irvin,
    Mary ------------- 19.
Isles,
    Mary ------------- 18.

Jackson,
    Ann -------------- 33.
    Celia ------------ 26.
    Elizabeth ------35, 64.
    Peggy ------------ 62.
Jack,
    Mary ------------- 27.

Jacobs,
  Amy ------------------ 60.
  Charity ------------- 56.
  Jane ---------------- 27.
  Salina W. ----------- 60.
  Sarah --------------- 25.
Jackson,
  Hannah -------------- 47.
Jameson,
  Mary ---------------- 26.
  Sally --------------- 27.
Jamison,
  Ann ----------------- 34.
  Hannah -------------- 75.
Jarrett,
  Leah ---------------- 28.
  Margaret ------------ 66.
Jenkins,
  Ann ----------------- 35.
  Elizabeth ----------- 49.
  Mary Ann ------------ 58.
  Patsy --------------- 61.
  Rachel -------------- 34.
  Rebecca ------------- 34.
  Susannah ------------ 36.
Jennings,
  Betsy --------------- 65.
  Nancy --------------- 56.
  Rebecca ------------- 27.
  Sarah --------------- 30.
Jewell,
  Margaret ------------ 30.
Jinkins,
  Elizabeth ----------- 65.
John,
  Susannah ------------ 22.
Johnson,
  Elizabeth ----------- 42.
  Harriet ------------- 21.
  Mima ---------------- 70.
  Minty --------------- 76.
  Rebecca ------------- 41.
  Susannah ------------ 44.
Johnston,
  Cynthia ------------- 55.
  Elizabeth ---- 70, 45, 52.
  Hannah -------------- 64.
  Jemimah ------------- 46.
  Mary -- 23,28^2, 33, 52.
  Nancy -----36,37, 44, 57.
  Penelope ------------ 43.
  Rebecca ------------- 41.
  Rosanna ------------- 36.
  Sidney -------------- 31.
  Susannah ------44, 49, 55.
Joice,
  Mary ---------------- 62.

Joliffe,
  Elizabeth ---------- 49.
  Lydia -------------- 22.
  Mary --------------- 41.
Jolly,
  Catherine ---------- 43.
Jones,
  Ann ----------- 26,62.
  Anna Payne ------- 72.
  Betsy ------------ 31.
  Catherine -------- 57.
  Deborah ---------- 64.
  Elizabeth -------- 70.
  Frances ---------- 69.
  Grace ------------ 18.
  Jemima ----------- 35.
  Judy ------------- 44.
  Keziah ----------- 48.
  Lizza ------------ 65.
  Mary ------------- 30.
  Margaret --------- 46.
  Nancy ------------ 20.
  Polly ---------43, 71.
  Rebecca ------ 31, 67.
  Sarah ------------ 35.
  Winnifred -------- 54.
  Winny ------------ 45.
Juell,
  Rebecca ---------- 37.

Kackley,
  Catherine -------- 34.
  Elizabeth -------- 53.
  Magdalene -------- 26.
  Margaret --------- 20.
  Rachel ----------- 49.
Kail,
  Mary ------------- 46.
Kaile,
  Elizabeth -------- 37.
Kain,
  Caty ------------- 54.
Kanara,
  Sarah ------------ 38.
Kean,
  Ann -------------- 59.
  Betty ------------ 34.
  Sallie ----------- 69.
Kearfoot,
  Margaret --------- 46.
Keary,
  Ann -------------- 45.
Keckley,
  Catherine -------- 38.

102.

Kortze,
   Mary --------------- 55.
Krebs,
   Catherine ----------- 59.
Kremble,
   Margaret ------------ 67.
Kremer,
   Esther -------------- 68.
   Mary E. ------------- 68.
Krouse,,
   Elizabeth ----------- 26.
   Polly --------------- 19.
Kurtz,
   Mary ---------------- 18.

Lafever,
   Eliza --------------- 43.
LaFollett,
   Ann ----------------- 50.
Lambkin,
   Sally R. ------------ 18.
Lamkin,
   Hannah M. ----------- 63.
Lamp,
   Catherine ----------- 53.
Lancaster,
   Sophia -------------- 35.
Lane,
   Martha -------------- 61.
   Rachel -------------- 66.
Lang,
   Nancy --------------- 66.
   Rebecca ------------- 74.
Lanham,
   Mary ---------------- 69.
   Sarah --------------- 17.
Lantz,
   Catherine ----------- 40.
   Maria --------------- 33.
Largent, (Sargent)
   Phebe --------------- 33.
Larick,
   Catherine ----------- 54.
Larrick,
   Leah ---------------- 28.
Larue,
   Hannah -------------- 63.
   Phebe -----------36, 55.
Lauck,
   Elizabeth ----------- 21.
   Maria --------------- 71.
   Patsy --------------- 21.
Lavender, (Tavender)
   Mary T. ------------- 52.

Lawrence,
   Elizabeth --------- 60.
   Martha ----------- 57.
Lawyer,
   Catherine --------- 30.
   Christiana -------- 23.
   Eve --------------- 30.
   Margaret -------18, 69.
   Mary -------------- 37.
Leach,
   Dolly ------------- 62.
   Margaret ---------- 33.
   Nelly ------------- 50.
Ledford,
   Molly ------------- 19.
Lee,
   Anna -------------- 28.
   Delphy ------------ 38.
   Lucy Peachy ------- 59.
   Phoebe ------------ 71.
Leeford,
   Molly ------------- 19.
Lehew,
   Mary -------------- 60.
   Rebecca ----------- 66.
Lehue,
   Rachel ------------ 75.
Leister,
   Lydia   59.
Leith,
   Martha ------------ 71.
Leizure,
   Nancy ------------- 36.
Lemley,
   Catherine --------- 25.
   Margaret ---------- 34.
   Sally ------------- 38.
Lemon,
   Hannah ------------ 36.
Lemons,
   Polly ------------- 71.
Lenox,
   Anna -------------- 30.
Leonard,
   Elizabeth --------- 35.
   Margaret ---------- 46.
   Mary -------------- 62.
Lentz,
   Margaret ---------- 42.
Lett,
   Betsy ------------- 68.
Levergood,
   Eve --------------- 76.
Lewis,
   Ann --------------- 64.
   Catherine --------- 20.
   Charity ----------- 16.

Loughland,
 Patty -------------- 29.
Lowry,
 Polly -------------- 44.
Loy,
 Elizabeth ---------- 20.
 Hannah ------------- 65.
 Mary -----------42, 65.
Loyd,
 Lydia -------------- 56.
Lucas,
 Elizabeth ---------- 17.
Luckey,
 Elizabeth ---------- 50.
Luckleiter,
 Mary -------------- 74.
Lupton,
 Elizabeth ---------- 24.
 Lydia -------------- 60.
 Mary -------------- 35.
Luke,
 Susannah ----------- 57.
Lyons,
 Mary -------------- 50.
Lynn,
 Jane -------------- 57.
Luttle, ?
 Lyddy -------------- 43.

McAll,
 Jane -------------- 45.
McBean,
 Rebecca ------------ 41.
McBride,
 Polly -------------- 76.
McCab, ___ -------------- 45.
McCabe,
 Mary -------------- 27.
McCall,
 Nancy ------------- 70.
McCann,
 Ann --------------- 37.
 Rebecca ------------ 31.
 Tabitha ----------- 72.
McCarty,
 Margaret ----------- 31.
 Sarah -------------- 34.
McCartney,
 Rachel ------------- 28.
McClung,
 Eliza -------------- 62.
McClure,
 Ann --------------- 70.
McConnell,
 Catherine ---------- 75.

McCoole,
 Anna --------------- 29.
 Catherine ---------- 29.
 Charlotte ---------- 40.
 Grace -------------- 17.
 Olivia ------------- 73.
McCool,
 Mary --------------- 19.
McCord,
 Ann --------------- 31.
 Rebecca ------------ 28.
McCormick,
 Hannah ------------- 71.
 Harriett ----------- 54.
 Jane -------------- 50.
 Mary -------------- 28.
 Margaret ----------- 22.
McCormack, (McCormick)
 Jane -------------- 50.
McCoughen,
 Mary -------------- 28.
McCrea,
 Isabella ----------- 27.
McCritten,
 Sarah -------------- 23.
McDaniel,
 Rebecca ----------- 26.
McDonald,
 Alice -------------- 38.
 Ann --------------- 76.
 Catherine ---------- 76.
 Eleanor ------------ 71.
 Elizabeth ------25, 26, 50.
 Jenny ------------- 66.
 Margaret ----------- 39.
 Mary -------------51, 57.
 Maza -------------- 38.
 Nancy ------------- 41.
 Sally ------------- 35.
McDowell,
 Rebecca ------------ 54.
McFadden,
 Elizabeth ---------- 16.
 Nancy ------------- 39.
McFarlane,
 Elizabeth ---------- 67.
McFarland,
 Nancy ------------- 36.
 Polly -------------- 65.
McFerson,
 Mary -------------- 33.
McGinnis,
 Ann --------------- 44.
 Arisby ------------ 55.
McGraw,
 Martha ------------- 26.
 Susannah ----------- 68.

Myers,
  Susannah --------------- 43.
Mytinger,
  Elizabeth -----------30, 42.

Nawcett,
  Jane ------------------ 38.
Neal,
  Peggy ------------------ 76.
Nebitt,
  Sarah ----------------- 59.
Neff,
  Diana ----------------- 48.
Neilson,
  Margaret -------------- 66.
Nelson,
  Catherine ------------- 54.
  Eleanor --------------- 62.
  Margaret -------------- 53.
  Mary ----------------40, 53.
Newbrough,
  Sarah ----------------- 74.
Newbury,
  Ann ------------------- 23.
Newcomb,
  Elizabeth ------------- 26.
  Mary ------------------ 66.
  Susannah -------------- 22.
Newell,
  Isabella -------------- 43.
Newman,
  Hannah ---------------- 41.
  Mary Ann -------------- 21.
Newton,
  Mary ------------------ 55.
Nicewanger,
  Elizabeth ------------- 59.
Nichols,
  Ann ------------------- 73.
Nicholls,
  Elizabeth ------------- 68.
Nicklen,
  Susannah -------------- 50.
Nicklyn,
  Mary ------------------ 68.
Nighswander,
  Lydia ----------------- 56.
Nisewander,
  Mary------------------- 68.
Nisewanger,
  Margaret -------------- 32.
  Rebecca --------------- 52.
Nixon,
  Elizabeth ------------- 34.
Nizberger,
  Magdalen -------------- 70.

Noble,
  Ann ------------- 70.
  Ruth M. ---------- 24.
Noke,
  Priscilla -------- 60.
Nolan,
  Catherine -------- 30.
Noland,
  Catherine -------- 66.
  Amelia ----------- 76.
  Mary Ann --------- 75.
  Hannah ----------- 71.
  Susannah --------- 21.
Nolen,
  Milly Ann -------- 75.
Noll,
  Elizabeth -------- 45.
Norman,
  Charity ---------- 20.
Norris,
  Lettice ---------- 46.
  Mary ------------- 59.
  Sarah G. --------- 59.
Northern,
  Abigail ---------- 73.
  Betsy ------------ 37.
  Elizabeth -------- 39.
  Margaret --------- 38.
  Mary E. ---------- 40.
  Peggy ------------ 62.
Norton,
  Catherine -------- 16.
Nottingham,
  Ann -------------- 54.
  Comfort ---------- 53.
Nowland,
  Mary ------------- 27.
Null,
  Susannah --------- 32.
Nutt,
  Elizabeth -------- 55.
  Jenny ------------ 24.
  Mary ------------- 16.

O'Boyle,
  Rhoda ------------ 27.
Oglesby,
  Nancy ------------ 39.
  Sarah ------------ 19.
Oglesvie,
  Docia ------------ 64.
Oliver,
  Mary ------------- 28.
  Nancy ------------ 72.
Olleman,
  Catherine -------- 32.

Olleman,		
	Mary	62.
Ong,		
	Nancy	72.
Opie,		
	Jane	25.
	Susan	42.
O'Rear,		
	Louisa	39.
	Malinoa	34.
Orey,		
	Betsy	28.
Orndorff,		
	Elizabeth	21.
	Rachel	36.
	Rebecca 21,	60.
Orr,		
	Elizabeth 21,	57.
	Jane	21.
	Martha	46.
Osborn,		
	Nancy	39.
O'Shackelford,		
	Evelina	71.
Otto,		
	Catherna	65.
Oubry,		
	Mary	48.
Overton,		
	Elizabeth	58.
Owen,		
	Jenny	60.
Owins,		
	Lucy	30.
Owgan,		
	Martha	32.
Owgen,		
	Susannah	74.
Padgett,		
	Catherine	42.
Page,		
	Elizabeth	22.
Pagett,		
	Elizabeth	62.
Paine,		
	Sarah	49.
Painter,		
	Bulah	21.
	Phebe	57.
	Rachel	44.
Palsor,		
	Caty	69.
Pangler,		
	Catherine	55.

Park,		
	Sarah	52.
Parker,		
	Eliza	52.
	Hannah	53.
	Mary	34.
	Polly	44.
Parks,		
	Betsy	34.
Parkins,		
	Deborah	54.
	Elizabeth	54.
	Lydia	49.
	Mary	21.
	Susannah	18.
Parlett,		
	Mary	73.
	Sarah	68.
Parrell,		
	Ann	23.
	Margaret	19.
Parscel,		
	Ruth	52.
Patch,		
	Leah	56.
Patterson,		
	Ruth	42.
Patton,		
	Betsy	66.
Peach,		
	Sidney	24.
Peacock,		
	Margaret	50.
Pearce,		
	Catherine	63.
Peck,		
	Rosannah	29.
	Sarah	67.
Pelter,		
	Nancy	27.
Penticost,		
	Margaret	17.
Pepper,		
	Arabella	44.
Perfater,		
	Debby	19.
Perine,		
	Sarah	25.
Perkeson,		
	Ann	51.
Perkins,		
	Eleanor	32.
Peroint,		
	Catherine	44.
Perrill,		
	Nancy	65.

Pritchard,			Raworth,	
Sarah	64.		Nancy	29.
Susan	18.		Rayon,	
Puffingerber,			Ann	74.
Susannah	56.		Rea,	
Pugh,			Ruth	44.
Betsy	61.		Read,	
Jane	62.		Elizabeth	55.
Sarah 33,	39.		Reader,	
Puller,			Polly	34.
Margaret	33.		Redd,	
Nancy	40.		Elizabeth	75.
Pulse,			Hannah	74.₂
Catherine	55.		Rachol	57.²
Elizabeth	74.		Redding,	
Purkhiser,			Delilah	64.
Elizabeth	41.		Reding,	
Purtlebaugh,			Susannah	31.
Barbara	52.		Redman,	
Mary	52.		Augusta	63.
Putney,			Dolly	63.
Mary	59.		Elizabeth	43.
Pyland,			Sarah	70.
Sarah	18.		Reed,	
			Elizabeth	50.
			Hannah	65.
			Harriet	23.
Raby,			Heany	61.
Mary	64.		Helen	26.
Ragan,			Jemima	65.
Cordelia	41.		Martha	53.
Mary	48.		Mary Ann	24.
Ralph,			Mercy	50.
Mary	65.		Rachel	45.
Rosamond	38.		Rebecca	40.
Ramey,			Sarah	51.
Lydia	72.		Rees,	
Mary	55.		Lydia	23.
Miriam	41.		Rebecca	75.
Sarah 27,	68.		Reese,	
Susannah	31.		Margaret	60.
Ramy,			Martha	52.
Mary 50,	69.		Reid,	
Randolph,			Margaret	25.
Sarah	26.		Reiley,	
Ranes,			Sybilla	16.
Lucy	37.		Reiser,	
Rankin,			Elizabeth	74.
Elizabeth	70.		Remey,	
Polly	38.		Lydia	27.
Ranolds,			Renner,	
Mary	39.		Magdalene	59.
Ranter,			Margaret	57.
Mary Ann	34.		Reynolds,	
Raworth,			Ann	38.
Charlotte	24.		Catherine	56.
Mary	58.		Frances	44.

Rhoads,
Ruth --------------- 57.
Rhodes,
Sara --------------- 20.
Rhomine,
Mary --------------- 39.
Rice,
Eliza --------------- 50.
Elizabeth --------21, 30.
Rebecca ------------- 45,
Sarah -------------- 27²
Richards,
Alice -------------- 65.
Catherine --------32, 44.
Frances ------------- 51.
Hannah ------------- 42.
Mary -------------38, 60.
Sarah -------------- 34.
Richardson,
Ann ---------------- 40.
Mary -------------31, 73.
Mrs. --------------- 70.
Susan -------------- 42.
Rickert,
Eva ---------------- 20.
Ridenour,
Nancy -------------- 63.
Ridgeway,
Ann --------------56, 60.
Clary -------------- 76.
Mary --------------- 47.
Miss. -------------- 46.
Phebe -------------- 17.
Shady -------------- 68.
Riely,
Elizabeth Ann ------- 73.
Mary --------------- 46.
Rife,
Christianna --------- 41.
Elizabeth ----------- 24.
Rigeway,
Mary --------------- 48.
Rigle,
Catherine ----------- 44.
Elizabeth ----------- 59.
Riggles,
Mary --------------- 47.
Riley,
Becky -------------- 44.
Clarkey ------------- 40.
Franky ------------- 19.
Matilda ------------- 66.
Parthenia ----------- 73.
Polly -------------- 40.
Sidney ------------- 19.
Rinker,
Barbara ------------- 29.

Rinker,
Elizabeth ----------- 41.
Samaria R. ---------- 60.
Sarah -------------- 51.
Risler,
Sarah -------------- 51.
Ritenour,
Susan -------------- 21.
Ritter,
Margaret ----------23, 32.
Polly --------------- 61.
Roach,
Catherine ----------- 51.
Roberts,
Mary --------~------- 33.
Priscilla ----------- 42.
Robertson,
Mary --------------- 68.
Robinson,
Anna --------------- 57.
Becky -------------- 36.
Eliza --------------- 61.
Hannah ------------- 39.
Katy --------------- 66.
Martha Maria Jacqueline 74.
Rockenbaugh,
Nancy -------------- 50.
Rodes,
Lydia -------------- 61.
Rodgers,
Hannah ------------- 37.
Roe,
Eleanor ------------- 45.
Rogers,
Catherine ----------- 25.
Eliza --------------- 24.
Elizabeth ----------- 76.
Esther- ------------- 24.
Fanny -------------- 67.
Hannah ------------- 42.
Mary ----------23, 35, 67.
Sidney ------------- 68.
Roland,
Elizabeth ----------- 43.
Romine,
Eleanor ------------- 67.
Elizabeth ----------- 25.
Hannah ------------- 62.
Lydia -------------- 32.
Mary Ann ----------- 19.
Rhody -------------- 57.
Ronemus,
Mary --------------- 63.
Ronimus,
Catherine ----------- 30.
Elizabeth ----------- 42.
Roper,
Nancy -------------- 60.

Sherrard,
Elizabeth ----------- 19.
Jane ---------------- 16.
Sherrer,
Susannah ------------ 33.
Shiner,
Eve ----------------- 37.
Shinn,
Ann ----------------- 31.
Shion,
Mary ---------------- 28.
Ship,
Eliza H. S. --------- 22.
Shipe,
Ann ----------------- 33.
Barbara ------------- 32.
Catherine ----------- 37.
Mary ---------------- 72.
Shipler,
Barbara ------------- 34.
Martha -------------- 61.
Shipley,
Mary ---------------- 60.
Rebecca ------------- 70.
Shipman,
Abigail ------------- 42.
Shivertaker,
Elizabeth ----------- 48.
Shiverteere,
Margaret ------------ 34.
Sholeberger,
Mary ---------------- 67.
Shores,
Mary ---------------- 16.
Sarah --------------- 41.
Short,
Ann ----------------- 62.
Eve ----------------- 27.
Jane ---------------- 33.
Showalter,
Polly --------------- 55.
Shown,
Elizabeth ----------- 55.
Shrack,
Molly --------------- 19.
Shraack,,
Sarah --------------- 48.
Shreck,
Elizabeth ----------- 26.
Shriver,
Catherine ----------- 43.
Elizabeth ----------- 69.
Shrock,
Elizabeth ----------- 48.
Shuler,
Polly --------------- 32.
Susannah ------------ 22.

Shull,
Ann Maria ------ 37.
Catherine ------ 34.[3]
Elizabeth ------ 65.[3]
Henrietta ------ 73.
Mary ----------- 53.
Rachel --------- 34.
Rebecca -------- 21.
Shultz,
Magdalene ------ 61.
Shumate,
Elizabeth ------ 64.
Shutt, (Shull)
Mary Ann ------- 17.
Sibert,
Sarah ---------- 53.
Siders,
Kitty ---------- 54.
Sidwell,
Rebecca -------- 70.
Sigler,
Mary ----------- 37.
Simons,
Phebe ---------- 58.
Simpson,
Ann ---------24, 61.
Charlotte ------ 54.
Elizabeth ------ 74.
Lydia ---------- 36.
Sarah ---------- 41.
Simrall,
Frances -------- 54.
Singhorse,
Catherine ------ 55.
Singleton,
Drusilla ------- 18.
Sinsinning,
Eve ------------ 19.
Skaggs,
Sarah ---------- 48.
Skilling,
Margaret ------- 38.
Slough,
Sarah ---------- 18.
Slusher,
Barbara -------- 22.
Catherine ------ 66.
Ingle ---------- 73.
Susannah ------- 42.
Juliana -------- 28.
Sly,
Margaret ------- 59.
Smallwood,
Liddy ---------- 62.
Smiley,
Martha --------- 52.

Steele,
 Florina ------------- 36.
 Isabella I. --------- 75.
 Margaret ----------26, 43.
 Rachel ------------- 41.
Steel,
 Mary ---------------- 19.
Steere,
 Mary Dinah ---------- 53.
Stein,
 Catherine ----------- 26.
Stephens,
 Eleanor ------------- 34.
 Gereta -------------- 32.2
 Elizabeth -----32, -- 76.
 Harriett ------------ 50.
 Mary --22, 25, 37, 58, 66.
 Tabitha ------------- 55.
Stephenson,
 Elizabeth ----------- 75.
 Nancy --------------- 62.
Stevens,
 Ruth ---------------- 25.
Stewart,
 Elizabeth ----------- 41.
 Lucy ---------------- 42.
 Mary ---------------- 20.
 Patty --------------- 51.
Steward (t),
 Mary ---------------- 38.
Stickley,
 Ann ----------------- 53.
Stigler,
 Catherine ----------- 38.
Stipe,
 Margaret ------------ 65.
 Mary ---------------- 42.
 Nancy --------------- 60.
Stillions,
 Maria --------------- 60.
Stokes,
 Elizabeth ----------- 48.
 Vina ---------------- 69.
Stone,
 Caty ---------------- 52.
 Elizabeth ----------- 34.
 Mary ---------------- 25.
 Susannah ------------ 68.
Stonebridge,
 Hannah -------------- 29.
 Rebecca ------------- 61.
Stonebrook,
 Catherine ----------- 26.
Stoner,
 Elizabeth ----------- 28.
Stonestreet,
 Elizabeth ----------- 30.

Stothard,
 Nancy ---------- 26.
Streit,
 Rosannah ------- 64.
Stribling,
 Ann ----------54, 55.
 Elizabeth ------- 70.
 Elizabeth T. ---- 46.
 Mary ----------- 28.
 Sarah ----------- 54.
Strickling,
 Elizabeth ------- 37.
 Fanny-------------65.
Striker,
 Sarah ----------- 31.
Strosnyder,
 Mary ----------- 52.
Stubblefield,
 Patsy ----------- 70.
 Susan ----------- 48.
Stump,
 Catherine ------- 18.
 Elizabeth ----72, 73.
 Mary ----------- 57.
Sturt,
 Jane ------------ 29.
Stype,
 Betsy ----------- 65.
Suberly,
 Catherine ------- 21.
 Mary ----------- 21.
 Susannah -------- 21.
Sugand,
 Lydia ----------- 50.
Sullivan,
 Sarah --------48, 72.
Summers,
 Keziah ---------- 64.
Sumption,
 Deborah --------- 36.
Sunit,
 Catherine ------- 27.
Supinger,
 Lydia ----------- 75.
 Nancy ---------- 56.
Sutherland,
 Jane ------------ 70.
Suter,
 Mary ----------- 59.
Sutton,
 Jane ------------ 69.
 Martha ---------- 16.
Suvilly,
 Milly ---------- 59.
Suverly,
 Rosannah -------- 63.

Swarts,		Taylor,		
Mary -------------	40.	Jane ---------- 44,	64.	
Swartz,		Judith -----------	63.	
Elizabeth --------	71.	Liddy ------------	28.	
Mary ------------	22.	Louisa T. --------	54.	
Swatz,		Mary ------33, 69,	74.	
Catherine --------	33.	Mary Catherine ---	41.	
Margaret ---------	30.	Margaret ---------	39.	
Swhier,		Rachel -----------	27.	
Mary ------------	59.	Sarah -----16, 33,	55.	
Swick,		Sarah Ann --------	58.	
Phebe ------------	69.	Susannah ---------	63.	
Swier,		Winny ------------	60.	
Catherine --------	34.	Temple,		
Swisher,		Jane -------------	30.	
Margaret ---------	50.	Phebe ------------	35.	
Switzer,		Templeman,		
Elizabeth --------	26.	Nancy ------------	49.	
Swope,		Teal,		
Mary -------------	71.	Catherine --------	40.	
Sydnor,		Teboe,		
Isabella ---------	58.	Rosanna ----------	75.	
Mary Ellen -------	58.	Tespers,		
Sylvia,		Mary -------------	47.	
Jane -------------	32.	Tewalt,		
Symson,		Leah -------------	69.	
Susannah ---------	38.	Thacker,		
		Mildred I. --------	33.	
		Thatcher,		
Talbot,		Mary -------------	43.	
Eleanor ----------	18.	Thomas,		
Talbott,		Darcus -----------	71.	
Eliza ------------	39.	Catherine --------	18.	
Taliaferro,		Hannah -----------	71.	
Elizabeth Sarah --	69.	Mary ----------45,	75.	
Tapp,		Thomlin,		
Elizabeth --------	19.	Catherine --------	25.	
Tapscott,		Thomson,		
Louisa -----------	18.	Elizabeth --------	69.	
Tarflinger,		Thompson,		
Catherine --------	34.	Elizabeth 21,28,35,	64.	
Tate,		Jane -------------	48.	
Ann --------------	38.	Hannah -------- 23,	49.	
Tavender,		Mary ---------- 66,	75.	
Mary -------------	52.	Mary Ann ------ 37,	69.	
Tay,		Margaret 28, 45, 45,	65.	
Susa -------------	47.	Milly ------------	56.	
Taylor,		Polly ------------	52.	
Ann ------------33,	36.	Sarah ---------51,	61.	
Betsy ---------34,	68.	Susannah ---------	60.	
Catherine -54, 66,	68.	Thorn,		
Catherine G. -----	52.	Rebecca ----------	57.	
Delilah ----------	54.	Thornborough,		
Elizabeth Ann ----	38.	Elizabeth --------	52.	
Elizabeth 36,41,43,	45.	Thrasher,		
Frances A. -------	51.	Mary -------------	58.	
Harriet ----------	73.	Throckmorten,		
		Ann --------------	63.	

White,
Ann ----------------- 21.
Anna ---------------- 16.
Catherine ---------- 60.
Elizabeth 25,35,44,71,72.
Elizabeth Lydia ---- 70.
Kitty -------------- 63.
Lydia -------------- 23.
Margaret ----------- 74.
Martha ------------- 58.
Mary --------------- 20.
Nancy -------------- 68.
Phebe -------------- 42.
Polly -------------- 74.
Rachel ------------- 36.
Sarah ------------40, 51.
Whiting,
Frances ----------48, 73.
Ann Beverly -------- 20.
Whitman,
Catherine ---------- 25.
Whittington,
Elizabeth ---------- 35.
Whittle,
Martha ------------- 28.
Whollian,
Mary --------------- 34.
Wholiham,
Margaret ----------- 39.
Wickam,
Mary --------------- 48.
Wickersham,
Rebecca ------------ 50.
Mary --------------- 29.
Wigginton,
Elizabeth P. ------- 60.
Jane --------------- 29.
Wilcox,
Abigail ------------ 22.
Amey --------------- 64.
Willcox,
Ruckey ------------- 68.
Wilfong,
Barbara ------------ 42.
Wilkenson,
Sarah -------------- 50.
Wilkerson,
Ethalinda ---------- 54.
Wilkey,
Ann ---------------- 75.
Frances ------------ 64.
Wilkins,
Ruth --------------- 63.
Wiley,
Nancy -------------- 21.
Wilkins,
Rebecca ------------ 64.

Willey,
Julianna ----------- 61.
Nancy -------------- 39.
Williams,
Ann -----21, 22, 24, 27.
Catherine ---59, 70, 71.
Eleanor ------------ 57.
Eleanor E. --------- 48.
Elizabeth ---46, 65, 74.
Frances ------------ 60.
Frances C. --------- 61.
Hannah ------------- 67.
Letitia ------------ 64.
Levi --------------- 17.
Louisianna --------- 35.
Martha W. ---------- 54.
Mary --------------31,63.
Mary Ann ----------49,64.
Mary Carson -------- 66.
Margaret ----------- 61.
Nancy -------------- 48.
Nancy Porter ------- 17.
Polly -------------- 53.
Rachel ------------- 44.
Rhody -------------- 52.
Sarah --------22, 27, 40.
Susannah -------- 63, 73.
Williamson,
Elizabeth ------- 55, 59.
Willington,
Jane --------------- 35.
Nancy -------------- 18.
Wilson,
Alice -------------- 49.
Eliza -------------- 34.
Elizabeth ---------- 46.
Harriett ----------- 67.
Jane --------------- 55.
Margaret ---------17, 42.
Mary Ann ----------- 75.
Mary K. ------------ 19.
Polly -------------- 73.
Ruth --------------- 75.
Sarah ---------42, 54,75.
Susannah ----------- 54.
Windel,
Mary --------------- 53.
Windle,
Ann ---------------- 45.
Windsor,
Elizabeth ----------38.
Margaret ----------- 37.
Sarah -------------- 47.
Winfield,
Lydia -------------- 61.
Wingfield,
Hannah ------------- 23.

Winn,
Kitty ------------- 53.
Winsel,
Elizabeth --------- 32.
Winser,
Mary ------------- 73.
Winterton,
Mary ------------- 62.
Wisecarver,
Barbara ----------- 61.
Christiana -------- 36.
Wiser,
Hannah ------------ 69.
Wissent,
Margaret ---------- 65.
Withers,
Evelina ---------- 44.
Martha ------------ 36.
Patience ---------- 68.
Wolf,
Mary -------------- 34.
Wolfe,
Nancy ------------- 39.
Wood,
Comfort ----------- 28.
Edy --------------- 67.
Lydia ------------- 29.
Rebecca ----------- 60.
Mary -------------- 56.
Mary Dorcas ------- 73.
Ruth ------------- 19.
Wolfe,
Elizabeth --------- 75.
Winifred ---------- 36.
Wolverton,
Margaret ---------- 70.
Woodrow,
Lydia ------------- 22.
Woodward,
Lethe ------------- 68.
Wormeley,
Arianna J---------- 55.
Susan B. ---------- 71.
Wrenn,
Nancy ------------- 31.
Wright,
Eliza ------------- 43.
Elizabeth --------- 69.
Hannah ------------ 28.
Jane -------------- 33.
Nancy -----------29, 32.
Phoebe ------------ 20.
Rachel ------------ 52.
Sarah ------------- 74.
Wroe,
Jane ------------57, 64.

Yakely,
Catherine --------- 61.
Yanders,
Eve --------------- 52.
Yats,
Jane ------------- 40.
Yoe,
Catherine -------47, 58.
Elizabeth --------- 18.
Young,
Airy -------------- 72.
Elizabeth --------- 66.
Jane -------------- 37.
Lucy -------------- 44.
Margaret ---------- 64.
Mary -------------- 35.
Nancy ------------- 53.

Zuber,
Christiana -------- 21.

OMITTED NAMES

Davis, Mary Ann -------- 56.
Groves, Anna ----------- 63.
McGann, Ann ------------ 37.

Helm, Mary Gibbs ------- 37.
Brooks, Elizabeth Lewis-- 41.

Men and women in the Marriage

Bonds other than husband and wife.

Abril,
    Elizabeth --------- 11.
Adams,
    William ----------- 2.
Aires,
    Judith ------------ 15.
Allensworth,
    Catherine Butler -- 1.
Allenworth,
    Philip ------------ 5.
Allensworth,
    Simon ------------- 1.
Anderson,
    Adam -------------- 5.
    Jacob ------------- 7.
Archy,
    Ann --------------- 13.

Babb,
    Blanche ----------- 5.
    Thomas ---------1,-5, 9.
Bailey,
    Margaret ---------- 8.
Ball,
    John -------------- 11.
Balmain,
    Alexander --------- 14.
Barrow,
    John -------------- 8.
Bean,
    Mordecai ---------- 12.
Beaty,
    David ------------- 10.
    George ------------ 9.
Beatty,
    Henry ------------- 13.
Bell,
    George ------------ 2.
Benett,
    Lewis ------------- 9.
Biggs,
    Thomas ------------ 11.
Blakemore,
    Thomas ------------ 7.
Bonham,
    Aaron ------------- 2.
Booker,
    Jacob ------------- 5.
Bowen,
    Bartholomew ------- 11.

Bowen,
    Thomas ----------- 11.
Boxell,
    John ------------- 2.
Boyce,
    Robert ---------- 7.
Brady,
    Captain John ----- 13.
Brecount,
    David ----------- 2.
Brenan,
    John ------------- 15.
Bridgers,
    Dillon ----------- 11.
Brinker,
    George ---------- 8.
Britain,
    Joseph ---------- 4.
Britton,
    Jesse ----------- 8.
    Wilson ---------- 2.
Bruce,
    James ----------- 7.
Burk,
    Abigail --------- 3.
Bush,
    Philip ---------- 13.
Burwell,
    Nat ------------- 2.

Cackley,
    John ------------- 10.
Cahoon,
    Daniel ----------- 13.
Campbell,
    Jane ------------- 11.
    John ------------- 11.
Carter,
    Arthur ----------- 9.
    Dale ------------- 13.
    Joseph ----------- 13.
    Rachel ----------- 14.
Cartmell,
    Martin ----------- 3.
    Nathan ----------- 3.
Cather,
    Joseph ----------- 9.
Catlett,
    Robert ----------- 1.

Glenn,
  Matthew ------------- 15.
Gilles,
  William ------------- 8.
Good,
  Peter --------------- 2.
Gordon,
  John ---------------- 5.
Gorley,
  Ann ----------------- 4.
  John ---------------- 4.
Gossett,
  Abner --------------- 1.
  William ------------- 5.
Grady,
  Michael ------------- 14.
Griffith,
  David --------------- 2.
  David Sr. ----------- 5.
Griffin,
  Samuel -------------- 5.
Grubs,
  Daniel -------------- 11.
  Elizabeth ----------- 11.
  Humphrey ------------ 11.

Hanshaw,
  Nicholas ------------ 7.
Harman,
  Mathias ------------- 13.
Harper,
  Mark ---------------- 5.
  Thomas -------------- 1.
  William ------------- 9.
Hayney,
  John ---------------- 11.
Helphenstine,
  Henry --------------- 6.
  Peter --------------- 2.
Helzel,
  Charles ------------- 3.
Henry,
  James -----------12, 15.
Heth,
  Henry --------------- 5.
Hicks,
  David --------------- 10.
Hickman,
  James --------------- 15.
Hoff,
  Morgan -------------- 12.
Holmes,
  David -------------3, 4.
Hotspeller,
  Stephen ------------- 14.

Huffman,
  Catherine -------- 1.
Humble,
  Michael ----------15.
Irwin, Joseph -------- 11.

Jackson,
  John ----------- 11.
Jamison,
  John ----------- 4.
Janant,
  Humbil ---------- 1.
Jennings,
  Edward ---------- 7.
  Isaac ----------- 3.
Jenkins,
  Jacob ----------- 12.^{2}
Jewell,
  William --------- 4.
Johnston,
  Hugh ------------ 13.
  Humphry R. ------- 7.
  Joseph ---------- 12.
Joliffe,
  Amos ------------ 8.
Jones,
  John ------------ 7.$_2$
  Thomas ---------- 9.^{2}

Kean,
  John ----------14,15.
Kearnes,
  Patrick --------- 7.
Kenny,
  Robert ---------- 1.
Kiger,
  Jacob ----------- 11.
Kline,
  Jacob ---------- 4.
Knester,
  John ----------- 10.
Kyger,
  George --------- 7.

Langley,
  Benjamin ------- 8.
Latty,
  Joseph --------- 6.
Lewis,
  Henry ---------- 2.
Lindsey,
  Edmond --------- 12.
  Jacob -------10, 12.
  Mary ----------- 12.

Names of Ministers with the abbreviations used in

this book.

Adams, Thomas ---------	T.A.	Linthicum, Archibald ----	A. L.
Allemong, John ---------	J.A.	Littleton, Thomas -------	T. L.
Ambrose, William -------	W.A.		
		McCann, James -----------	J.McC.
Baker, Joseph ----------	J.B.	Monroe, John -------------	J.M.
Balmain, Alexander -----	A.B.	Monroe, William ----------	W.M.
Barnes, Robert ---------	R.B.	Montgomer, John ----------	J.M.
Bond, John -------------	J.B.	Moriety, John ------------	J.M.
Broadus, William -------	W.B.	Mosely, William ----------	W.M.
Buck, Thomas Jr. -------	T.B.Jr.		
Bunn, Seely ------------	S.B.	Northern, William --------	W.N.
Carson, Joseph ---------	J.C.	Paynter, James -----------	J.P.
Chapman, Robert H. -----	R.C.	Phelps, Elisha -----------	E.P.
Chastain, Lewis --------	L.C.	Pickett, John ------------	J.P.
Collin, Nicholas -------	N.C.	Polk, John ---------------	J.P.
Corbin, Lewis ----------	L.C.	Pollard, C. Perry --------	C.P.
Dagg, John L.------------	J.L.D.	Raynolds, George H. -----	G.R.
Dalby, Joseph -----------	J.D.	Reed, George -------------	G.R.
Davis, Daniel ----------	D.D.	Robertson, J. J. ---------	J.R.
Davis, William F.R. ----	W.D.	Roswell, Stephen G. ------	S.R.
Dawson, Benjamin -------	B.D.		
Dorsey, Thomas J. ------	T.D.	Sanson, James ------------	J.S.
		Sansford, Isaac ----------	I.S.
Ferguson, Robert F.-----	R.F.F.	Sine, Christy ------------	C.S.
Finnell, Reuben --------	R.F.	Shannon, Andrew A. --------	A.S.
Foote, W. H. -----------W.H.F.		Ship, Edward G.-----------	E.S.
Fristoe, William -------	W.F.	Stone, Benjamin ----------	B.S.
Frye, George M. --------G.M.F.		Streit, Christian --------	C.S.
Frye, Joseph -----------	J.F.	Swift, Richard -----------	R.S.
Groves, Ezra -----------	E.G.	Tilden, John B.----------J.B.T.	
Haar, Simon ------------	S.H.	Walls, James -------------	J.W.
Harper, George W.S.------	G.H.	Walls, Jennings ----------	J.W.
Harvey, William --------	W.H.	Weeks, Alderson ----------	A.W.
Hendron, Samuel O.-----	S.O. H.	Williams, William -------	W.W.
Hickman, John ----------	J.H.	Winter, Thomas ----------	T.W.
Hill, William ----------	W.H.	Withers, James ----------	J.W.
Hinkle, Ely ------------	E.H.		
Hoge, Moses ------------	M.H.		
Huffman, J. C. -------	J.C.H.		
Hutt, John -------------	J.H.		
Ireland, James ---------	J.I.		
Jefferson, Hamilton ---	H.J.		
Kennerly, Thomas -------	T.K.		
Krauth, C. P. ----------	C.K.		
Legrand, Nash ----------	N.L.		